# SOCIAL
# GROUP WORK

**GISELA KONOPKA**

THIRD EDITION

# SOCIAL
# GROUP WORK

## *A Helping Process*

*Prentice-Hall, Inc., Englewood Cliffs, New Jersey 07632*

**Library of Congress Cataloging in Publication Data**

KONOPKA, GISELA.
  Social group work.

  Bibliography.
  Includes index.
  1. Social group work.  I.  Title.
HV45.K63  1982      361.4      82-7695
ISBN 0-13-815787-1            AACR2

Printed in the United States of America

10  9  8  7  6  5  4  3  2  1

Editorial/production supervision: Jeanne Hoeting
Manufacturing buyer: John Hall
Cover: "Hands" by E. Paul Konopka
Cover design: Diane Saxe

ISBN 0-13-815787-1

PRENTICE-HALL INTERNATIONAL, INC. *London*
PRENTICE-HALL OF AUSTRALIA PTY. LIMITED, *Sydney*
PRENTICE-HALL CANADA INC., *Toronto*
PRENTICE-HALL OF INDIA PRIVATE LIMITED, *New Delhi*
PRENTICE-HALL OF JAPAN, INC., *Tokyo*
PRENTICE-HALL OF SOUTHEAST ASIA PTE. LTD., *Singapore*
WHITEHALL BOOKS LIMITED, *Wellington, New Zealand*

To people all over the world
who believe human dignity
can become reality for everyone

*and*

to my husband, E. Paul Konopka,
who fought for it all through his life.

# CONTENTS

# INTRODUCTION TO THE FIRST EDITION

The foolishness of my writing in comparison with what I wanted to write infuriated me for years. Greatness, greatness, greatness is what I wanted and insisted upon, only to notice that everything I wrote was small and miserable. I couldn't understand it. My soul was great, it was astonishingly great, and yet, it was captured in a little, feeble body and could not get itself free. I had in my soul the greatest truths to tell but when I came to the work of telling them I couldn't do it, I couldn't find a starting place. . . . Where could I begin?

I was long years discovering the secret that it does not matter at all where one begins, and that it is not necessary for anything one writes to be instantly great, the important thing is for a man to resign himself to the truth that he is only a man, and to work. . . .[1]

---

[1] William Saroyan, *The Bicycle Rider in Beverly Hills* (New York: Scribner's, 1952), p. 99.

To start a book which is some kind of textbook with such a quote must seem strange. These words had been written in the anguish of the creative writer, not by the scientist or instructor. Yet in writing this book, the same anguish is present, partially because of the always creative process of writing, but mostly because of the vastness and importance of the subject of social group work. Any endeavor directed toward helping people in whatever area is an audacious undertaking, since human beings are powerful and weak creatures at the same time, regardless of whether they are the helper or the one to be helped. Helping people in a group and through a group is especially demanding and difficult. Groups are the basic expressions of human relationships; in them lies the greatest power of man. To try to work with them in a disciplined way is like trying to harness the power of the elements and includes the same kind of scientific thinking, as well as serious consideration of ethics. Like atomic power, groups can be harmful and helpful. To work with such power is a humbling and difficult task.

The group work process—as developed in the last forty years—has great promise. To write about it so that both actual practice and theory become alive presents more than one problem. The writing must be logical and scientific; at the same time it must paint the picture of a work of art. Every writer, every practitioner, in this helping endeavor called social group work, has written parts of this book. The thinking of other writers from different disciplines is also incorporated. Insight has come from those being served as well as from lay people in the communities. All the contributions by others are gratefully acknowledged. This book is an attempt to present this intricate subject as a whole piece of cloth; the threads from which it is made are not always recognizable, but they are there. Without them, without the untiring work of others, it could not be written.

Recent years have seen a great increase in interest in the group approach to treatment of a variety of problems. It is time to pull together our existing knowledge. Several years ago Gertrude Wilson and Gladys Ryland wrote the first comprehensive book on social group work.[2] In the meantime, the method has been developed and has entered many additional fields of practice. New knowledge has arisen. This does not detract from the importance of the first pioneering work, and the contribution of its authors is gratefully acknowledged.

The reader must be prepared for the fact that he will miss not only extensive quoting, but also a complicated scientific language. The avoidance of such language does not mean that the subject is simple or that the approach to it will be simplified. It is the author's conviction that thoughts—especially in the field of human relations—must and can be

[2]Gertrude Wilson and Gladys Ryland, *Social Group Work Practice* (Boston: Houghton Mifflin, 1949).

expressed in the clear language of good literature. This is no easy task and, without question, this writer will not always achieve the necessary simplicity. Yet the clearer the thought the less involved and obscure the language will be.

A professional effort means translation of thought into action, and the conversion of highly complicated knowledge into seemingly effortless doing. Knowledge and skill are constantly in the state of development.

> The best of us, however vigorous our search for truth, will always leave at the outer reaches, frayed edges of knowledge or uncertainly grasped truths, and will at the last recognize how true it is that our greatest contribution to and through education is the excitement and development of students, who, becoming equally interested in the search for truth, can complete what we imperfectly begin.[3]

It is hoped that the student, the practitioner, and the teacher who read this, will read the book in this spirit.

## ACKNOWLEDGMENTS

Thanks for help go to so many: to teachers, colleagues, students, group members, and clients. Yet they cannot all be named. I want to mention those who gave special help and encouragement.

Thanks go to:

my teachers, Gertrude Wilson; Ruth Garland, who died too early, and Grace Coyle who had wanted to see this writing, but who, unfortunately, passed away before the manuscript was finished;

my colleagues, Ruby Pernell, Miriam Cohn, and Frances Guzie, who were willing to discuss the many problems of social group work and who offered case material;

many of my former students, among them Sarah Churchill, Perry Roth, and Vernon Bloom who also helped with a supply of pertinent case material.

No manuscript can be written without painstaking attention to detail. Very special thanks for help with this and editorial comments go to Vernie Mae Czaky who read and reread the manuscript and the footnotes.

And few books can be written without some encouragement and the support of people close to the writer. For both I thank Dr. Theodore H. Blegen who, through the many years he was the dean of the graduate school at the University of Minnesota and after his retirement, has given me help and warm, constructive criticism, especially supporting me in the

---

[3]O. Meredith Wilson, "A Message from the President," *The Minnesotan*, XIV, No. 1 (Oct. 1960), p. 2.

use of a simple language. I wish to acknowledge the assistance of Professor Walter R. Friedlander and Professor Herbert Blumer.

And finally, the deepest thanks—as always—to my patient and thoughtful husband who lived with the endless hours, nights, weekends, that must be taken to write a book.

This acknowledgment was written for the first edition in 1963. Twenty years have passed. New ideas, new contexts have emerged. My additional thanks go especially to group workers, group work teachers, and group members, young and old, in many countries all over the globe. Their questions and thoughts have deeply influenced my thinking.

Bayanihan—What It Means
*Bayanihan is an ancient Filipino custom, symbolic of the Filipino way of group work. The word as found in the "Vocabulario de la lengua Tagala" (1754) by P. Juan de Pedro de Sanlucar is derived from the word* bayani *meaning "obra commun" or "group work."* Bayanihan *means getting-together to push through a common project.* Magbabayani *refers to the people getting together to execute a common job.*

*The moving of a whole house borne on the shoulders of a working group of neighbors symbolizes the true spirit of the Bayanihan.*[1]

# INTRODUCTION TO THE SECOND EDITION

The decade after publication of the first edition of this book was a stormy one, not only in the United States of America, but all over the world, and the storm continues while this is being written. The amazing and almost awe-inspiring point is that this storm is directly related to the problem of human relations, to the intense wish of more and more people on this earth to translate lofty ideals about justice, dignity of the human being, caring for each other, and brotherhood into reality. This has been the struggle of mankind as long as it has existed, but it now reaches farther into every fiber of societies. Century-old cultures begin to feel the shaking

[1]From program notes *Bayanihan*, Folk Arts Center, "Glimpses of Philippine Culture," Sept. 9, 1970.

of the belief that one has to accept whatever state one lives in and that one can be part of decision-making regarding one's own destiny. Blissful complacency with whole systems that perpetuate a relationship of "superior" and "inferior" among people is shaken—whether in relation to ethnic groups, or races or nationalities, or sex, or age, or economic status. Mankind searches for ways to truly relate individuals and groups in a basically positive and human way—and the road to this end is strewn with errors, pain, and lives. There is obviously no panacea. Yet in rereading what I wrote about ten years ago, it struck me again that the 1920s pioneers—and they are the ones we must thank for this—in the same zeal for humanization of life, did work out *one* way that is at least a part of coming closer to the goal mankind strives for. Group work *is* a "venture in sanity," as Eduard Lindeman said and far more than that if it is taken seriously and not practiced as a routine technique. It is based on a philosophy of deep respect for the individual and the individual's being limited by his or her consideration of others, a serious and not easily learned limitation, but a most exciting and positive one. Group work includes the yearning of human beings for strength in common action, for individual assertion within a community, and for intimacy so necessary to nourish warmth and joy in face of the stern demands of life.

I have been asked by colleagues and students which model of group work I adhere to—the Social Goals Model, the Remedial Model, or the Reciprocal Model. Aside from my revulsion against such atrocious terminology, my answer is clearly: Neither one, nor all of them together. I find it impossible to exclude the aims of any one of them. To state it succinctly: I believe that *social work* is *one* among the human relations professions that tries to translate the basic philosophy of individual dignity combined with responsibility for the human group into reality. It must be definitely goal- or problem-oriented. According to whatever situation the social worker meets, his responsibility is always to the individual as well as to the group and the total system in which they move. He is a supporter, an enabler, a change-agent in relation to both, individual and environment. This applies to all of social work. He works sometimes in the context of the one-to-one, sometimes in the context of the small group, and sometimes in the context of the wider community. Social workers must learn to work in all those relationships. The better they understand what they are doing the more effective they will be. Group work is *one* of the methods used predominantly in the context of the face-to-face group and which uses the group also as a medium of action. It may be used in groups of children or young people or adults, of remedial or action groups. It may be practiced in closed institutional settings or in the open community to develop a neighborhood, a school system, a village. I see group work as one of the major helping processes of such wide range. I do not consider it the *only* one. It is inseparable from an underlying philosophy, from human compassion and the fire of wanting to change whatever harms people.

In this book I have placed group work mostly in the field and the profession of social work, because it was and still is mostly taught within social work education.

I think that the cycle of group work's historical development begins to close though: Group work started within education, informal and formal, youth services, adult education and social action. It developed significant ways of working within the fields of therapy, corrections, and the fight against social deprivation. It again will be most significant to those fields and the various professions working in them. In fact, it widens its use to many other fields: community development, the ministry, youth movements, wherever people want some help with gaining self-confidence and effectiveness while living, working, thinking, and feeling with each other.

I personally find great hope in our troubled world, because of the self-assertion of people as groups and individuals. To enhance this, it is my additional hope that the group work method will make its contribution far beyond the efforts of one profession alone.

"Paternalism has created—or cultivated—the roles of 'giver' and 'receiver,' both inadequate in a cooperative society. I see a definite role for Social Group Work to overcome this attitude."[2]

[2]Carola de Ruzo, Group Work Educator, Latin America, in a letter to the author, 1970.

# INTRODUCTION TO THE THIRD EDITION

Much has been written about group work, with many theorists trying to categorize the various concepts of the helping process. My views have been labeled at different times, "psychiatric," "traditional," or "general"; none of these apply. My perception, practice, research, and teaching of social group work comes from a complex perspective based on a wide variety of resources. I define social group work as a practice with people in formal and informal educational settings; a wide variety of social services; therapy and community action based on a particular philosophy; and a basic understanding of individual, small group, and larger community forces.

The *philosophy* of social group work has as its most significant touchstone a deep concern for the *dignity of the human being*.

The *understanding of the human being* is based on several theories. Summarized, it recognizes that people are physical, intellectual, and emotional creatures, a "Ganzheit" (wholeness) influenced by both conscious and unconscious motives.

The human being is neither born good nor bad, but has the potential to be both.

Human beings are not only "related" to each other, but are intertwined with other people and their physical, economic, and human environment. No human being can live separated from others. Human relations are most significant to the development of each person, again physically, intellectually and emotionally. Most important are therefore small groups, including the family, friendship, and other face-to-face groups.

Sometimes, but not always, a person is needed who is able to understand thoroughly and explicitly this philosophy and theory in order to translate it into significant action for individuals, groups, and communities. This person is the professional group worker. Many sensitive and well-motivated lay persons may act in the same capacity. The professional is only distinguished by (1) the *conscious* use of philosophy, knowledge, and skill; and (2) a heightened sensitivity to others and his or her own self. The group worker is not allowed to "manipulate" (in its negative sense) individuals or groups, but must be able to help them develop themselves, contribute to others, and to the totality of the system in which they live.

The social group worker is a *person* whose special skills lie in the use of his or her knowledge to help others through a warm, honest, and capable relationship.

My philosophy and view of the human race come from theory, but they are also influenced by life events. I grew up in a poor Jewish family in Berlin, born to parents who, when they were young, had already experienced the horror of pogroms and persecution in Poland and had immigrated to Germany, the country of freedom at that time. Very early I experienced the terrible pain of war when my father was called into the Army. I also experienced the competence of a young woman, my mother, who made it possible for us to eat, by working day and night. I remember her tears, the poor food, and her exceedingly warm reception of "people on welfare" who came to our little store. This was in contrast to the demeaning way in which the social worker, whom I met, treated the same people. I read a great deal; along with the classics, there was a vast literature of the early socialist writers available to me whose names would mean little to people in the United States. My basic concept of "justice with a heart" was born early through those readings and experiences. Dante's *Divina Comedia* overwhelmed me with its beauty and tragedy, Schiller's *Don Carlos* gave me a rationale for a search for freedom and friendship, Lessing's *Nathan the Wise* taught me religious tolerance and the story of *Savonarola* introduced me to the complex question of the difference between fighting for a cause and dogmatism. I could go on and on with this, but I will not.

As a teenager I experienced great social reformers such as Karl Wilker, who completely changed public attitude toward delinquents, and Walter Friedlander, who helped shape new policies to serve the poor. I belonged to a Youth Movement, which wanted to change the world for the better. I experienced the enormous significance of group support, both as support for myself, the individual, as well as a force to strengthen social action. The Youth Movement had to combine concern for the individual and the group with concern for political action. This is one of the reasons that I have always found the controversy in social work between "micro" and "macro" intervention—atrocious words anyhow—absolutely irrelevant, and I have never understood how my contribution to and my concept of group work could be understood by some writers as being exclusively concerned with the individual. One of my earliest articles was just as concerned with racial injustice as with the emotional tortures to which the children that I worked with were exposed.[1] My book on *Eduard C. Lindeman and Social Work Philosophy* (Minneapolis: University of Minnesota Press, 1958, 220 pp.) makes explicit the dual focus of my concept of a helping profession and social group work as individual—and social action-oriented.

The advent of the Nazis; the experience of demeaning human cruelty; my active involvement in the underground movement against fascism in three countries (Germany, Austria and France); and the experience of being spat at, imprisoned, and almost raped by a prison guard, as well as living in abject poverty, intensified my goal direction and my unshakable concern of making any work related to people directed toward human dignity.

Now, to the understanding of my view of the human race: I have been called a neo-Freudian or an Adlerian, but these labels do not fit. Certainly I have studied intensely Sigmund Freud, Alfred Adler, and Karl Marx long before I came to the United States. I did not accept them totally, but I admired their contribution to the understanding of human motivation. Sociologists (e.g., Weber and the Fabians); anthropologists (e.g., Clyde Kluckhohn); and psychologists (e.g., William Stern and Kurt Lewin) added to the picture. I see the human race, individuals and the systems within which they move, and their relationships as most complex. It is important to realize that human beings are acting and acted upon as individuals, but never in isolation. I consider any theory, if used dogmatically, simplistic and false. Those who work with people should have knowledge of a wide variety of theories, be capable of intertwining them, and have a fresh

---

[1]Gisela Konopka, "Group Therapy in Overcoming Racial and Cultural Tensions," *American Journal of Orthopsychiatry*, XVII, No. 4 (Oct. 1947), pp. 693–99.

outlook about each problem that arises. There is always the possibility that we discover new facets of human behavior we have not known.

When I came to the United States and learned about group work from Gertrude Wilson, it seemed very familiar to me, since it was the method we, in the European Youth Movement before Hitler, were talking about in school reform and especially in work with delinquents.[2] When I read Grace Coyle and Clara Kaiser, I was delighted to find their strong interest in the labor movement and social action. I was not especially interested in welfare in its bureaucratic and authoritarian sense, but I was excited about the group work component in social work because it talked of "members" and not "clients," and because the goal of the group worker was constantly to enhance the strength of individuals *and* groups, and never one or the other. I was also impressed with the fact that social group work did not simply accept group pressure as something positive (as it had been done under the Nazis and is again now being done in some group practices, especially in corrections). The recognition that the specific role of the group worker is to safeguard the potential of the individual within the group, while at the same time strengthening the groups as a whole, is a most exciting and significant aspect of any work in human relations. I realized the importance of social group work to individual therapy, community development, community action, group living, and education, and to international relations as well.[3] In those first years of my awareness of group work, I saw it as one of the major methods that would help to develop more positive social relations and services in the United States.

I am excited about the revival of social group work, especially if it is not in terms of an empty technique, or a dogmatic application of just one theory or another. If we will be able to revive social group work as one of the exciting attempts of putting into practice the concerns for human dignity and the extraordinary capacity of human beings to develop their strength, then I feel that my particular perspective of social group work makes a significant contribution.

[2]Gisela Konopka, "Reform in Delinquency Institutions in Revolutionary Times: The 1920s in Germany," *The Social Service Review*, 45, No. 3 (Sept. 1971), pp. 245–58.

[3]Gisela Konopka, "The Application of Social Work Principles to International Relations," paper presented at the National Conference of Social Work, Cleveland, Ohio, 1953. Published in the *Social Welfare Forum*, 1953 (New York: Columbia University Press) pp. 279–88.

*Social work's secret tool is the infinite untapped, unused, unsuspected capacity for growth in the sovereign individual personality. . . . Of all types and breeds of social worker, the social group worker most consciously accepts this democratic premise in his work.*[1]

# ONE
# HISTORY OF SOCIAL GROUP WORK

In the 1980s it is exciting to read the words above, written about twenty-five years earlier. Today the cry everywhere in the world, sounded by all those who have felt discriminated against, is for participation and the use of every individual's own capacity to grow and be effective. Seeing the social group worker as a significant force in helping persons to achieve that self-realization is important.

To discuss group work, a definition of this approach must be given, Since its conscious beginning the practitioners using the social group work method have searched for a simple definition. This definition has changed

[1]Louis Towley in Frank J. Bruno, *Trends in Social Work, 1874–1956* (New York: Columbia University Press, 1957), pp. 421–422.

1

somewhat in the course of history, and there is not yet a generally accepted one. The most abstract and encompassing concept expressed can be found in the *Curriculum Study* where Marjorie Murphy defined *social group work* as a method of social work and as "enhancement of persons' social functioning through purposeful group experience."[2] This definition parallels closely the one given by Helen Harris Perlman when she describes casework, the oldest method in social work:

> Social casework is a process used by certain human welfare agencies to help individuals to cope more effectively with their problems in social functioning.[3]

Neither definition—as is always the case with definitions—gives a total and complete picture; both need interpretation and amplification.

Let us consider the first part of the group work definition. This part places social group work within the context of social work as one of the methods through which this profession renders its service. Group work as a *method of social work* is only a recent concept. Originally it was conceived of as a movement, a way of democratic action, and a part of several fields of social services. Foremost among these were informal education, youth services, recreation, camping, the labor movement, settlement houses, and community centers. We must understand the historical development of what is today called the group work method in order to appreciate its underlying philosophy, to understand this particular form of working with people and the way in which it has contributed to widen the concept of social work—a fact still disturbing to those who want to limit severely the functions of this profession. We will return to this after we have tried to trace the historical evolution of the present concept of social group work.

Group work did not spring up suddenly as Athena from the head of Zeus. It was not discovered like a new drug, which can be dated, at least, according to the day of its publication. It cannot even be traced to a certain person, as is the original formulation of the other method of social work, casework, which usually is credited to Mary Richmond. Casework too has changed in the course of history, but it owes its inception to one person in the service of one particular organization, the Charity Organization Societies.

The history of the development of modern group work is part of the history of social agencies evolving within a changing society. Industrialization brought with it slums, movement of the farm population into the cities,

[2]Marjorie Murphy, "The Social Group Work Method in Social Work Education," *A Project Report of the Curriculum Study,* XI, Werner W. Boehm, Director and Coordinator (New York: Council on Social Work Education, 1959), pp. 39-40.

[3]Helen Harris Perlman, *Social Casework* (Chicago: University of Chicago Press, 1957), p. 4.

and large-scale immigration to the United States. The older social services distinguished sharply between the giver and the receiver. Yet among the newer services there were the beginnings of an idea turned into action: self-help, self-help of a group nature. "Whereas philanthropy was generally of middle class origin, mutual self-help, as the name implies, developed from the need for mutual aid and support."[4] There were the beginnings of the labor movement, related not merely to improvement of wages, but having a strong cultural aspect, with beginnings of adult education, and with camp vacations for their children financed by the workers' own efforts. There were the brotherhoods, which developed their own centers, such as the Jewish centers. The Jewish centers were developed partially by the older, more privileged immigration for the new poor Eastern Jewish immigration, and they partially presented the effort of the new immigrants to help themselves. These were nationality groups, helped by the "outsider" in the settlement houses, but increasingly taking on their own responsibilities. And there were youth agencies with strong and significant participation by youth and adult volunteers. In all these groups burned a fire of "citizen action," either to improve their own lot or to help improve that of others, by involving those others, not by acting for or in behalf of them. The proud preamble of the *Girl Scout Constitution* expresses the approach to many social problems, found in all of these different movements:

> We maintain that the strength of the Girl Scout movement rests in the voluntary leadership of its adult members, in the cooperation and support of the community, and in the affiliation with Girl Guide and Girl Scout movements of other countries through the World Association of Girl Guides and Girl Scouts.
> We declare that the democratic way of life and the democratic process shall guide all our activities.
> We hold that ultimate responsibility for the Girl Scout movement rests with volunteers.[5]

The recreation movement, too, was a vital root of group work. At the turn of the century it was a social movement. It was closely related to the unions' fight for the eight-hour day, for the right to a creative life after long hours of deadening mechanical work. It opened new outlets for the "culturally and educationally disadvantaged." The recreation movement fought for playgrounds for children in the slums, for summer camps and swimming pools. It was not a movement for "entertainment," but for vital necessities of body and soul, especially for children. Most of the activities

[4]Peter Kunstler, Social Group Work in Great Britain (London: Faber and Faber, 1955), p. 40.

[5]From the Preamble to the Constitution of the Girl Scouts of the United States of America and used by permission.

were conducted in groups. Eventually, group interaction itself became the dominant concern. For many years group work and recreation/informal education were erroneously considered synonymous. In fact, even in the present day, this confusion often persists despite the change in the concept of group work and the changes in the field of recreation.

The organizations that built the foundations of group work were the self-help and informal recreational ones: settlement houses, neighborhood centers, Y's, the Scouts, Camp Fire Girls, Jewish centers, and camps. Later they were designated as "group work agencies," but at their inception they worked separately.

Participation in small groups, the democratic way of life, community responsibility, and membership in a worldwide effort were new concepts that united these services and movements without their being aware of it.

In the period after World War I, social casework, used predominantly in the Charity Organization Societies, gained additional insight from psychoanalytic theory. This was necessary and valuable to its practice, but it was sometimes over-used.

At that time, the social group work method was hardly consciously developed, yet the services from which it grew increased, not only in number, but also in significance. This was the period when most European monarchies tumbled, when countries in central Europe without any experience in self-goverment tried hard to develop a democratic society, and when the emancipation of women radically changed family relationships. In the United States there was disappointment that the war had not made the world "safe for democracy," but the picture of the roaring twenties is very incomplete if it omits the enormous growth of voluntary associations and their impact on a rapidly changing society. It was during this time that an investigation into the unexplored area of group association started, not as a dispassionate research into small group behavior (this occurred later, after World War II), but as a way of achieving a better society and developing a true "democratic way of life." This is the reason why social group work was not conceived of as a method but as a goal, a philosophy, a movement, a psychology, and a profession all rolled into one.

The settlement's goal was described by Robert Woods:

> The social worker thus serves to unite the new scattered industrial, racial and religious elements that are thrown together to make up the population of our great city communities.[6]

And the function of Workers Education was seen as:

---

[6]Robert A. Woods, *The Neighborhood in Nation Building* (Boston: Houghton Mifflin, 1923), p. 94.

Workers Education will stimulate the student to serve the labor movement in particular and society in general, it is not education to be used for selfish personal advancement.[7]

This was the period that saw the beginning of research into the phenomenon of group behavior. Mary Richmond wrote in 1920:

.. a tendency in modern casework which I seem to have noted and noted with great pleasure. It is one which is full of promise, I believe, for the future of social treatment. I refer to the new tendency to view our clients from the angle of what might be termed small group psychology.[8]

And Mary Parker Follett, the political scientist and active settlement worker, who saw the possibility of a new and just society on the horizon, wrote:

The great cosmic force in the womb of humanity is latent in the group as its creative energy; that it may appear the individual must do his duty every moment. We do not get the whole power of the group unless every individual is given full value, is giving full value.[9]

The goal again was the democratic society as a means to provide for the highest fulfillment of the individual and allow him to take his place as a responsible member of the human race.

These movements and thinkers increasingly realized that *a way of working with groups* could hinder or help this goal. The insights and concepts did not come mainly from the social work profession. They came more from education, especially the ideas of John Dewey, and from sociologists who were active in these self-help movements and entered schools of social work as teachers.

Mark Starr described Workers Education in 1937:

This training is often a learning-by-doing process. It engages in a great number of educational activities which are not "courses" at all, but projects created spontaneously out of problematic situations "here and now." . . . The aim is to preserve the balance of "ideas and fun," to remember "ultimates" as well as "immediates."[10]

[7]President's Report, 5th Convention Workers Education Bureau, 1927, quoted in Mark Star, *Workers Education Today* (New York: League for Industrial Democracy, 1941), p. 3.

[8]Mary Richmond, "Some Next Steps in Social Treatment," *Proceedings of the National Conference of Social Work, 1920* (New York: Columbia University Press, 1939), p. 258.

[9]Mary Parker Follett, *The New State*, 4th ed. (New York: Longmans, Green and Co., Inc., 1934), p. 342.

[10]Mark Starr in Theodore Brameld, ed., *Workers Education in the United States*, Fifth Yearbook of the John Dewey Society (New York: Harper & Row, Pub., 1941), p. 91.

Workers Education utilized these concepts of the group work method: the "learning-by-doing," the "starting where the group is," and the use of informality. They clearly showed the influence of John Dewey.

Eduard C. Lindeman developed in his book, *The Community*,[11] the important technique of allowing conflict to come into the open in groups. Clara Kaiser offered the first course of group work in the School of Social Work at Western Reserve in Cleveland. When she left for New York in 1935, Grace Coyle continued to develop the course. It was taught partially as a method and partially as a field of practice.

Despite the fact that group work was taught early in a school of social work, its integration into the social work profession was not an easy one. Group work seemed like a foreign body in social work. Social work, after all, had grown out of the Charity Organization Societies, which were geared to the relationship of helper to the one being helped. They were proud of their highly formalized approach and of their new-found focus on the individual and the inner forces influencing the individual.

Group work, by contrast, grew out of neighborhood approaches and self-help movements. It considered informal relations one of its basic approaches. It focused strongly on group interaction and group strength. It hardly seemed concerned with individual dynamics, but was vitally concerned with environmental and social impact. Group work was also highly action-oriented, but was not well-developed as a conceptual system. It was only partially identified with the profession of social work, whose field of interest seemed, to group workers, too limited.

Group work in the years after the 1920s was developed mainly through increasingly conscious group efforts of people from different professions, especially education, psychology, and social work. In 1936 the American Association for the Study of Group Work was founded. Its aim was to "clarify and refine both the philosophy and the practice of group work."[12] Yet, as late as 1939, group work was treated as a separate subject at the National Conference of Social Work. Its relationship to the field and the profession of social work was still tenuous. Group workers still saw themselves as a separate profession, and social work could not yet envision the group approach as an integral part of its function. Mary Richmond's insight seemed to be forgotten, while Lindeman's words sounded like a plea:

> A group is a specific form of human interrelation, namely a collection of individuals who are experimenting for the purpose of determining whether their needs are more likely to be satisfied by means of collaboration than

[11]Eduard C. Lindeman, *The Community* (New York: Association Press, 1921).

[12]Harleigh B. Trecker, ed., *Group Work Foundations and Frontiers* (New York: Whiteside, Inc., 1955), p. 3.

through individual effort. I cannot see why, then, groups and group experiences do not stand at the very center of social work's concern.[13]

The period immediately preceding World War II and the war years themselves had a strong impact on the development of group work, and hastened its identification with the social work profession.

The advent of the Nazis in Germany emphasized the importance of a constant and conscious work for democracy, not only as a political form of government, but also as a way of life. Eduard C. Lindeman wrote in 1939:

> ... the roots of democratic culture do not lie in theories and conceptions, but rather in conduct, in experience and its satisfactions. If these roots do not strike deep into the "soil" of human personality, they will be easily destroyed by their external enemies, or they will wither away and die for want of nutriment and exercise. Whenever in history the people have thought and felt and lived democracy there has been cast upon human experience a sharp luminosity. Fears were dispelled and hopes renewed and, whenever in history tyranny and despotism have succeeded to power, human experience has been shadowed by suspicion, anger and bitterness.[14]

The shadows of fascist Germany intensified the light that those interested in group work had tried to shed on the importance of qualitative group life, which meant increased participation by citizens in community life; of strength that grows in the individual and in the group from the feeling of "self-help"; and of the need to work with intelligent leadership in all strata of the population and in all groups. On the other hand these shadows reminded people of the disastrous power of group associations and of the skilled misuse that could be made of them.

Unfortunately this awareness of the power of group association for negative purposes often has been forgotten and therefore has led to the misuse of group power, even by professionals. In the field of corrections especially, forms of practice were developed and given the deceptive title of "treatment." Such practices use the power of the group by simply coercing people in a most authoritarian way while allowing the person in power to pretend that he or she did not exercise undue mistreatment. They force group confrontation and give prisoners, for example, the license to select victims and demean them, all under the pretence of "group therapeutic pressure." Often the confrontations are only verbal, though even those "mangle the soul" as Fritz Redl called it. At times confrontations are translated into physical action. In one of the so-called treatment centers for

---

[13]Eduard C. Lindeman, "Group Work and Education for Democracy," *Proceedings of the National Conference of Social Work, 1939* (New York: Columbia University Press, 1939), p. 344.

[14]Eduard C. Lindeman, "The Roots of Democratic Culture," in Trecker, ed., *Group Work Foundations*, pp. 24–25.

adult offenders I visited, one of the major group sessions consisted of having a prisoner who had offended the group lie on the floor while the other prisoners held him down, forcing him to strain against them. The prisoners, including the selected offender, did this voluntarily. Group pressure—by people who have themselves little hold of their emotions—led to those practices. Shaming before a group and torture by groups to achieve conforming behavior are old practices and have been used in smaller and larger societal institutions for centuries. What is new, in this latter part of the twentieth century, is that it is labeled *therapy* or *treatment*. In the 1940s, fortunately, the knowledge of such misuse taught group workers, who at times had considered group activities a value in themselves, that these activities, too, could be used to enslave youth as well as to help them freely participate in a human society. It forced them to look deeper into human movement to learn about the unique forces within each individual and not to rely alone on programs and group process. The insanity that was gripping whole societies at this time seemed to bring about, among caseworkers, a greater appreciation of the group and, among group workers, a greater appreciation of individual dynamics.

There were other reasons for this rapprochement. War services, on the home front and in the armed forces, brought caseworkers and group workers together as practitioners on a larger scale than ever before. The psychiatric professions, which had strongly influenced social casework and which were accorded high status in the eyes of social caseworkers, began to experiment with groups as a therapeutic device. This in itself did not yet bring more appreciation of social group work, but the idea of using the group as a helping element did impress many.

Perhaps one must also mention the influence of refugees from central European countries on the use of group work for the purpose of therapy.[15] This author's first public presentation at the National Conference of Social Work dealt with this subject, and it was considered a new beginning.[16] A total misunderstanding following this paper was that I meant to say that one should only look at inner, psychiatric motives in human behavior.

Refugees came with a combined tradition of psychoanalytic thinking and group experiences that had been of deep significance to them; they

---

[15]See the works of such social workers as Morris F. Mayer, director of Bellefaire, an institution for disturbed children, who has written extensively on casework and institutions with much appreciation of the importance of group work; Henry Maier, who writes in the same field; Susanne Schulze, who emphasized group work and casework in the total child welfare field; Fritz Redl, who has strongly influenced development of group therapy; Bruno Bettelheim and his work with disturbed children; Walter A. Friedlander's sympathetic treatment of group work in his basic texts; and myself. This should not detract from the great or greater influence of American-born social workers in this same field (e.g., Samuel R. Slavson, Gertrude Wilson, Grace Coyle, Margaret Svendsen, or Raymond Fischer).

[16]See Frank Bruno, *Trends in Social Work as Reflected in the Proceedings of the National Conference: 1874-1946* (New York: Columbia University Press, 1948, p. 276.

had practiced in a milieu in which groups played an important part in education and therapy. Having grown up in an authoritarian family culture—and having resented it—they realized the significance of voluntary group participation to individual development. Psychoanalysis had neither the dramatic nor the exclusive impact on them that it frequently had on the person reared in a highly individualistic and puritan culture such as that of the United States. Analytic therapy was seen by many middle European refugees as only one form of treatment among others; it was to be used with discrimination. They had grown up with the beginnings of the psychoanalytic movement; they accepted the theory as valuable, but not as dogma. Added to this were their own painful experiences in Nazi Germany and Austria, which intensified their motivation to work on human relations.

For myself, if I represent at all—at least in some ways—this group of immigrants, I must say that my first encounter with social group work in 1941 was a revelation. Having just come from a society that seemed to present an inescapable gulf between the individual and the group—which insisted that the individual be sacrificed to the interests of the group—I found the concept of individualization in and through the group exhilarating. Sallie Bright, in 1948, called this "individual development within the group" the answer to a "national dilemma." She also saw in it the potential of a method to combine two purposes: the therapeutic goal of mental hygiene related to the individual, and the society-directed goal of keeping a democracy alive. In her own words:

> True, the settlement house group may not be able to affect the Turkey and Greece situation directly; but a democratic nation is the sum total of democratic neighborhoods and communities, and what you are doing in group work is to give people a chance to practice the methods of democracy in their own backyards. And, from a mental hygiene point of view in a frustrated nation, you are relieving the frustration of the citizen who can't make himself heard on a global scale by giving him a chance to make himself heard in the neighborhood. It is a thrilling thing to realize, then, that if the citizen can be heard in all the neighborhoods, his collective voice will, in the end, have global carrying power.[17]

This dual focus on democracy in action and mental health is very significant in the development of the group work method itself. It has led to controversy within the ranks of group work practitioners. Practitioners from the traditional field of informal education and recreation feared that the concern with mental hygiene and the focus on therapy would detract from the valuable use of the group work method to help with citizen action and services to normal youth. Actually, both foci were kept, even during

---

[17]Sallie E. Bright, "Letting the Public in on Group Work Objectives," in Trecker, ed., *Group Work Foundations,* p. 48.

the period when the healing power of the group was first recognized and used by social group workers. This occurred with sufficient emphasis in the late years of the 1930s. Papers on the use of the group work method for therapeutic purposes appeared in the *Proceedings of the National Conference of Social Welfare.*[18] The dual goal direction is symbolized by a paper presented by the author at the Annual Meeting of the American Orthopsychiatric Association and entitled, "Group Therapy in Overcoming Racial and Cultural Tensions."[19]

During the war years the members of the rapidly developing American Association for the Study of Group Work (AAGW) still hesitated to identify themselves with any specific profession. In 1940, William Heard Kilpatrick, the great educator and friend of John Dewey, wrote in a book published under the auspices of the AAGW:

> This group work is, however, not to be thought of as a separate field of work, but rather as a method to be used in all kinds of educational effort. "Group Work" in this sense is now more or less of a movement, and as such deserves support and success. But its success will be achieved when, and to the degree that, effective working in groups has established itself as an essential part of any adequate education of youth, however and wherever conducted.[20]

Kilpatrick thought that group work should be identified with the profession of education. Yet the agencies from which it had grown; the developments described on the preceding pages; the change in social work itself, which had moved away from its strong emphasis on psychiatry; and the fact that group work was taught in a few schools of social work identified it more closely with social work. Although it is almost impossible in the development of the method itself to name an individual who alone "invented" group work or to cite a certain point in history when it was first employed, the turning point in the identification of group work with social work can be dated and credited to a person. The date that is recognized is 1946; the person, Grace Longwell Coyle.

At the meeting of the National Conference of Social Work in Buffalo, New York, in 1946, the members of the AAGW met in the auditorium of

---

[18]See Gisela Konopka, "Therapy through Social Group Work," *Proceedings of the National Conference of Social Welfare* (New York: Columbia University Press, 1946), pp. 228–236; see also Samuel R. Slavson, "Group in Development and in Therapy," *Proceedings of the National Conference of Social Work, 1938* (New York: Columbia University Press, 1938), pp. 339–349.

[19]Gisela Konopka, "Group Therapy in Overcoming Racial and Cultural Tensions," *The American Journal of Orthopsychiatry*, XVII, No. 4 (Oct. 1947), 694–699; also in Arnold M. Rose, ed., *Race Prejudice and Discrimination* (New York: Borzoi Book, Knopf, 1951), pp. 565–572.

[20]William Heard Kilpatrick, *Group Education for a Democracy* (New York: Association Press, 1940), p. vii. The author became aware of this statement through an especially perceptive article dealing with the development of group work written by William Schwartz and entitled, "Group Work and the Social Scene," in Alfred J. Kahn, ed., *Issues in American Social Work* (New York: Columbia University Press, 1959), pp. 110–137.

the Kleinhaus Music Hall. It was only a year after the end of World War II. Hopes were high for a "new society" and civic responsibility was strongly felt. The audience listened to the "dean" of social group work, Grace Coyle, who had helped develop objectives and methods. Her subject was "On Becoming Professional." Her presentation was not concerned with the privileges or the status of a profession; rather, it was concerned with the responsibilities and the prerequisites of a professional endeavor. Her first sentences established the seriousness of such a claim:

> Within the ten years since the American Association for the Study of Group Work was born, there has been increasing evidence that group workers were coming to regard themselves as professional and that other groups were demanding of us the assumption of such responsibilities. As the founders of the organization will, I am sure, all agree, this was not our intention in the beginning. . . .[21]

She proceeded to discuss the attributes of a profession, each time evaluating with strict honesty whether group work came up to the required standard. She then entered the controversial discussion of group work's alignment:

> One baffling problem has plagued the development of professional consciousness among group workers over this decade. It is usually phrased in terms of alignment, and a dilemma is presented. We must, it seems, be either educators or social workers. . . .[22]

She discussed the great variety of agencies grouped under health and welfare services. They were more or less bound to social work through tradition. She continued:

> A large part of our difficulty in knowing what we are has come out of the words "social work." To many people they connote relief, or dealing with the poor, or uplift, or some other unpleasant facet of life. We need to realize that not only we but other people are changing. . . . My own hope is that the emerging definition of social work may define it as involving the conscious use of social relations in performing certain community functions, such as child welfare, family welfare or health services, recreation and informal education. Casework, group work, and community organization have this common factor, that they are all based on understanding human relations. While the specific relations used in each are different, the underlying philosophy and approach are the same: a respect for personality and a belief in democracy. This we share with caseworkers and expert community organization people. It is for this reason that I believe group work as a method falls within the larger scope of social work *as a method* and as defined above.[23]

[21]Grace L. Coyle, "On Becoming Professional," in Trecker, ed., *Group Work Foundations*, p. 328.

[22]Ibid., p. 338.

[23]Ibid., pp. 339–340.

When the assembly accepted this reasoning and decided to become a professional membership organization, group work entered the family of social work. This process was finalized in 1955 when the AAGW joined the newly formed National Association of Social Workers.

One of the insights gained from work with groups is that any person entering a group constellation changes through his or her interaction with others; conversely, the given group changes in turn by the entrance of a new member. The same happens in the realm of ideas and organizations. Social group work changed through its close association with the profession of social work and also with the older method, social casework. In turn, it changed the profession and widened the concept of the social welfare field. It took insight and certain concepts from the earlier method and added concepts and approaches, not only to the total profession of social work but also to the practice of casework. The trend toward a more aggressive and more outgoing approach in casework is related, for example, to the original, more informal, and neighborhood-related practice of group work, while the more conscious purposefulness seen in modern group work practice is influenced by the clear and more formalized approach of social casework. (Caseworkers and group workers do not always credit each other for the help they gain from each other. Sibling rivalry also exists in the realm of ideas.)

With the new concept of group work as a *method of social work,* the integrative process had only begun. The years after World War II placed demands on the development of the method through actual practice and through better conceptualization and formulation of theory. The process is in no way finished. The years after the war saw an immense rise in group work literature.[24] Gertrude Wilson's *Social Group Work Practice* (1949), Harleigh B. Trecker's *Social Group Work* (1949), Grace Coyle's *Group Work with American Youth* (1948), and Gisela Konopka's *Therapeutic Group Work with Children* (1949) appeared in a time span of only two years. These books all made the attempt to clarify the orderly process of social group work as part of the helping function of social work on the wide scale from healthy to sick individuals and groups. Definitions were sought for, but not easily formulated. In 1949 a committee of the AAGW published a report entitled "Definition of the Function of the Group Worker." To define the method alone seemed to be too difficult. The report showed the interrelation of goal, function, method, and required underlying knowledge. It was for years the official definition of group work. Though loosely conceived, it did show many concepts that are worked out more thoroughly today. It is therefore reproduced here:

[24]This writer studied social work with a specialization in social group work during the war years, 1941–1943. At that time no textbook in group work was available; in fact, most of the literature consisted of articles.

The Group Worker enables various types of groups to function in such a way that both group interaction and program activities contribute to the growth of the individual, and the achievement of desirable social goals.

The objectives of the group worker include provision for personal growth according to individual capacity and need, the adjustment of the individual to other persons, to groups and to society, and the motivation of the individual toward the improvement of society; the recognition by the individual of his own rights, abilities, and differences of others.

Through his participation the group worker aims to effect the group process so that decisions come about as a result of knowledge and a sharing and integration of ideas, experiences and knowledge, rather than as a result of domination from within or without the group.

Through experience he aims to produce those relations with other groups and the wider community which contribute to responsible citizenship, mutual understanding between cultural, religious, economic or special groupings in the community, and a participation in the constant improvement of our society toward democratic goals.

The guiding purpose behind such leadership rests upon the common assumptions of a democratic society; namely, the opportunity for each individual to fulfill his capacities in freedom, to respect and appreciate others and to assume his social responsibility in maintaining and constantly improving our democratic society.

Underlying the practice of group work is a knowledge of individual and group behavior and of social conditions and community relations which is based on the modern social sciences.

On the basis of this knowledge the group worker contributes to the group with which he works a skill in leadership which enables the members to use their capacities to the full and to create socially constructive group activities.

He is aware of both program activities and of the interplay of personalities, within the group and between the group and its surrounding community.

According to the interests and needs of each, he assists them to get from the group experience the satisfactions provided by the program activities, the enjoyment and personal growth available through the social relations, and the opportunity to participate as a responsible citizen.

The group worker makes conscious use of his relation to the group, his knowledge of program as a tool, and his understanding of the individual and of the group process, and recognizes his responsibility both to individuals and groups with whom he works and the larger social values he represents.[25]

Another committee of the AAGW worked on the new relationship to therapeutic services. Its work deepened the concept of group work as a method to be used in many different agencies if it was used purposefully and with increased skill in diagnostic thinking about individuals and their situations. Its final report strengthened the bond with the entire profession of social work and prevented the danger of creating a hierarchy in the use of the method according to the function it had to fulfill. The statement, as presented by Gisela Konopka, the committee's chairperson read:

[25]Trecker, ed., *Group Work Foundations*, pp. 4–5.

The word "psychiatric" has taken on prestige value in social work for a long time though pioneers in psychiatric casework have fought this for years. Helen Perlman said that it is not "frosting on the cake." Ethel Ginsburg said, "In our simple-minded fashion, we try to explain that the 'psychiatric' in psychiatric social work does not mean that we know more psychodynamics than the other fellow. It just means that we know how to work as social workers in a psychiatric setting with psychiatric patients and their relatives, as partners in a team."

And I repeat here Grace Weyker's statement that we presented at the meeting last year when our committee on similarities and differences between group work and group therapy made the first statement.

"Psychiatric social work has gone through a series of stages which might be listed as (1) early recognition of a distinct self, (2) the play-by-myself age, and (3) the know-all, superior age. It seems to me that psychiatric social work should now be ready to enter a fourth stage, to be a stable adult member of the social work family. Probably one of the biggest blocks to such adult stability for psychiatric social work is confusion over the label. Much of this confusion is tied in with a mistaken connotation of glamor or superiority which has been accepted tacitly among groups who should know better.

"Psychiatric social work according to the official and accepted definition is simply 'social work practiced in direct and responsible relationship to psychiatry.' Part of the misunderstanding of psychiatric social work lies in the area that a psychiatric social worker has some peculiar skill in working with people or understanding the dynamics of behavior. This should not be true. Certainly any social work training which aims to prepare people for casework or group work cannot be considered satisfactory if it does not include this understanding of behavior. Certainly the entire field of social work has taken over from psychiatry a great many concepts regarding personality development and causation in behavior. In other words, it would seem obvious that any practice of social case work or social group work would require a psychodynamically oriented social worker.

"A concept that met general approval was that psychiatric social work requires all of the equipment of the social worker and in addition, (1) a deepened knowledge of psychopathology and of the various settings in which mental and emotional disorders may be treated, and (2) a clear delineation of the social worker's place in and contribution to, the collaborative treatment of a clinical team. . . ."

We defined psychiatric group work or therapeutic group work as "the use of the social group work method in working with groups of patients in a psychiatric setting." In casework this is often designated as "casework in a foreign setting" and this applies to group work too. It was underlined that in such a setting the group worker is part of the psychiatric team and the responsibility is a medical-psychiatric one under guidance of the psychiatrist. In the general group work setting the group worker is primarily responsible for the work done. Much of what he does is also therapeutic.

*Knowledge Needed:* Both general group work and psychiatric group work are a social work method of working with people in groups. Basic to both of them are understanding and skill in working with individuals in groups.

*Goal:* Goal of the general group worker is the adjustment of the individual to the group and the group as a whole to society. Its focus is an educational, socializing, democratic one—and is on individual growth *through* group growth. Psychiatric group work has the same goal of adjustment of the individual. Focus is on helping the individual move toward health and emotional development.

*Diagnosis:* Both are concerned with recognition of sickness and strength in the individual.

*Role of the Worker:* The general group worker moves from the central role as soon as possible, enabling the group to determine its own goals and leadership. The psychiatric group worker is the central figure in the group, often assuming the role of mother- or father-figure. He may always remain in this role.

*Impact of Social Values on the Role of the Worker:* The group worker in the general setting as well as in the psychiatric setting deals with social values. Yet a neighborhood group will be more influenced by neighborhood status values than a group in a psychiatric setting. The difference again is more and less, not in terms of not at all. One of the values of the group in a psychiatric setting is the possibility for the member to get away from established status situations and to start comparatively as a "blank" in relation to others.

In the general group setting the group worker has also a greater educational responsibility in terms of social values.

*Type of Group:* The group worker in the general setting works with formed or natural groups. The psychiatric group worker always works with formed groups.

*Grouping:* In general group work the agency determines groupings in relation to social goals and individual preferences. In psychiatric group work grouping is an important factor in helping the individual. The agency[26] determines and controls groupings on the basis of individual therapy needs only.

*Duration of Groups:* In general group work the group worker may work with a group over a long span of time helping the individuals and the group move into different projects and relationships according to their changing age group. In psychiatric group work the time limit is set in relation to the therapeutic goal determined by the psychiatrist and the rest of the team.[27]

While the impact of psychoanalysis on social work had been strong after World War I, group work accepted its insights somewhat critically and tempered them—partly because it entered the social work family at a time when psychoanalytic thinking had begun to change and partly because the underlying concepts of group work were derived from such early sociologists as Simmel and Weber.

The postwar years showed a great increase in research in small group behavior done mostly by representatives of a new specialization, social psychology. New insights also came from the field of cultural anthropology. These developments helped strengthen the integration of knowledge (which we will discuss in a following chapter); they also hindered the development of the group work method through the unfortunate phenome-

---

[26]The committee meant hospitals or child guidance clinics, although it was not spelled out in the original report.

[27]Gisela Konopka, "Similarities and Differences between Group Work and Group Therapy," Report of the Group Therapy Committee, A.A.G.W., mimeographed, ST-451-8, undated; also in *Selected Papers of the National Conference of Social Welfare,* 1951, pp. 51-60.

non of "fadism" in our society. *Group dynamics*, misunderstod as a form of method instead of "the study of forces underlying the behavior of groups," as clearly stated by one of its foremost experts,[28] became a mechanistic device in working with groups. In general, however, this development in the social sciences enriched group work and ultimately all social work, as seen in the Curriculum Study of the Council on Social Work Education.[29] Louis Towley foresaw this trend when he wrote:

> ... Then came a dynamic kind of sociology—anthropology: the concept of status, role, casts, and pattern, and the influence of the situation on conduct. Social group work responded to these sympathetic, explanatory, group-rooted ideas. Many workers shared Cohen's belief that the social group work field is closer to these developments than is casework and therefore should bring the ideas to social work as a whole.[30]

The historical development of an approach to one of the basic problems of human society—such as relationships among people and their individual development over such a comparatively short period of time—cannot yet produce agreement among all those who practice group work. In her volume on the curriculum study, published in 1959, Marjorie Murphy tried to summarize some generalizations on social group work on which there is agreement at the present time. I will present only the first three points:

1.  Social group work is a method of rendering service to persons, through providing experience in groups. Development of the person towards his individual potential, improvement of relationship and social functioning competencies, and social action are recognized as purposes of social group work. The worker functions within a framework of ethical and social values.
2.  Social group work is a generic method which can be used in different settings.
3.  The method includes conscious use of worker-member relationships, relationships among members, and of group activity. The worker simultaneously uses relationships with individual members and with the group as a whole. He works as an enabler with both, helping members and the group to use their capacities and strengths. He uses himself differently in accordance with specific objectives and his assessment of members' needs, interests and capacities.[31]

And, as previously stated, there is agreement that group work is a method of social work. Method is an orderly way to achieve an objective.

---

[28]Leon Festinger, "Current Developments in Group Dynamics," mimeographed, undated, New York: A.A.G.W., p. 1.

[29]Werner W. Boehm, Director and Coordinator, *A Project Report of the Curriculum Study,* Vols. I–XIII (New York: Council on Social Work Education, 1959).

[30]Bruno (with chapters by Louis Towley), *Trends in Social Work,* pp. 426–427.

[31]Murphy, "The Social Group Work Method ... ," *A Project Report of the Curriculum Study,* p. 78.

Social work methods are helping processes. They cannot be separated from the function the profession as a whole sees as its own; from the specific purpose to be achieved in each case, whether individual or group; from the deep understanding of the one who needs help; from an understanding of oneself; and from the total ethos and value base of the profession.

A helping method cannot be mechanical. It is the heart of the profession because only its competent use can truly fulfill the ends for which a humanitarian profession stands. For example, preventing recidivism among criminals may be a goal. The *way in which it is done* determines whether one follows the precepts of a humanitarian profession or those of another value system. One can, for example, shoot the offender or cut off his hand, certainly ways to achieve the goal of "preventing recidivism." The example is used to show the intricate and inseparable relationship between goal, function, philosophy, and method. This makes the use of the group work method a professional effort, which includes knowledge and judgment. It cannot be used mechanistically. There have been voices raised that social work should consider the goals more and should forget about methods. Yet one cannot supersede the other. Practice is the heart of the social work profession and this necessitates the use of a method congruent with the ends. No one said it better than Gandhi:

> ... The means may be likened to a seed, the end to a tree; and there is just the same inviolable connection between the means and the end as there is between the seed and the tree....[32]

We traced the historical development of the concept of social group work and saw it change from the designation of a field, a movement, a goal to a social work method, part of the "means" of social work. To understand it today, we must therefore understand the goal and its function in society as part of the function of the total social work profession. Beyond understanding group work as a social work method, the tenor of the 1960s and 1970s with the clamor for putting professed values of respect for human beings into practice, with the increased emphasis placed, especially by young people, on mutual help, less competition, and learning by doing and experiencing, group work re-enters the wider fields of education, community developments, and youth work. It seemed that group work was no longer exclusively affiliated with social work and that it was becoming a legitimate method in other helping, educational, therapeutic, and general human relations professions. This must be emphasized. In the ten years following the "youth revolt" and a heightened social consciousness regarding the poor and minorities, group workers were deeply involved in the movements of their time. It has become far more accepted, following this

---

[32]Gandhi in Rudolph Flesch, ed., *The Book of Unusual Quotations* (New York: Harper & Row, Pub., 1957), p. 167.

period, that human beings of all ages need support groups for individual help, for educational purposes as well as for social action. Group work has spread without being always designated as such, but social work professionals frequently have not seen this. In 1979, at a meeting in Cleveland on Perspectives on Group Work, I stated:

> I have to say that many hopes I had for the social group work method were fulfilled. I think, though, today, that the affiliation with social work with which I agreed at the given time, probably was a mistake. The roots of social work are too closely anchored in authoritarian and bureaucratic historical developments. The acceptance of something as revolutionary as social group work was too hard for this profession. It was well recognized in the Settlement Movement, youth-serving agencies, and later in mental health, corrections and community development. Yet, as a whole, the social work profession wanted its practitioners to be totally "in charge." This prevented the profession, and especially its educational establishment, from giving fullest recognition to social group work—certainly always with exceptions. Possibly social group work needs to be part of many professions, such as education, social work, nursing, psychology, psychiatry, political science, etc.

Group work, as defined throughout this book, should help to humanize services. It is a method of social work that helps persons to enhance their social functioning through purposeful group experiences and to cope more effectively with their personal, group, or community problems. I do not conceive of it as an empty technique or a gimmick to make people do what some "superior" person has decided for them. Group work is a method based on the premise of the dignity of each individual.

## *BIBLIOGRAPHY*

BRIGHT, SALLIE E.,   "Letting the Public in on Group Work Objectives," in Harleigh B. Trecker, ed., *Group Work—Foundations and Frontiers,* pp. 35–49. New York: Whiteside, Inc., 1955.

BRUNO, FRANK J.,   *Trends in Social Work 1874–1956.* New York: Columbia University Press, 1957.

COHEN, NATHAN E.,   *Social Work in the American Tradition,* pp. 10–13; 144–145; 189–193. New York: The Dryden Press, 1958.

COYLE, GRACE L.,   "On Becoming Professional," in Trecker, ed., *Group Work—Foundations and Frontiers,* pp. 328–342.

——————,   "Social Group Work," *Social Work Year Book, 1954,* pp. 480–486. New York: American Association of Social Workers, 1954.

FINK, ARTHUR E., EVERETT E. WILSON, and MERRILL B. CONOVER,   *The Field of Social Work,* (3rd ed.), pp. 500–528. New York: Holt, Rinehart & Winston, 1942.

FOLLETT, MARY PARKER,   *The New State* (4th ed.). New York: Longmans, Green, 1934.

FREUD, SIGMUND,   *A General Introduction to Psychoanalysis,* English translation by Joan Riviere. New York: Liveright, 1935.

HENDRY, CHARLES E., ed.,    *Decade of Group Work.* New York: Association Press, 1948.

KAISER, CLARA A.,    "The Advance of Social Group Work," *Social Welfare Forum 1955*, pp. 35-47. New York: Columbia University Press, 1955.

——————, "Group Work Education in the Last Decade," *The Group*, XV, No. 5 (June 1953), 3-10; 27-29.

KLEIN, ALAN F.,    *Social Work Through Group Process.* School of Social Welfare, State University of New York at Albany, 1970.

KONOPKA, GISELA,    *Eduard C. Lindeman and Social Work Philosophy.* Minneapolis: University of Minnesota Press, 1958.

——————, "Group Therapy in Overcoming Racial and Cultural Tensions," *The American Journal of Orthopsychiatry*, XVII, No. 4 (Oct. 1947), 694-699.

——————, "Group Work: A Heritage and a Challenge," *Social Work with Groups 1960*, pp. 7-21. New York: N.A.S.W., 1960.

——————, "Group Work with Adolescents," *Mental Health in Virginia*, 16, No. 4 (Summer 1966), 5-12.

——————, "Knowledge and Skill of the Group Therapist," see "Group Therapy," Round Table 1948, Harry M. Little, Chairman, *American Journal of Orthopsychiatry*, XIX, No. 1 (Jan. 1949), 56-60.

——————, "Social Work as an Active Cultural Change Agent," *Proceedings of the Minnesota Academy of Science*, Vol. 28 (Nov. 1960), 146-152.

KUNSTLER, PETER,    *Social Work in Great Britain.* London: Faber and Faber, 1955.

LIEBERMAN, JOSHUA, ed.,    *New Trends in Group Work.* New York: Association Press, 1938.

LINDEMAN, EDUARD C.,    "Group Work and Education for Democracy," *Proceedings of the National Conference of Social Work*, 1939, pp. 342-347. New York: Columbia University Press, 1939.

——————, "The Roots of Democratic Culture," in Harleigh B. Trecker, ed., *Group Work—Foundations and Frontiers*, pp. 13-25.

MALONEY, SARA E. and MARGARET H. MUDGETT,    "Group Work—Group Casework: Are They the Same?" *Social Work*, 4, No. 2 (Apr. 1959), 29-36.

MURPHY, MARJORIE,    *The Social Group Work Method in Social Work Education*, Vol. XI, *A Project Report of the Curriculum Study*, Werner W. Boehm, Director and Coordinator. New York: Council on Social Work Education, 1959.

NORTHEN, HELEN,    *Social Work With Groups.* New York: Columbia University Press, 1969.

PERLMAN, HELEN HARRIS,    *Social Case Work.* Chicago: University of Chicago Press, C. 1957.

PHILLIPS, HELEN U.,    *Essentials of Social Group Work Skill.* New York: Association Press, 1957.

RICHMOND, MARY,    "Some Next Steps in Social Treatment," *Proceedings of the National Conference of Social Work*, 1920, pp. 254-258. New York: Columbia University Press, 1939.

SCHWARTZ, WILLIAM,    "Group Work and the Social Scene," in Alfred J. Kahn, ed., *Issues in American Social Work*, pp. 110-137. New York: Columbia University Press, 1959.

——————, "The Social Worker In the Group," *New Perspectives on Services to Groups*, p. 17. New York: N.A.S.W., 1961.

SLAVSON, SAMUEL R.,    "Group in Development and in Therapy," *Proceedings of the National Conference of Social Work*, 1938, pp. 339-349. New York: Columbia University Press, 1938.

TRECKER, HARLEIGH B., *Social Group Work: Principles and Practices* (rev. ed.). New York: Whiteside, Inc., 1955.

WHITTAKER, JAMES K., "Models of Group Development: Implications for Social Group Work Practice," *Social Service Review,* 44, No. 3 (Sept. 1970), 308–322.

WILSON, GERTRUDE, *Group Work and Case Work—Their Relationship and Practice.* New York: Family Welfare Association of America, 1941.

_____, "Social Group Work—Trends and Developments," *Social Work,* 1, No. 4 (Oct. 1956), 66–75.

WILSON, GERTRUDE and GLADYS RYLAND, *Social Group Work Practice: The Creative Use of the Social Process.* Boston: Houghton Mifflin, 1949.

WOODS, ROBERT A., *The Neighborhood in Nation Building.* Boston: Houghton Mifflin, 1923.

*... that the conception of the field of social work should above all be kept fluid in order to maintain in this profession at least an open mind toward humanity's changing needs and the best methods for meeting them.*[1]

# TWO
# SOCIAL GROUP WORK AS A PART OF SOCIAL WORK

Social group work is today very necessary in a variety of professional endeavors, but in this chapter we will focus on it only as part of social work. In the course of history the term *social work* has meant a type of service, a certain function to fulfill, a method of practice, and a profession. Today we conceive it to be a profession, just as we consider teaching or medicine. It is practiced in the large field of social welfare, which encompasses all services whose defined social goal is to promote the social welfare of individuals and groups in the community. These services include, among others, public education, hospitals, and playgrounds, and they all require the skills of many different professions.

[1]James H. Tufts, *Education and Training for Social Work* (New York: Russell Sage Foundation, 1923), pp. 30–31.

The particular functions of these different professions are determined by the role society has ascribed to them, and they alter with the passage of time. We can see this in the profession of teaching, which has widened its function since the time it was limited to the teaching of simple skills such as reading and writing. It also has different functions in different societies; it varies according to the development and the culture of a given society. Teaching has broadened its scope from the education of a few belonging to the clergy and the nobility in the Middle Ages to virtually every member of society in modern-day America. Social work too has changed its function during the course of history. It started with almsgiving (a function seen as its sole or major purpose in only a few societies at the present time). Today it serves all people regardless of their social or economic status and works on a wide variety of individual, group, and community problems. The common purpose is "help with social functioning." Admittedly this encompasses a wide area of human behavior, but no wider than "physical functioning," which has been for a long time the main concern of the medical profession. Without question this social work function overlaps in part with the function of other professions.

In the complicated web of human society many efforts have been and are being made to replace its defective fibers. They are made to improve the environment as well as to help the individual. As long as human beings have existed, they have been striving to understand and master nature and to improve the relationship among all members of the human race. These goals include the efforts of the common laborer, the artisan, and the highly trained professional. The more complicated a society becomes, the more these efforts are separated according to the specific function they have to fulfill as well as according to the skill needed to fulfill them. They become increasingly specialized. In our present society each individual who is gainfully employed carries out a specialized function during working hours. Yet, outside of these hours the individual engages in a large, undifferentiated range of human efforts and skills in the roles of parent, friend, and citizen in a democratic society. As a parent or friend a person is physician, nurse, teacher, social worker, dressmaker, laborer, counselor, typist, baker, cook, and so on. As a citizen in a democratic society, he or she is also legislator and policy-maker. Any vocation or profession utilizes only a few of the functions that every human being can and must fulfill. It refines skill; it adds and uses specific knowledge. This applies to dressmaking and cooking as well as to nursing the sick, teaching the young, and helping the distressed. Every profession, therefore, must by necessity overlap at points with other professions and it *always* overlaps with certain functions every human being does. For far too long this has been of concern to the profession of social work as if it were something that should not be. Too often social workers were worried lest their functions were also carried out by others. This should not concern us. What social work has to offer—and this is true of every other profession—is specific knowledge and skill to be employed in one of the many areas other people are also concerned with.

Even if we do not concern ourselves with these gray areas of overlapping responsibilities, we must establish the core function of social work, and derive from this the goal of each individual effort in the profession. Otherwise the discussion of method is futile. Since method is an orderly way of procedure, it must have a specific aim. For a long time that aim was expressed in agency efforts, described, for example, as "giving relief" or "preventing juvenile delinquency" or "providing services to youth." Yet each of these goals involves the services of many professions. It is not easy to determine this core function. Herman D. Stein, professor of the New York School of Social Work, hastened to state in an address given at the Annual Forum of the National Conference of Social Welfare in 1961:

> I do not have the temerity nor the slightest intention of attempting to answer the question "What is the function of social work?" but will continue the process of addressing this central and never-ending question for our profession.[2]

The words of Dr. Tufts, written in 1923 and quoted at the beginning of this chapter, warn against a too early or too narrow definition. Early definitions, sometimes still used today, are often too limited.

The social worker is expected by society to be able (1) to assess, clarify, and help individuals with the integration of their inner motives and the demands of their social environment, and (2) to help change social environment if it is detrimental to the social development of individuals. This is a far cry and quite different from an earlier concept of "social adjustment," which implied conformity and submission to any demand of the social environment—a concept that stigmatized the social work profession as primarily an effort to maintain the "status quo," contrary to its tradition of social reform. What it does mean is the assessment of individuals, their capacities and motivations as well as their environment, and helping with acceptance or change of one or the other, depending on who or what needs help. To repeat: Professional responsibilities always overlap at the outer edges. Their core practice, task, or function differs.

Two basic needs of the human being—besides the physical one of survival—are the needs for self-respect and for belonging, which is the acceptance of the "I" and the "you" and the finding of the bridge between these two. Only in this way can a person live up to his or her greatest potential and make contributions to an imperfect society within the limita-

[2]Herman D. Stein, "Observations of the Function of Social Work: A Discussion Based on Dr. De Jongh's Paper at the International Conference of Social Work in Rome," Jan. 1961, p. 1, mimeographed. (Published version of this paper, contained in *Community Organization,* 1961, published in New York by Columbia University Press, 1961, does not contain this quotation.)

tions of the individual's particular capacity. This means the development of many capacities: the capacity to fulfill different tasks at different stages of development; to learn to accept frustration or to deal with it in a constructive way; to postpone gratification—a difficult art; to express anger and fear, yet to express them in a way that does no harm to others or to oneself; to be able to work and play; to think and feel; and, above all, to love and to accept love. These capacities are all learned only in interaction with others. In a healthy community they are learned naturally in the family and through relations with neighbors and friends. Yet modern society is complex. The demands of the social environment bring many problems: increasing loneliness produced in large urban centers, greater mobility that does not always allow easy access to friendship ("What is the use of making friends?" a teen-ager said. "Whenever we are close to someone, they move or we do!"). People must learn new skills: to make new friendships quickly; to deepen the ones already formed, and to bear the frustration of loss; to meet the members of groups that look at each other with suspicion—racial, religious, or nationality groups; to cope with economic deprivation, which means not only having no money but also experiencing the agonies of failure and bitterness; to cope with marital problems; to accept and adjust to the fast pace of modern life with the resultant gaps of misunderstanding between generations; to maintain the wish to succeed, but also to know the limits placed upon each person by both internal and external factors; and much more. Sometimes these problems too can be worked out with the assistance of neighbors and friends. Often they need the help of the social worker, who will not always do the work alone, but might skillfully enlist the aid of members of the community. Social group work services therefore cover the wide range from individual to community problems, from working with healthy, capable leadership to working with the sick and rejected. Werner Boehm, in his *Curriculum Study,* classified the tasks of social work under "restoration" (work with a breakdown, either of an individual or a group or community), "prevention," and "provision of services," an indication of the widened range of social work functions.

The *group work method* is one of several methods used to fulfill social work functions whenever its particular approach is most appropriate. The matrix of the group work situation is the *group,* individuals in interaction. This differentiates the specific helping process from that of casework, another basic social work method. Helen Perlman designated the components of the casework situation as the *Person,* the *Problem,* and the *Place.* The group work situation is more complex: its components are the *Person in the Group,* the *Group,* the *Problem*—sometimes of this particular person, sometimes of the particular group, sometimes of the total community—and the *Place.*

This complex situation includes also diverse "points of entry" of group work services:

1.  Individuals in distress ask for help or are referred to group work services because of their problems. We find this in family services, mental health services, school social work, corrections, agencies working with the handicapped, and others.
2.  Groups ask for help to better fulfill their members' needs and purposes. Such situations include groups discriminated against in the community, parents' groups concerned with the upbringing of their children, and community service and action groups wanting to find better solutions to community problems.
3.  There is no specific request for help, either by a group or an individual, but the community as a whole has recognized needs for services to either prevent problems or promote a healthy group life. Examples of this are group work with street corner gangs, and youth work, which helps children and young people with their developmental tasks. It includes also the still neglected services to people (children and adults) in institutions.

Overlapping functions with other professions have led to confusion in terminology and have, in turn, influenced group work practice. The most significant example of this is the confusion and conflict around the terms of *group work* and *group therapy*. They need clarification as part of the discussion of the function of social group work.

There are a few representatives of social work who use the term group work as a synonym for "recreation" or "informal education." For them, the terms group work and group therapy are completely separated, since they believe that group work is exclusively concerned with the leisure time needs of healthy children and adults. This concept of group work has practically disappeared. It is today a method of social work with its threefold functions, previously mentioned. Recreation and education are seen as fields of service in which group workers function as social workers with their group work skill.

If we therefore eliminate the outdated concept of group work as equaling recreation, the confusion between the terms group work and group therapy needs serious consideration. The following is an attempt at clarification:

Among board members of the American Association for Orthopsychiatry in which the major professions of the psychiatric team are represented (i.e., psychiatry, psychology, and social work), it was for a time a joke to suggest that a meeting should be held regarding "Who does What to Whom and Why and When" because of differences of opinion over who is qualified to perform what therapeutic duties. There is confusion also in terminology pertaining to individual treatment, as seen in the interchangeable use of "casework treatment," "casework therapy," "therapy," "treatment," and "counseling." Yet this is multiplied when it comes to work with groups. The cause of this may be due to the more recent success of group work as a method for therapeutic treatment after many years of being considered an inferior tool by the helping professions—including social work. Corsini wrote that these group methods represent "a revolution in psychotherapy and may well be the answer for some up-to-now unsolved problems, . . ."[3]

Yet which group methods are we talking about? What is the definition? *Social group work,* as presented in this book, is a method of social work which helps persons to enhance their social functioning through purposeful group experiences and to cope more effectively with their personal, group, or community problems. This means that it is based on the competence a social worker develops in his training and education and that it is concerned with mental health and social problems. Its beneficiaries are both the sick and the healthy. The agencies in which it is practiced span the wide arc of health, education, welfare, and other community organizations. Its specific means and approaches will be discussed in detail in the following chapters.

What, then, does group therapy mean? Corsini, who has given us one of the most comprehensive and clear presentations of the whole complex question of group therapy, starts out by confronting the reader of his book on *Methods of Group Psychotherapy* with the fact that there exists no simple, inclusive and yet exclusive definition. He states:

> What contributes to the confusion is that the term group psychotherapy[4] may be used in two specific ways. It may be thought of as a generic term, encompassing a variety of procedures. It may also be thought of as a name for a single procedure. If by group psychotherapy therapist A means method X and if therapist B understands that group psychotherapy means method Y, then it is obvious that the two are not communicating. The complexity of this problem becomes evident when it is realized that more than 25 specific methods have been described in the literature.[5]

Corsini points out that definitions can be too wide or too narrow. An example of the former is a statement he quotes from a War Department bulletin:

> In a broad sense any procedure which tends to improve the mental health of more than one individual is group psychotherapy.[6]

And the example of a too narrow one is, according to Corsini, this remark made by one of his colleagues:

---

[3]Raymond J. Corsini, *Methods of Group Psychotherapy* (New York: McGraw-Hill, 1957), p. 3.

[4]Corsini uses this term interchangeably with group therapy. This is frequently done in the literature.

[5]Corsini, *Methods of Group Psychotherapy,* p. 4.

[6]Ibid.

This is not group psychotherapy, because the members do not sit in a circle and talk.[7]

Corsini's own definition is more inclusive and more precise:

Group psychotherapy consists of processes occurring in formally organized, protected groups and calculated to attain rapid ameliorations in personality and behavior of individual members through specified and controlled group interactions.[8]

One edition of the *Journal of Social Issues* was devoted exclusively to group methods in psychotherapy, social work, and adult education; in it, Jerome D. Frank gave his definition of group therapy. It is a fairly elaborate explanation:

The term group therapy refers to all methods of treating psychiatric patients in groups under the leadership of a psychotherapist. Therapeutic groups may consist of children, adolescents or adults in or out of institutions who are in emotional distress presumably arising in large part from chronic disturbances in their relationships with other people. The goal of these groups is to ameliorate the suffering and improve the personal and social functioning of their members. The means to this goal are the emotional interactions of the members with the leader and each other. . . .[9]

If we compare the two definitions, we find that neither confines group therapy to the method of one profession alone, but leaves it open as to what kind of professional shall conduct the groups. They both stress the purposefulness of the action and the goal of amelioration of suffering or stress in individuals. Frank adds "social functioning" as a goal, but this may also be implied in Corsini's definition without being specified. The only difference between the two may lie—although this is not necessarily so—in some differentiation of clientele. Jerome Frank limits group therapy to psychiatric patients, while Corsini includes an apparently wider group.

If we compare these two definitions with the one used for social group work, we realize that group work practice directed toward groups with emotional or mental problems would fall within the same definition. The difference lies only in the fact that group work is also concerned with groups consisting of healthy individuals and with social action groups.

In recent years, two other attempts have been made to delineate and clarify terms that designate group treatment. Both show that practice of group work and group therapy are difficult to sort out. Differences are

[7]Ibid.
[8]Ibid.
[9]Jerome D. Frank, "Group Methods in Psychotherapy," *Journal of Social Issues*, VIII, No. 2 (1952), 35.

seen mostly in fields in which the methods are practiced, but in recent years these two overlap frequently. For example, group work—as well as group therapy—is practiced in psychiatric hospitals.[10]

The logical conclusion seems to be that the terms used for purposeful use of the group are interchangeable, as long as the purpose includes—as Fritz Redl said once in a letter to the author—"a repair job"; that means some help with emotional or mental problems. That would mean *group therapy* is practice which is aimed at ameliorating suffering and improving the personal and social functioning of its members through specified and controlled group interaction aided by a professional person. This definition of the term group therapy does not limit it to any specific professional identification, nor to adherence to a certain technique. It includes aim and function. This is in accordance with the thinking of Corsini and Spotnitz. This is also the way the public understands the term group therapy. Group work practice, therefore, when directed toward amelioration of personal and social functioning, may rightfully be called group therapy.

This does not mean, however, that the practice of the social group worker will be or should be the same as the practice of the psychiatrist. Corsini speaks about the fact that therapist A may mean a certain method X and therapist B, another method Y. These differences in group therapy methods occur within the same profession, according to differing theories or assumptions. Beyond this there is a difference in method related to the professional background of the group therapist. Ethics and professional discipline require the therapist to stay within the framework of his or her own competence.

Increasingly, knowledge of individual dynamics and group process becomes common knowledge for several professions, yet in differing degrees and appropriate to their own tasks. The social worker, for example, learns them in the context of reality interactions, of cultural background and economic conditions; the psychiatrist learns about them in the context of medical knowledge and pathology. The twentieth century is caught in a dilemma. On the one hand, all sciences are becoming more and more aware of their interrelatedness, a trend requiring more people with broad, general knowledge. But on the other hand, since knowledge in each field of science has increased tremendously, more specialization and scientists with more specialized knowledge are required within each field. The only answer is close teamwork. It is the purpose of team members to supplement one another and to constantly learn from each other. In group therapy each practitioner must realize that this method requires a certain tolerance

---

[10]See *Journal of Social Issues* mentioned above; see also Philip Zlatchin, Clara A. Kaiser, and Saul Scheidlinger, "The Group in Education, Group Work and Psychotherapy," Round Table, 1953, Harris B. Peck, Chairman; Edward D. Greenwood, Discussant; *American Journal of Orthopsychiatry*, XXIV, No. 1 (Jan. 1954), 128–152.

toward group behavior, which is different from that encountered in individual-to-individual contacts. The analyst, Spotnitz, suggests that:

> a higher degree of emotional preparation is needed to conduct analytic psychotherapy comfortably in a group than in individual practice.[11]

It is part of the preparation for social group work to gain, through supervised field work, this emotional preparation Spotnitz talks about. The group worker brings to group therapy specifically an understanding of environmental pressures, knowledge of group process, and skill in working with it. This means that the group worker will help group members focus on their present situation and their functioning in the various systems in which they move. With this guidance, group members will be able to handle necessary changes in themselves, and they will be better equipped to work on changes in the systems and relationships that they are involved in. William Glaser in *Reality Therapy* stressed focus on the "Here and Now."[12] His writing has helped to undergird further the approach considered most helpful by social group workers.

Another aspect of the controversy between group work and group therapy should be discussed, namely the question of *status*. It seems unpardonable that in the field of human relations this problem of competition has added to the confusion and sometimes has prevented progress. For some reason—probably because of the then high status of psychiatry on the North American continent—the term therapy seemed to indicate something more precious and more important than the term originally used in social work. This applies to both the individual and group approaches. Group work fought this prestige value from the beginning.[13] This was in accord with the value system of the social group worker who resisted any class system, even in the theoretical or interprofessional realm. To indicate that they were talking about the same method in the framework of their own social work profession and of equal importance and skill, regardless of whether it was practice with healthy or sick people in groups, most social group workers consciously avoided the term group therapy to describe their practice; instead, they called it social group work. The decision to do so has maintained the unity of group work and has enhanced its general status. It has at times confused the public and, unfortunately, has led to confusing terminology in social work itself. Social workers trained in a period when group work was practiced predominantly in the field of recreation and who had not kept up with its changing focus frequently disregarded the specialization in group method developed within their own profession. They turned to other professions to learn group therapy or

---

[11]Hyman Spotnitz, M.D., *The Couch and the Circle* (New York: Knopf, 1961), p. 227.

[12]William Glaser, *Reality Therapy* (New York: Harper & Row, Pub., 1965).

[13]See pp. 13–15.

practiced it without help in handling a group. The confusion of terms grew. Such verbal monstrosities as "group case work" were added. This writer will adhere to the term social group work to designate a basic method practiced in many different settings directed at a variety of interpersonal/environmental problems.

## SUMMARY

The function of social group work is seen as part of the function of social work and the fields in which it is practiced. This does not exclude the use of the group work method by other professions.

Social work's function at the present is not finalized. Its core tasks are (1) to assess, clarify, and help individuals with the interaction of their inner motives and the demands of their social environment, and (2) to help change social environment if it is detrimental to the social development of individuals. Functions of each particular field, organization, or agency in which social work is practiced are more limited and specific.

Social group work functions within the fields of health, welfare, education, and recreation as a helping method used in groups with varied purposes and consisting of members on a wide scale from healthy to sick.

Functions of professions in a complex society overlap partially.

To clarify one of the major confusions in function and terminology, the relationship between group work and group therapy is discussed.

Definitions used in this text are:

*Social Group Work* is a method of social work that helps persons to enhance their social functioning through purposeful group experiences and to cope more effectively with their personal, group, or community problems.

*Group Therapy* is practice that is aimed at ameliorating suffering and improving the personal and social functioning of its members through specified and controlled group interaction enabled by a professional person.

*Group Work* includes work with groups consisting of healthy as well as of sick individuals. When the group worker uses professional training and skill to work with groups of individuals who have problems in personal and social functioning, this worker enters the practice of group therapy. The individual does it in a particular way based on the extent of his or her professional qualifications.

To avoid status conflicts and to clearly keep the identification with social work, this practice is called *social group work* (a parallel to social case work, another method of social work).

The summary would not be complete if the reader were not also reminded of the fact that there are numerous other terms for group work and group therapy, i.e., group counseling, group guidance. They are used interchangeably with the other two terms and, therefore, will not be discussed separately. Terminology is very confusing. In recent years the terms *family counseling* or *family therapy* have been used in the social service field. The family is a group, however, and as such also belongs within the realm of group work.

## BIBLIOGRAPHY

American Association of Group Workers, "Definition of the Function of the Group Worker," *The Group,* XI, No. 3 (May 1949), 11–12.

BRUNO, FRANK J., *Trends in Social Work 1874–1956.* New York: Columbia University Press, 1957.

CORSINI, RAYMOND J., *Methods of Group Psychotherapy.* New York: McGraw-Hill, 1957.

COYLE, GRACE L., *Group Work with American Youth.* New York: Harper & Row, Pub., 1948.

_____, "Social Group Work: An Aspect of Social Work Practice," *Journal of Social Issues,* VIII, No. 2 (1952), 23–34.

FESTINGER, LEON, "Current Developments in Group Dynamics." New York: *Amer. Assoc. of Group Workers,* mimeographed, undated.

FRANK, JEROME D., "Group Methods in Psychotherapy," *Journal of Social Issues,* VIII, No. 2 (1952), 35–44.

GLASER, WILLIAM, *Reality Therapy.* New York: Harper & Row, Pub., 1965.

KONOPKA, GISELA, *Adolescent Girl in Conflict.* Englewood Cliffs, NJ: Prentice-Hall, 1966.

_____, "Group Treatment of the Mentally Ill: Education for Life," *Canada's Mental Health,* Supplement No. 54 (Jan.-April 1967).

_____, "Similarities and Differences between Group Work and Group Therapy," Report of the Group Therapy Committee, A.A.G.W., mimeographed ST-451-8, undated; also in *Selected Papers of the National Conference of Social Welfare,* 1951, pp. 51–60.

_____, "Team Relationships and Operations in Social Group Work," Appendix C in Marjorie Murphy, *The Social Group Work Method in Social Work Education,* Vol. XI, *A Project Report of the Curriculum Study,* Werner W. Boehm, Director and Coordinator, pp. 106–114. New York: Council on Social Work Education, 1959.

_____, *Therapeutic Group Work With Children.* Minneapolis: University of Minnesota Press, 1949.

MURPHY, MARJORIE, *The Social Group Work Method in Social Work Education,* Vol. XI, *A Project Report of the Curriculum Study,* Werner W. Boehm, Director and Coordinator, New York: Council on Social Work Education, 1959.

SPOTNITZ, HYMAN, *The Couch and the Circle.* New York: Knopf, 1961.

TRECKER, HARLEIGH B., ed., *Group Work—Foundations and Frontiers.* New York: Whiteside, Inc., 1955.

_____, *Group Work in Psychiatric Settings.* New York: Whiteside, Inc., 1956.

WILSON, GERTRUDE and GLADYS RYLAND, *Social Group Work Practice.* Boston: Houghton Mifflin, 1949.

ZLATCHIN, PHILIP, CLARA A. KAISER, and SAUL SCHEIDLINGER, "The Group in Education, Group Work and Psychotherapy," Round Table 1953, Harris B. Peck, Chairman; Edward D. Greenwood, Discussant; *American Journal of Orthopsychiatry,* XXIV, No. 1 (Jan. 1954), 128–152.

# THREE
# THEORIES OF HUMANS AND THEIR LIFE CYCLE UNDERLYING SOCIAL GROUP WORK

In this simple sentence, Kluckhohn and Murray have expressed their view of humans as beings who have many characteristics in common with each other and yet who occur in an infinite variety of patterns. The view of humans underlying group work practice is derived from many theories of personality and society; it takes account of their human, natural and socioeconomic environment, since it seems increasingly impossible to speak of the human being as an entity separated from all other influences. With the exception of the very unusual occasion of a hermitic existence, the human being must always interact with others, changing them and being

[1]Clyde Kluckhohn and Henry A. Murray, "Personality Formation: The Determinants," *Personality in Nature, Society and Culture* (New York: Knopf, 1949), p. 35.

changed by them. This concept of interaction in no way contradicts the concept of individuality and each person's essential difference.

The following is an attempt to present the human life cycle by integrating understanding of the individual with understanding of the natural group. Students of human behavior and dynamics are constantly trying to formulate a basic theory of this integration. Underlying this somewhat new and unorthodox view of developmental needs and tasks and the ways in which they are fulfilled are assumptions derived from a modified dynamic psychology, best expressed by Erik Erikson and from years of research and experience of the author.[2]

As indicated in the introduction, the author does not adhere to a specific "school of thought." The student of social group work should understand that this method combines philosophy, ethics, psychology, sociology, and a deep search of life's meaning, which translates into the reality of human service. The dignity of each human being is the major touchstone.

Different from the early exclusive emphasis on the individual—and therefore the dominance of casework in social work—my concept of the individual stresses his or her interrelatedness with others. The great theologian, Edward Schillebeekx, summarized this superbly:

> No individual can be understood; (a) independently of the course of the past events that have surrounded him, that undergird and confront him and elicit his critical reaction; (b) independently of his relations with those about him, contemporaries who have received from him and in turn have influenced him and touched off specific reactions in him; (c) independently of the effect he has had on subsequent history or of what he might have intended to set in motion by direct action of his own. In other words, an individual human being is the personal focal point of a series of interactive relations to the past, the future and his or her own present.[3]

This view of man combines the recognition of man's inevitable relatedness to his own past and aspirations for the future (how wrong, therefore, the fashionable "finding oneself" by isolation from others and the total ignoring of the past in some therapies.)

The underlying philosophy of social group work as presented in this book is that it cannot be a mechanistic deterministic concept of human

---

[2]The reader is urged to read Erik H. Erikson, *Childhood and Society* (New York: W. W. Norton & Co., Inc., 1950) and social role theories, especially as presented by Richard A. Cloward and Lloyd E. Ohlin, *Delinquency and Opportunity* (Glencoe, Il: Free Press, 1960) and by Robert K. Merton, *Social Theory and Social Structure* (Glencoe, Il: Free Press, 1949). See also Helen L. Witmer and Ruth Kotinsky, eds., *New Perspectives for Research on Juvenile Delinquency* (Washington, DC: U.S. Department of Health, Education and Welfare, Social Security Administration, Children's Bureau, 1956); and Gisela Konopka, *Young Girls: A Portrait of Adolescence* (Englewood Cliffs, NJ: Prentice-Hall, 1976).

[3]Edward Schillebeekx, *Jesus* (New York: The Seabury Press, 1979, p. 44).

development—neither Pavlov nor Skinner seem to recognize the infinite complexity of human motivation, aspiration, and behavior.

Combined with Freud's recognition of the many irrational forces within the psyche of the human being, one needs to understand the view of human existence expressed in the writings of the early existentialists. I do concur with them regarding how very varied and inexplicable each individual is; I therefore abhor the response of many social workers or therapists to the suffering of others with definite "diagnoses" and the rash response, "Yes, I understand." It must be clear to us that we can only *try* to understand. I also agree with the existential concept of anguish in each person's life born out of the inevitable need to make decisions about one's own fate, and the ever-present doubt as to whether the right choices have been made. There is loneliness in the life of all human beings. The assumption that constant happiness should be the goal of human existence is misleading. That does not mean that we have to prepare human beings only for suffering. Yet, we should not deny the courage one needs to live, and the agony of having to make decisions.

Basic needs of human beings grow out of their physical, mental, emotional, and spiritual natures. They cannot be separated. The theory of the Greeks, which hypothesized a soul within but separate from the body, is no longer acceptable. Even the recent concepts of dynamic psychology, which rest on the assumption that the human being is a whole but separate entity, are no longer completely acceptable. Our present theory holds that the individual is not a *separate entity* but is a *whole individual interrelated with others.* A person reacts to, is influenced by, and can influence a variety of complex systems. The need for food and shelter, for love and tenderness, for accomplishment, and for fulfillment of the thirst for knowledge are all dependent on the interaction of humans with each other. Next to the biological necessities, the deepest human longings are to be loved and to be important—important to someone. It is from these that all other needs spring. An inseparable connection exists between self-respect and a freely-given relationship with someone else. Throughout life, humans struggle to gain or to retain this sense of self by reaching out to the *you*—to the one who gives importance and warmth and tenderness to his or her own self. When this bridge is built a person can give love to others and can accomplish whatever he or she is capable of doing. At that point a person can feel fulfillment and achieve sacrifice. But without the bridge between the *I* and the *you*, the human being crumbles. It is the assumption of social group work that human beings have not only the basic need to be loved, but also the capacity and strength to love in return. But this is not achieved without the constant struggle to overcome other tendencies and to counteract environmental forces that may prevent, suppress, or diminish this capacity.

The practicing group worker, whether working with young or older people, whether encountering severe developmental problems in therapeutic situations or with the developmental process should always remember:

1. The infinite variety of human beings.
2. The existence of anguish as a normal occurrence in everybody.
3. The inevitable interrelatedness of all human beings.
4. The crucial interrelatedness of past, present, and expectation of the future in each person.
5. The significance of the past, yet not in a deterministic sense.
6. The capacity of human beings to grow and change in any age period.
7. The understanding that human beings are partially influenced by conscious, unconscious, and preconscious motivation, but that they have the potential to recognize these motivations and act rationally.
8. The significance of expectation in human motivation.
9. Significance of concepts, such as defense mechanism and projection. Those are some irrational ways of handling human relationships, common to all people.
10. The vital significance of giving and receiving affection for the development of each person.

Related to the understanding of *interdependence* of each individual with others is the understanding that every person achieves healthy development through a healthy and appropriate group life throughout the life cycle. It is important to clarify what is meant by a healthy group life. A healthy group life has the following ingredients:

1. Provision for the identification with equals.
2. Provision for the warmth of belonging to more than one person. Fear of the threatened loss of the one and only beloved person is always present and becomes overwhelming if a wider relationship is not established in the course of life.
3. Freedom to be and to express one's self and to be different in the presence of others.
4. Freedom to choose the friends one prefers combined with a responsibility to accept others if they need to be accepted, even though no close friendly relationship has been established.
5. Opportunity to try out one's own individuality while at the same time permitting the enjoyment of the uniqueness of others.
6. Opportunity to exercise independence and to be allowed to be dependent when this is necessary and indicated, as in childhood or in distressing situations in adulthood.
7. Opportunity to give to others as well as receive from them.
8. Opportunity to feel that as an individual or as a group, one has the strength to influence one's own fate.

It is only in very early infancy that the human being is not related to or has no need for such a group situation. In the first weeks of life an infant responds only to the warmth and protection of an individual stronger and more powerful than him- or herself—the mother or the substitute mother, which may be any other member of a healthy family. The infant certainly has an impact on the family group situation, but the new family member is involved only with one person. If the basic need for a one-to-one relationship is not fulfilled at this period, the child will be an exceedingly disturbed person in later life. It is then impossible to give help through the medium of the social group work method. The only help, as far as we know, can come from an intensive therapeutic one-to-one relationship. Fortunately, these situations are comparatively rare.

Such damage was seen after World War II, especially in Germany, when abandoned infants were placed in separate cribs and left isolated, only to be fed by a bottle placed close to their mouth. They had no warm body contact with anyone. Some who experienced this have suffered in later life because of this early experience. Individuals in prisons with a history of violence have been reported to have experienced similar early deprivation of affection. I warn—as always—against a deterministic view. We know little of why some people keep their basic health in spite of very destructive experiences.

Very early in the life cycle individuals begin to interact with others, not just with single persons other than the mother, but in group situations as well. The characteristics of this interaction, though, show as much change as any other characteristics of the developing human being. In the healthy development of a child, the family provides this early satisfaction of group needs. The earliest group experience of interaction within the family circle gives the child a valuable mental and emotional learning experience that can be applied as the child grows and begins to reach out beyond the intimate family group to peers. Comparatively recent psychological observation has shown that even at an early age a child needs to reach out to contemporaries, even though the predominant need at this stage is the need for adult protection and care. A young child cannot tolerate a large group or enter into a complicated group relationship, but even the 2-year-old shows increased animation and delight when he or she discovers and reaches out to another "baby." This is the beginning of one's need to relate to contemporaries. The greatest need for a child is still for adult protection. Yet, different from what was thought only a few years ago, the need to "participate" starts very early in life.

With increased awareness of the *I*, the child's need for interaction with persons outside the family group (i.e., with peers) increases and gradually becomes more complicated. At the same time, however, adults, and specifically both parents, must provide a sense of security and protection for the whole period of childhood. The parents are the significant adults in the nuclear family. In some cultures other adults fulfill this role, either in addition to the parents or substituting for them. In the extended families of the Orient, grandparents and other relatives are as important as the parents and so is the *metapeleth* (teacher-educator) in the kibbutz. In some of the newly developing communes on the North American continent, all adults who belong play additional parental roles.

The child's sense of importance, then, develops through the influence of these two sets of relationships: relationships with family members and relationships with contemporaries outside the family group. Two-year-olds frequently play "alone together," enjoying each other's presence, but rarely relating closely to each other. Three- and four-year-olds, however, interact with each other and try out their own personalities and a whole range of conflict-solving in group situations. The provision of a healthy group life both within and outside the family becomes essential to healthy development. Dynamic psychology has stressed for years the importance of family relationships and the working out of interpersonal conflicts and dependencies between parents and children. It has stressed the way these influence the child's identification with societal values and his or her development of trust and self-respect. The helping methods of psychiatry and social casework have been founded on an understanding of these relationships. Social group work also bases the theory of its understanding of the human being on the importance of the parent-child relationship, but it goes beyond this and recognizes that this relationship plays only one part in producing the healthy or unhealthy development of the individual, that group life outside the family also influences the development of the child.

Case histories of disturbed or delinquent children too frequently omit any reference to such group associations. It is the opinion of this author that only by taking them into consideration can additional light be shed on the understanding of such children or adults. For too long the family has been credited for all positive development or blamed for all shortcomings in the mental health of children. Without question the climate of the family group is a very important factor, but it is not the only one. A handicapped child, for instance, who is exposed to the torments of other youngsters can be only partly protected by the family group—he or she may still suffer serious emotional disturbance as a result of contacts outside the family. If the knowledge of these outside contacts is not available to those who want to help this child at a later stage, treatment may be based on the wrong factors and the experts will be puzzled because they cannot find the reasons for the disturbance in the close family environment.

Social group work is making a real contribution to the understanding of individual dynamics by insisting upon the importance of group life outside the family group. "I had my first seizure on the playground when I was 9 years old," recalled an adult seizure patient. "I woke up and saw the kids staring at me and heard them shout, 'Ida had a fit! Ida had a fit!'

Mother rushed out and held me in her arms, and she has supported me ever since, but I can only see the kids! I never felt I was worth anything." "Don't ever get a child that looks like me," said a pretty dark-skinned 10-year-old black child to her beloved white group worker. She had a loving family, but she had experienced the cruel selectivity of a society that discriminates against Blacks. Both these children had experienced not only hurt, but also a breakdown of their self-esteem. In each instance this had occurred through harmful group experience outside the family. Help with this could come only through experience with positive relationships in another kind of group situation.

"You know that I had a terribly weak mother, and a father who did not care one hoot about his family," said a young man who enjoyed at this time his own wonderful, warm, and loving family and was carrying a responsible position. "But I will never forget what it meant to me to have friendships in my youth group, to have your understanding (this was directed to the group worker) and to be able to do things that made me not only forget my dismal home, but gave me the feeling that I was an important being, not just someone on this earth to be slapped around." Here the group life outside the family provided the necessary ingredients for a healthy development, in spite of family breakdown.

The importance of group experiences increases at the time the child enters school. It is not purely an accident that school life usually starts when the child no longer has an intense need for parental protection. In general, children can move into a wider circle of outside relationships, although adults remain the most significant objects of identification as well as protectors and stimulators. Emotional and intellectual growth occur in part through group interaction and in part through stimulation emanating from inanimate objects and play. Stimulation through things and activities occurs throughout the human life cycle, from early childhood to old age, but it is especially significant in the early school years. The concern with these objects is rarely expressed in solitary occupation; more often it is expressed in games with other children or in efforts directed toward other human beings, as in gift-giving or in demonstrations of accomplishment: "I made this; look at me!" The group worker's efforts in working with children of approximately 8 to 11 years, whether they are healthy or sick, are based on this particular characteristic of that age. The group worker's efforts will include a great deal of use of materials and activities in the context of group relationships. In general, children of this age talk less than they do at a later age and need less direct human interaction than in the preschool years.

The importance of group life is probably strongest in adolescence. This is closely related to the physical maturation process and the movement away from adult protection. To become an adult the adolescent must discover the path toward independence from those who have sheltered, protected, and taught him. During this period the adolescent cannot yet give these up completely. Family ties are actually very important if the adolescent feels that they are not interfering with any attempts at independence. The insecurity at this age is almost pervasive. The biological change is dramatic and the youth must come to terms with the fact that biologically he or she is a fully-grown man or woman while emotionally and socially the adolescent is neither ready nor permitted to fulfill this function. This alone is an immense task fraught with conflict and anxiety. Doubts of one's identity increase with the awareness of adult responsibilities while one is still a child. Even the healthy, well-balanced adolescent goes through this period of fear of adulthood's demands while at the same time thrilling to the prospect of the privileges that come with emancipation. Mentally, insecurity and confusion are expressed in the re-evaluation of values that seemed absolute at an earlier age. While identification with parental values seemed important during an earlier period, doubts about their validity arise in the adolescent period. Some adolescents express their doubts by completely rejecting parental values; others, by constantly questioning them. This has been described in most of the literature as *rebellion.* It was taught that rebellion is a necessary attribute of adolescence. Increasingly it has become clear that youths rebel only in the context of relationships with authoritarian adults. In a more participatory environment, whether it be in the family, school, or any other institution in which the adolescent moves, the adolescent does not necessarily rebel. Yet he or she is always "re-evaluating values," and questioning.

This pervasive insecurity needs some balance, and it is found usually in identification with and relation to the contemporary group: other adolescents are not only "co-sufferers," they are also mirrors that help one to learn about one's own image. They are people with whom one can share everything, even feelings of degradation, guilt, or shame, without losing one's self-respect because they, too, are living through these same emotions. They give support to one's own development of individuality despite the influence of the previous generation, which by necessity wants and must try to mold the young in its image. They provide an outlet for the wide swings in mood so frequent in adolescence. They cry and laugh with one another when to do so would seem silly or exaggerated to anyone outside the in-group. Association with other adolescents also permits actual "trying out" of unexplored territory and fulfillment of the consuming thirst for adventure. Sometimes this appears in forms tolerable to society and sometimes in forms dangerous to it. Yet, adolescents must be provided with this "trying-out period," which Erik Erikson calls the necessary "moratorium." The society that does not provide for it invites the development of a youth population that is not only docile, unimaginative, and conforming but also hostile and seriously delinquent. Modern society, with its tight rules, is in danger of doing this. The rigid authoritarian system of

Nazi Germany is a classic example of a society that was ideal for fostering conformity and hostility. With no room for harmless adventure and with no toleration of mistakes, young people brought up under this regime became hateful and antisocial. The diabolical Hitler regime understood this and nurtured it: German youth, impressed by the doctrines of racism, were sent into Jewish homes to destroy property and to torture and abuse the adults; they were provided outlets for promiscuous sex relations which were reserved for those selected by the state.

In recent years, the fear of permissiveness has created in the United States and in some other Western countries an atmosphere of fear of youth and a tightening of rules related to adolescents that might easily lead to rebellious hate. This sentence was written in 1962 and reads now like a prophecy. Meanwhile we had the "youth revolt," "generation gap," and the "drug scene" in most Western and some Eastern countries. It is very evident that it is not permissiveness that created those tensions. Every historian or sociologist studying youth movements will find that they did not develop in societies that genuinely accepted the importance of each age period. They developed in the period before World War I, especially in very authoritarian countries like the German or Austrian monarchies and were directed against the rigidity of schools and the absolute power of the fathers. In the United States too much was taken over from European cultures, especially in the Caucasian part of the population while the political intent of the country was increasingly participatory. As in all youth revolts the criticism of the older generation was also directed against any inconsistency of behavior compared with avowed values. While the values expressed demand love of one's neighbor, compassion, respect for individual dignity, and honesty, the actual behavior shows very different traits. Youth is sensitive to this individually, but even more so when cultures begin to change and communication becomes increasingly possible among those who do not agree with the status quo. Certainly there are also many adults who agree that values should be put into practice. The basic need is obviously not only for communication between the generations but especially for finding a significant place for young people in the total network of society and its segments and for an outlet of the strong need of youth for adventure and excitement. During the height of floods in the typhoon season a group worker in Calcutta, India, pointed to bands of young people cheerfully and noisily collecting clothes and food for flood victims: "Those are usually our most difficult gangs, stealing, fighting, sullen and hateful. Now they have found a significant task which is appreciated by the whole community, they can run trucks legitimately—it is exciting." It is tragic that one must wait for disaster to enlist such youthful energies. It is imperative to find ways of involving youth in living. A youth who loses a sense of significance can become very destructive. In the United States, this is mostly expressed in individual or small gang delinquencies; in Europe, it is frequently expressed in terror organizations.

With adolescence, the child enters the arena of wider societal group relations. He or she begins to consciously experience group acceptance and/or group discrimination. An adolescent may experience discrimination by or exclusion from a group because of belonging to a particular racial, religious, economic, or social status group, and the experience may create deep scars and resentment. Legitimate ambitions of a young person are thwarted for the same reason. If acceptance cannot be found, rejected adolescents will band together not only to find some sense of security and worth, but also to openly defy or undermine the adult world that stands against them.

During adolescence, the need for intensive group life reaches its peak. Adulthood does not have as strong an emotional drive for this since developmental tasks are not as much in the foreground then as they are during childhood. It is a mistake, though, to assume that developmental tasks are ever completely fulfilled.

By necessity, psychology in the twentieth century had to focus on the child; the adult was usually seen as a finished product with only remnants of unfinished childhood traits to be ironed out. At the present, psychological theory underlying social group work views adult life, including old age, as a continuous developmental process. The process is slower than in childhood and does not involve as much an active helping person. Yet, there always must be a growth-conducive climate in the community and outlets for the constant need to belong and to participate.

Most adults find partial fulfillment of these needs in the family; this time, however, they function in a role different from that of childhood. They are now in the responsible position of forming a healthy group life in their own families. Dependency needs, which never completely cease, are fulfilled by the marriage partner, a person chosen from outside the previous intimate circle of the first family constellation. The need to contribute can be fulfilled in responsible care of children and in participation in wider community groups.

In general, the healthy group life of the adult pivots around these two major group constellations. With the increase of the small family unit in our Western society, limited to parents and children, adults increasingly long for an additional group constellation, the friendship group outside the family circle. The wider family in other cultures, and in some part of our culture, provides for the continued need of friendship, of relating intimately to people of one's own sex and one's own age group. If relatives do not provide this, adults must reach outside of the family circle for such friendships. Such relationships give them an opportunity, when it is necessary, to move away from the demand for competency, for status, or for responsibility. This need to be a "child" at times or "to let down one's hair" is again fulfilled frequently by the marriage partner. But most adults need another such outlet. This is especially important for those adults who are not married or who have lost their spouse. The need for adult friendship was too frequently overlooked in individual psychology. It is not a need for large or for high activity-centered groups. A businessman in a small community expressed it best by saying, "We feel so alone when we have only our family or acquaintances based on prestige and business association. What can we do? We run to psychiatrists because we can't have friends." Our culture at present offers comparatively good opportunities for outlets for the need to participate and to gain importance in adulthood, but it provides little fulfillment of the need to belong outside the narrow confines of the family. A solution certainly will not lie in the formation of "friendship clubs"; it will lie more in the direction of a *cultural acceptance of the friendship needs of adults to be dependent as well as independent,* and provision for opportunities to "belong."

The interdependence needs of the aged fall into the same range as those of the adult in general. There was a time when it was assumed that the aged wanted only to be dependent and that this desire was accompanied by a withdrawal from others. It has become evident that these assumptions were false. At no time in a person's life cycle, with the exception of the very first weeks of infancy, does the human being want to be completely dependent. Dependency realistically may increase because of decreased physical or mental capacity, but it never again becomes emotionally satisfying in the normally developed adult. The aged continue to want to be active and to participate and belong to a community of people. If all other faculties remain intact, an elderly person continues to be a developing, learning, and contributing member of the community. This is only impossible if the community climate does not allow for such continued creative effort. The aged whose faculties are not intact, either physically or mentally, have the same needs but they are tinged with deep anxiety and a feeling of frustration.

During that time of life very deeply cutting personal changes may occur, specifically the death of spouses or beloved friends. Though this may happen at any time in life, it is experienced generally more often in that age period. The need for support by equals, and without sentimentality, is especially great. Yet, as in every age group, each individual will have different experiences from another one and will react differently. Services geared to the aged should be as highly individualized—within group context—as those designed for any other age group.

Group work services for the aged are shaped increasingly by this changed understanding of the aged.

### SUMMARY

Group work practice is based on a concept of human beings as constantly developing individuals in necessary and significant interaction with each other. People are shaped by others and in turn are involved in shaping others. The human being presents an inseparable unit of physical, mental, and emotional forces, again in interaction with others.

Development does not cease with childhood but continues all through the life cycle. The basic needs beyond the biological ones are the needs to belong, to be an important individual, and to participate.

In the life cycle these needs must be fulfilled in a variety of changing small group associations. These associations have specific characteristics in different age periods. At each stage of development individuals must find fulfillment through qualitative group associations or they will be damaged in one way or another.

No individual goes through the life cycle without some damage. Human beings have various capacities to deal with dissatisfactions and frustrations on their own. They need help at different stages of their development with their developmental tasks or with overcoming hurdles to them.

Group work practice is directed towards provision of such help and takes as its rationale the use of its method from this view.

Because of its strong emphasis on viewing the individual in interaction and therefore the importance of qualitative group life, its practice is also based on a thorough understanding of the dynamics of face-to-face groups. This will be presented in the next chapter.

## BIBLIOGRAPHY

*Dialogue on Youth,* University of Minnesota: Center for Youth Development and Research, Seminar Series No. 1, 1970.

ERIKSON, ERIK H., *Childhood and Society.* New York: Norton, 1950.

HOEBEL, E. ADAMSON, *Anthropology: The Study of Man* (3rd ed.). New York: McGraw-Hill, 1966.

KLUCKHOHN, CLYDE and HENRY A. MURRAY, "Personality Formation: The Determinants," *Personality in Nature, Society and Culture.* New York: Knopf, 1949.

KONOPKA, GISELA, "A Healthy Group Life—Social Group Work's Contribution to Mental Health," *Mental Hygiene,* 45, No. 3 (July 1961).

——————, *Eduard C. Lindeman and Social Work Philosophy.* Minneapolis: The University of Minnesota Press, 1958.

——————, "Resistance and Hostility in Group Members," in Harleigh B. Trecker, ed., *Group Work—Foundations and Frontiers.* New York: Whiteside, Inc., 1955.

NORTHEN, HELEN, "Interrelated Functions of the Social Group Worker," *Social Work,* 2, No. 2 (Apr. 1957), 63–69.

SCHILLEBEEKX, EDWARD, *Jesus.* New York: The Seabury Press, 1979, p. 44.

WILSON, GERTRUDE, "Human Needs Pertinent to Group Work Services," *Proceedings of the National Conference of Social Work,* 1942, pp. 338–360. New York: Columbia University Press, 1942.

*Self-respect—the survival of the soul*
Spranger.

# FOUR
# THEORIES OF GROUP PROCESS UNDERLYING SOCIAL GROUP WORK

In the helping process of group work the client is the group member and the group as a whole. This dual focus changes the psychological climate fundamentally from that in a one-to-one relationship. In the individual interview, the person who needs help is confronted by the "strong" and "capable" one, and a psychological "distance" can develop between these two people. Helen Perlman wrote:

> Whatever the nature of the problem the person brings to the social agency, it is always accompanied, and often complicated, by the problem of being a client.[1]

[1]Helen Harris Perlman, *Social Casework*, (Chicago: University of Chicago Press, 1957), p. 37.

44

A similar relationship may exist between the individual group member and the group worker, but at the same time the person is surrounded by equals, by people "in the same boat." The relationships of the members to each other have much meaning. They are never static. They change in time, and in relation to specific situations, even if a helping person such as the group worker is not present. This changing movement is called the group process. Marjorie Murphy defined it as "the totality of the group's interactions, developments and changes which occur in the group's life."[2]

As in the preceding chapter, where an attempt was made to integrate understanding of individual dynamics with the changing group needs during the life cycle, this chapter will try to integrate our knowledge of group dynamics with an understanding of the individual. This will not and cannot be achieved perfectly, since such integration must come from the concerted effort of many disciplines. There is increasing drive in this direction, as symbolized in the rise of social psychology. Muzafer Sherif, one of the early investigators of social process, began to build such a bridge in his book, *The Psychology of Social Norms.*[3] Erich Fromm's *Escape from Freedom,* was perhaps one of the deepest integrative efforts of combining psychoanalytic theory with an understanding of group relations and group needs.[4] The following presentation must be short—by necessity. It is based on concepts derived mainly from the older sociologists—Simmel, Eubank, and Durkheim; on research done by Kurt Lewin and his followers, and on writings by representatives of group work such as Coyle, Wilson, Trecker, Somers, and Konopka (see bibliography at the end of this chapter). The theories and key ideas presented will always be placed within the context of the kind of groups the social group worker encounters.

Before we describe those concepts theoretically, let us see some short "snapshots" of the impact of group relations:

### Example

Janie, an 11-year-old girl, had been referred to the group in a Child Guidance Clinic because of her excessive silence, almost amounting to muteness. Individual interviews could not reach her. In the first meeting the girls were discussing why they had come to the clinic in an informal way, while they were doing some handicraft. When one of the girls told about her feelings of being odd, different, Janie burst out with a "You think you are crazy too?" She had seemed completely detached from the group until this moment.

Identification with another group member had freed Janie to speak up.

[2]Marjorie Murphy, "The Social Group Work Method in Social Work Education," *A Project Report of the Curriculum Study,* XI, Werner W. Boehm, Director and Coordinator (New York: Council on Social Work Education, 1959), p. 32.

[3]Muzafer Sherif, *The Psychology of Social Norms* (New York: Harper & Row, Pub., 1936).

[4]Erich Fromm, *Escape from Freedom* (New York: Holt, Rinehart & Winston, 1941).

**Example**

In a summer program the black 12- and 13-year-olds showed a sullen hostility but did not express themselves. Leo had the least status in the group, was always pushed or scorned. Leo usually was very quiet. But early one morning he turned to the camp counselor, "Oh, stop calling us kids—it sounds like 'boys' to us." Others joined in. "You said it, Leo. We are men. You said it!" Leo turned, saw himself surrounded by friendly faces. The counselor apologized and said he wanted to learn more. The whole group became more animated and Leo was very outspoken.

The group had given support and a beginning new self-concept.

**Example**

Johnny was only five years old. He was intellectually far above this age level and was treated like a 10-year-old by his family; in fact he was constantly pushed toward more achievement. He was hostile to other children, destroyed what they cherished, and attacked them. His group associations, chosen by his parents, were always with older children. The group worker suggested a group of children his age. He first wandered around, seemingly forlorn and incapable of relating to the active play of the four- and five-year-olds. No pressure was placed on him, either by the group worker or the other children. He idly joined two children exploring a plant. The sure, gentle hands of one of the children took the leaves apart without breaking them. "How do you do that?" came from Johnny. The two began to work on other plants. After awhile they started to race, to laugh. Johnny became a little boy among others, he relaxed.

The group had given back the opportunity to Johnny to be a *child* in his natural social relations.

There could be many more such examples in which we can see and observe the strength of the group process. The dynamics in this process are the relationships of the members with one another, produced by the individuality of each member. The members change within themselves while contributing to the changes of the others.

The groups with which the social group worker is concerned are *face-to-face groups that allow for individualization.* No specific size can be given, because the number of people who can make up such a group depends on the age of the members (young children cannot relate to as many persons as adults), on the capacity for relationships among the members (emotionally deprived people can relate only to very few at a time), and on the content of the group meetings that might prove most significant to the members (intimate discussions will require fewer members than will active work on projects). We must distinguish a "group" from the concept of "mass," which implies parallel action, but not interaction among the members. It must also be distinguished from a loose, small or large assembly of people who happen to be in the same place. *Interaction* and *some feeling of common goal* or *concern* are attributes of a group. A simple collection of people can change into a group under certain circumstances.

### Example

At the beginning of a flight in a commercial airplane, the passengers were isolated individuals, who only happened to be in the same plane. There was little or practically no communication. Then an emergency developed. The plane had to make a forced landing. During the wait for another form of transportation, the unrelated passengers became a group. There was inter-change of feelings—what they had thought when the pilot announced the necessity to land; interchange of concern for what meaning the delay had for each passenger. Strangers tried to find solutions for those who were seriously inconvenienced by the delay. There was a shared appreciation of the pilot's skill and a wish to express this. When he boarded the bus that was to take the passengers to another airport, all those aboard spontaneously cheered him.

A group had emerged under the pressure of a common strong experience.

The original *formation* of groups does influence group relationships and group behavior. Often group workers become involved with groups that existed before the practitioners met them. It is necessary to know each group's formation to be able to understand its present needs. Sociologists have distinguished between *natural* and *formed* groups. Natural groups are those organized by the members themselves; formed groups are those brought together by a person outside the group membership. The primary natural group is the family. Other examples of such groups are friendship groups, gangs, and professional groups. Formed groups are therapy groups or groups brought together for educational purposes, such as a school class. Inside such groups, natural sub-groups may emerge.

Most natural groups form around causes, traditions, or people. Yet the purpose for which such groups were originally formed may change in time. If a social group worker is called upon to help with an ongoing group, the knowledge of its original purpose may be an important clue to the group's present functioning:

### Example

A group worker was asked to work with a neighborhood group of adults that met weekly in a settlement house. It was a *social group* whose members con-stantly fought with each other and with everyone else in the house. Members of the group had a powerful influence in the neighborhood and succeeded in fanning hostilities. The behavior of this group was puzzling until the group worker learned that it was originally not a social group, not a friendship group, and that it had been formed around a *cause*—the improvement of the neighborhood—a number of years prior to its meeting with the group worker. Members had met with high hopes and enthusiasm, but they encoun-tered many difficulties and received no help. Their frustration turned into resignation and, finally, they gave up the cause. Several strong members refused to disband the group and so it continued to meet without a specific goal and held together only by a diffused hostility.

Knowing this helped the group worker to approach this group differently from the way he would have worked with it had it always been a friendship group.

Group workers *form* groups frequently in social agencies, court services, clinics, hospitals, and schools. There is a large variety of common denominators around which group formation has proved itself effective: Groups may be built around specific symptoms (groups of enuretic children); a certain behavior (groups of highly acting-out children or groups of withdrawn ones); diagnosed illness (groups of diabetics or multiple sclerotics); or specific forms of treatment (patients who receive physical therapy). Groups may be formed around the common concern of people for others: parents seeking or needing help with problems of their children; relatives trying to understand their mentally sick spouses or parents; and citizens working on specific community problems such as the need for housing, playgrounds, old-age homes, better mental health facilities, and so forth.

Group constellation influences vitally group process and may mean the difference between a helpful, ineffective, or harmful group.

The dynamics of the group process are determined by the *kind and quality of the interaction among members*. To understand this network of relationships—to be helpful to individuals in it—we must understand this constantly changing process. What we observe in a group is the basic and immense power human beings have over one another. It is the power of acceptance or rejection; of pulling people into the group or leaving them outside; and of making people feel that they are valuable rather than shunned, ignored, or mishandled. By knowing the position of a person in the group or the role taken by or assigned to him or her, we do not yet know the "why" of this position, but we do have a valuable observation that might lead us to the "why," and in this way determine the kind of help needed. Sometimes an understanding of the network of relationships in the group is sufficient to gain insight into a certain position of an individual and the actions accompanying the position—yet most of the time we must combine this knowledge with an understanding of him or her as an individual. The reverse is also true: It is impossible to understand the individual without knowing the positions in groups that are significant to him or her (e.g., the family, the work group for an adult, the play group for a child).

Moreno developed a way of taking a "snapshot" of relationships in a group, of drawing the acceptance-rejection pattern; it is called the *sociogram*.[5] It is a graphic way of becoming more aware of the constellations in a

---

[5]See Jacob L. Moreno, *Who Shall Survive? Foundations of Sociometry, Group Psychotherapy and Sociodrama*, revised edition (Beacon, NY: Beacon House, 1953). See also use of the sociogram in the context of working with delinquents in Gisela Konopka, *Therapeutic Group Work With Children* (Minneapolis: University of Minnesota Press, 1949), pp. 42–45.

group: the *subgroups,* the *leader,* the *isolate.* It must be understood that the sociogram gives only the picture of a given phase in the group process— only a moment in time. The picture is constantly changing. It cannot give the reasons for the observed phenomena. Action—helping intervention— cannot simply follow out of the observation. It is an instrument for observation; it is not intended for use in making decisions in regard to treatment.

Most groups show the phenomenon of *subgroups.* They are part of the natural workings of the group process. Rarely will we find a group where all members have exactly the same relationships, qualitatively and quantitatively, with all other members. This does not even exist in the primary group, the family. The parents form by nature a separate pair—a subgroup distinguished from the rest of the family. Beyond this, every family, even the happy and healthy one, will have some additional subgroup formation, changing in time.

Subgroups may consist of two (pair or dyad), three (triad), or more members of the group. Aside from the diagnostic value their recognition has for the one who works with groups, the emotional acceptance of the inevitability and legitimacy of subgroups is a prerequisite for good and skillful group work. If this is not forthcoming, the group worker who works against the subgroups usually loses the whole group. People working with groups used to assume that a "good" group must do everything together and must show equally strong bonds among all members. Group leaders became tense when subgroups emerged. Teachers, for instance, began to relax in the schoolroom and became more effective when they accepted and recognized the subgroups in their classrooms and began to work with them instead of against them. Subgroups may enhance the quality of the total group when they feel part of the group and contribute to its strength and growth. Examples of this are the strong ethnic groups that contribute to the unity of a whole nation.

Subgroups may become dangerous to the group—and to their own members—when they begin to separate themselves out of the group. These are the subgroups with "walls," frequently called cliques. Work with such subgroups for the purpose of integration is difficult. Part of the group worker's task is to prevent or control these subgroups before they develop into full-blown entities.[6]

Most members of a group belong to one or another subgroup. Yet there are two group positions or roles that need special attention: the position of the *isolate* and the *leader.* The isolate is a member either neglected or highly rejected by the group, yet present in it. *Neglected isolates* are in the most lonely situation. These people are tolerated by the group,

---

[6]Administration deals to a considerable degree with group behavior. It is not the task of this book to go into detail regarding this. It should be mentioned here, however, that this distinction between subgroup and clique often becomes vital in the administrative process.

but they are surrounded by a glass wall. They may be seen, and may see through it, but there is no communication, no bridge. We find such isolates frequently in groups that are formed by necessity, as living groups in institutions, school classes, or work groups of adults in prisons. They are there, but not of their own volition. Yet we do find neglected isolates in voluntary groups where they could leave, but instead they come to each meeting. Why? The answer will be different in each case. It must be found in the individual *and* the group situation. Most isolates suffer desperately. They are frequently people who are most in need of group acceptance; they yearn for nearness to others. They have a low self-concept and they cannot reach out. They find tenuous satisfaction in just being tolerated by the group or in pretending to themselves that they are truly a part of the group.

### Example

In a group discussion, Miss A. described how she had never felt comfortable in a group. She had always belonged to several groups—"I could not just be by myself all the time"—but she could not remember that she ever talked to anyone or that anyone talked to her. She had always pretended she was quite busy when she was in those groups, she had helped in the kitchen at parties or had done just what the others did, but nobody seemed to see her and nobody ever met her outside the group. She always felt like crying. One of the members asked, "Why did you not start talking?" "I could not," said Miss A. "Why the heck did you come back?" "I was afraid to be alone, and sometimes I thought I was just imagining all this, and everything really was all right...."

Miss A's overwhelming need to be with others because she could not tolerate herself, made her choose to stay with the group even in the uncomfortable position of the isolate. This was less painful than being alone. And she had found an additional way out: to pretend everything was all right. And why was she in this isolate position? Group members expressed their disgust with her "footmat" quality. In this particular group the need of all members for attention was great, and their capacity to reach out spontaneously was limited until they began to talk over some of their problems. Similar dynamics may have been present in other groups Miss A. had joined. This is also an example of why conscious help with these relationships is so necessary.

The *rejected isolate* is more actively involved in the total group situation. These individuals usually reach out to other members of the group or to the group as a whole, but find themselves rebuffed. The reasons for this may be again inside the rejected individuals, as for instance the boy who provokes others, who never wants to do what the others want to do, who starts fights, and so on. It may also lie in the specific group constellation and the group "climate." A sensitive, artistic boy may become the rejected isolate in a group of little "he-men." The person who violates the mores of his or her group, willingly or unwillingly, may be isolated in this manner.

Examples of this are the enuretic child who "smells," the camper who has head lice, the youngster who "tattled" on some planned illegal activity of the street corner gang, or an adult who stands for racial integration in a neighborhood group opposed to it. The rejected isolate sometimes becomes the *scapegoat* of the group. Such people are not rejected for something they are themselves, but for something the group projects on them—group projection frequently being as unconscious as individual projection.

### Example

Carol was constantly attacked by her group of 14- and 15-year-old girls, because she was, according to them, "a bad girl," and "over-sexed." The girls were themselves very curious about sex. Unconsciously they envied Carol's mature figure.

The irrationality and usually unconscious motivation of "scapegoating" makes work with it especially difficult.

*Leadership* in a group is perceived differently today from the way it was perceived in the early days of social group work. Early textbooks characterized the leader as a person possessing a certain list of qualities that made him or her a leader in every group. Today, however, leadership is seen as being related to the purpose and the situation in the group. Leadership may change in the same group in the course of development of a group. Personalities who take on leadership roles in groups cover a wide range. The young men or women who fire the imagination of their community action group in the discussion of an effort to work in a high delinquency area and stimulate the carrying through of a plan are different personalities from the slow-moving, hesitant, soft-spoken patient on the mental hospital ward who always succeeds in coaxing copatients into some active involvement, thus keeping alive in them the spark of sanity. They are leaders in their particular groups.

Helen Jennings, in her early investigation into leadership and isolation, described in her book of the same name several personalities who showed completely different characteristics, yet who were clearly accepted as leaders in the institution for girls that she studied.[7] They fulfilled different needs of the group. Jennings found only one quality they had in common: They were more interested in others than they were in themselves. Even this characteristic would not apply to all leaders in groups. We need only to think of the highly authoritarian gang leader, whose interest is frequently only personal and who uses the group members for selfish reasons.

Indigenous leaders grow out of the group. They are accepted by

[7]Helen Hall Jennings, *Leadership and Isolation, A Study in Personality in Interpersonal Relations* (New York: Longmans, Green, 1943).

group members as the leader because they fulfill the purpose of the group, because they can be helpful to them, or because they have usurped power and are ruling by fear. The social group worker is *not* considered and must not take the role of the leader in the modern concept of group work. The group worker is an outsider who *helps* the group and each member, including the leader. At times he or she must help a group to become strong enough to withdraw from an authoritarian leader or to help alter the form of leadership being used.

Leader, isolate, and member of a subgroup are all positions individuals take in the group by virtue of their interaction with others. The concept of *role* has been added to the understanding of individual behavior. It indicates the *expected behavior of an individual in a group,* usually defined not by the person alone, but by the group and by the culture in which he or she grows up. Each human being is expected to perform many roles, often simultaneously. A young man must be parent to his child and at the same time, child to his own parents, two highly diverse roles, difficult to hold at the same time, and frequently a cause for conflict. Yet to become what is expected of him, he must be able to learn to combine these roles, and many additional ones. He may have to be learner in one group context—an evening class, for instance—and a teacher, either to his own children or as a professional, in another. The capacity to carry roles of often very different nature competently and without great inner conflict is part of a healthy personality. One of the attributes of a healthy society is to make demands on its members that are not too contradictory. Yet, few do this. The present culture of the United States, for example, asks for highly divergent role behavior among women, ranging from the role of wife and mother, with focus on the home, to the one of breadwinner and citizen, with active participation in the affairs of the country. Where these expectations are not regarded as mutually exclusive and where the woman can accept the role appropriate to her own specific situation, no breakdown occurs. Some women can combine all these roles successfully. When the role expectation is such that it allows no flexibility and where a particular subgroup (i.e., the family, the profession, or the neighborhood) insists upon the exclusive value of one or the other role, the woman may then develop feelings of guilt or conflict.

Role conflict may also be produced by an individual's faulty perception of what is expected of him or her.

### Example

In a group of parents discussing mental health needs in the family, Mr. D. constantly injected complicated terms and their definitions. The group became increasingly impatient with him, and finally "told him off." Mr. D. was bewildered. "I thought it was expected of me to bring in my knowledge," he said. (He had worked in a mental hygiene clinic.)

Mr. D. had not realized that, by joining the group of parents, the others expected him to participate as the father of his children, not as a teacher.

Helen Padula described dramatically how role expectation can influence behavior so strongly that it prevents recovery:

> Patients may reflect the expectation that they are sick as long as they are in a mental hospital. Throughout many years of hospitalization, a young man in a V.A. hospital was never known to walk forward; he always navigated backward. A nurse ran into him on the street, on his first trial visit. He was walking forward, quite normally. Amazed, she asked him, "How come?" "Oh," said he, "outside you are not allowed to walk backward."[8]

The concept of role is a valuable one in adding to the understanding of the individual as well as of group mores. It must never be used rigidly, though, and it must always be used with the full knowledge of the great variety of roles an individual can and must play, as well as the many cultural differences expressed through role behavior. Much harm has been done by stereotyped assumptions of roles based on preconceived value systems or limited understanding and experience with the richness and variety of the many roles human beings can take. The word role is a rather unfortunate one. The variations of individual's behavior are genuine, not "played."

A group becomes a group—more than the sum of its individuals—when it develops a certain relationship, a tie, a force that gives the individual a feeling of belonging. This feeling of belonging is called the group *bond.* A bond may change in time; it may become stronger or weaker. Natural groups usually start with some bond; formed groups frequently have no feeling of a bond in the beginning, but develop it in the course of treatment or by working together. A group cannot exist for long without a bond. This does not mean, however, that a strong bond is always beneficial to group members or that a weak one always indicates a poor group experience.

In post-World War II Germany, a young American tried to discuss with a group the great importance of *Gemeinschaft,* a group with a bond; he extolled its virtues. He could not understand why his audience froze. He learned later that this had been one of the major propaganda slogans of Nazi Germany: the Nazis had fostered a strong bond among Germans to enhance the exclusiveness of the German "Aryan" and to bind them closely to one another. Bond in itself does not present a value. It can serve constructive or destructive purposes. A delinquent gang may have a strong group bond. The purpose of the group—stealing—is well served by this.

---

[8]Helen Padula, "Releasing the Human Potential in Chronic Mental Patients through Social Work Services," paper presented at the Workshop conducted by Ontario Department of Health, May 25-26, 1961, mimeographed; subsequently published in *The Social Worker,* 29, No. 4, Canadian Assn. of Social Workers (Oct. 1961), 13-25.

Group work with the gang may mean help with a change of its purpose while keeping the bond strong; yet it may also lie in helping to dissolve the bond, depending on the dynamics of a particular gang. In a therapy group, the worker usually will help the group to develop some bond, otherwise the individual shells cannot be broken. Yet the worker will be wary lest the bond become too strong and the group not allow its members to join other healthy community groups even if they are capable of this. A responsibility of the helper is to help diminish bond when the group has served its limited purpose. The great emotional significance of bond among members must be kept in mind and they must not be forced to give it up abruptly: This has been done too frequently when group dynamics were overlooked in the treatment and the group was regarded as a collection of individuals. The group worker will have to help the group members to be "weaned" from the bond among themselves, just as the baby is weaned, by allowing for some pleasure and substitution in the process. This may mean referral to new satisfying groups or a conscious return to groups that had meaning to the patient prior to being sick.

Bonds can also become damaging when their strength prevents members from seeking any associations outside the group.

### Example

The group worker encountered a group of middle-aged women who had met since they were teen-agers. They enjoyed their meetings. They guarded their relationship so strongly that any member who had tried to break away was considered a "traitor." The women had stayed unmarried and had made no friendships outside this club.

One may argue that these women apparently were enjoying the life they wanted—which may be true. It was apparent, though, that the strong bond had severely limited their horizons. A similar dynamic can sometimes be observed in professional groups or in agency staffs that are proud of their strong sense of unity, but it severely limits members to their own particular group. The members interpret a movement away from the group—a change of profession or agency affiliation, for example—as a rejection of the total group; they react toward anyone's leaving with hostility and a complete severance of relationships.

The group worker's aim is toward a bond that gives warmth and security to its members and that allows them to move with relative freedom to or away from the group. The degree of strength of the bond must vary according to each individual group's constellation and purposes.

The move into a group which has developed a bond is not easy. The position of the *newcomer*, the one who enters an already formed group, needs special attention. It is a basic law of groups that the total "gestalt" of the group changes when a new person enters. This applies also to the family, the primary group. Any additional child changes the total family situation. The smaller the family the more intense is this change. Groups react to the newcomer in a way different from the way they react to any other member. At entrance into the group the newcomer becomes the receiver of the group's hopes or its anxieties or hostilities. The exaggerated acceptance that an "expert from far away" (for instance, the consultant in a foreign country) usually experiences is produced largely by his being "the stranger in the group." If he has high status all expectations and hopes are thrown upon him. He does not enter the daily concerns of the group—their more intimate relationships—and therefore he is exempt from certain strains and stresses among the members. He enjoys a "moratorium" in group relationships, thus making him very effective for a limited time, but excluding him from real acceptance. Only when his "feet of clay" are allowed to show, does he become a member of the group. If a consultant or expert is not aware of this, he may have the wrong idea of his true capacities and get a rude awakening.

The anxiety and hostility are usually encountered by the newcomer who has no high status introduction. This occurs often in children's groups—especially in institutions where group composition changes frequently—if no special help is given to change this damaging aspect of the group process. Since the newcomer, whether adult or child, is usually insecure and afraid when entering an already formed group, such help is a necessary function of group work. The newcomer is not only afraid of the others in the group, but he or she is also concerned about meeting personal expectations.

### Example

John had been on a trial visit to the treatment center and had met the other children. That day he had moved in "easily," almost with bravado. At noon he arrived to stay. He ate little. The other children—very occupied with themselves—either ignored him or showed a certain coldness. In the rest period after lunch I found John lying on the floor of his room with his head sticking out into the corridor—he was obviously trying to hear what others were saying and yet did not dare to join them.

All individuals in the group change constantly through their interactions with others. Most people feel a healthy ambivalence in regard to this. They wish to be involved, but at the same time they resist change and desire to keep their identity as it is. This struggle in the individual between status quo and change has its parallel in the processes of *conflict* and *solution* in the group. A group that shows no conflict (this includes again the family) is a dead one, indicating either an extinction of its member's individuality or a pretense at it—with underlying deep cleavages. A group that is in constant conflict with no way of solving it is a sick one, giving no satisfaction to its members and keeping them in a state of insecurity and hostility. Conflict-solving is a major task of groups, whether it concerns the sharp clash between inmates in a penitentiary, the hurting differences in a family, the gang fights of teen-agers, the racial conflicts in a neighborhood, the nagging accusations in a secluded group of institutionalized people, or the differences of opinions in a community leadership group. The various types of conflict-solving can be classified as follows:

1. *Withdrawal* of one part of the group. Examples of this are the "We don't play with you any more" in a children's group or desertion in a family.
2. *Subjugation.* A willful silencing of one part of the group either by the leader of the opposition or by a subgroup. This can be accomplished by violence, including murder, or through threat, ridicule, or any display of superior power on the part of a particular subgroup within the total group.
3. *Majority rule.* This is also a form of subjugating the minority, although it is not quite as arbitrary as other forms of subjugation.
4. *Minority consent to majority rule.* Here the factor of subjugation is ruled out since deliberations must have preceded the final solution and the minority has agreed to abide by the majority decision.
5. *Compromise.* Neither side gets full satisfaction, but each agrees to the limits to be set on its own suggestions.
6. *Integration.* A rare and highly complicated form of conflict-solving that presupposes thoughtful deliberations with a desire on both sides to arrive at a common decision, even though the final decision may be quite different from that originally proposed. Integration occurs, for example, in Quaker meetings where the required period of silence is a recognition that each side must somehow work through its own desire to be "victor." (Being human, they do not always succeed.)

These solutions lie on an ascending scale of capacity in conflict-solving. Group maturity can be measured partially in the way a group solves its conflicts and arrives at decisions; conflict-solving and decision-making are similar processes since both involve a choice between alternatives.

Group workers must use this knowledge, as helpers, to give the individuals in the groups they work with an opportunity for conflict-solving and decision-making. They must recognize that deprivation of this opportunity can bring about or increase pathology within any group. This is evident in hospitalized mental patients, particularly those in institutions where there is little understanding of the significance of a normal group living situation conducive to interaction among people, participation in decisions, and expression of concern for others.

### Example

In adapting to the insular mores of the mental hospital the patient loses his capacity to deal with the world outside. Already afflicted by dissociative and depersonalizing influences inside himself, he is exposed to a culture in which these very symptoms are powerfully reinforced. Conditioned by a sick, empty, and routinized world; *deprived of any necessity or right to make decisions* [italics by author]; enervated by monotony; separated from family, friends, and normal associations, the patient is gradually shorn of whatever courage, capacity, and resources he ever had. He becomes socially crippled in addition to, or in place of, his illness.[9]

The problem of deprivation also exists in prisons, and—unfortunately— also in some community-based facilities which rarely give an opportunity for decision-making in a group. (And this in a population that particularly needs learning in this area!)

When a group moves away from irrational behavior in the way it makes decisions and learns a new—and more rational—way of solving conflicts, individuals in the group begin to feel an inner strength and a pride in themselves as well as in the group. Self-discipline does not grow out of the effort an individual makes alone; it is helped through group interaction. Thus discipline is no longer felt by the individual as rigid confinement, but rather as a breath of freedom from overwhelming forces.


## SUMMARY

The *dynamics of the group* are deeply intertwined with the dynamics of each individual in it. The movement of the group—the group process—is seen in the relationships between its members. It changes in time; its quality depends on the degree of health and the maturity of its members and on the purpose of the group. Group workers must understand group formation. They must understand the necessity for subgroups and assess the place of subgroups in the total group. They must know about the positions of members as *isolates, leaders,* or *members of subgroups,* for the role of each member is related to the expectations of the group and to its values and mores. Group workers must recognize *bond* as a vital part of every group and realize that its degree is intrinsically related to *group formation* and *goal.* Finally, they must recognize *conflict-solving* and *decision-making* as specific functions of groups, with a strong impact, in turn, on individual development.


## BIBLIOGRAPHY

ADLER, DAN L., RONALD LIPPITT, and RALPH K. WHITE,   "An Experiment with Young People Under Democratic, Autocratic and Laissez-faire Atmospheres," *Proceedings of the National Conference of Social Work,* 1939, pp. 152-158. New York: Columbia University Press, 1939.

[9]Helen Padula, "Releasing the Human Potential in Chronic Mental Patients ... ," Workshop paper, p. 1.

BAXTER, BERNICE and ROSALIND CASSIDY, *Group Experience: The Democratic Way*. New York: Harper & Row, Pub., 1943.

BORGATTA, EDGAR F., "What Social Science Says About Groups," *Social Welfare Forum, 1957*, pp. 212-235. New York: Columbia University Press, 1957.

BERNSTEIN, SAUL, "There are Groups and Groups," *The Group*, XIII, No. 1 (1951).

BRADFORD, LELAND P. and RONALD LIPPITT, "Building a Democratic Work Group," *Personnel*, 22, No. 3 (1945).

CARTWRIGHT, DORWIN and ALVIN ZANDER, eds., *Group Dynamics—Research and Theory*. Evanston, Il: Harper & Row, Pub., 1953.

COOLEY, CHARLES H., "Primary Groups," in A. Paul Hare, Edgar F. Borgatta, and Robert F. Bales, eds., *Small Groups—Studies in Social Interaction*, pp. 15-20. New York: Knopf, 1955.

COYLE, GRACE L., "New Insights Available to the Social Worker from the Social Sciences," *Social Service Review*, XXVI, No. 3 (Sept. 1952), 289-304.

_____, *Social Process in Organized Groups*. New York: Richard R. Smith and Co., 1930.

_____, *Studies in Group Behavior*. New York: Harper & Row, Pub., 1937.

DURKHEIM, EMILE, "Division of Labor," in Hare et al., eds., *Small Groups*, pp. 5-9.

FELDMAN, RONALD A., "Group Integration, Intense Interpersonal Dislike and Social Group Work Intervention," *Social Work*, 14, No. 3 (July 1969), 30-40.

FESTINGER, LEON, "A Theory of Social Comparison Processes," in Hare et al., eds., *Small Groups*, pp. 163-187.

FROMM, ERICH, *Escape From Freedom*. New York: Holt, Rinehart & Winston, 1941.

GARLAND, JAMES, HUBERT JONES, and RALPH L. KOLODNY, "A Model for Stages of Development in Social Work Groups," in Saul Bernstein, ed., *Explorations in Group Work*, pp. 12-53. Boston: Boston University School of Social Work, 1965.

HAIMAN, FRANKLYN S., *Group Leadership and Democratic Action*. Boston: Houghton Mifflin, 1950.

HENDRY, CHARLES E., ed., *Decade of Group Work*. New York: Association Press, 1948.

INKELES, ALEX, "Personality and Social Structure," in Robert K. Merton, Leonard Broom, and Leonard S. Cottrell, Jr., eds., *Sociology Today*, pp. 249-276. New York: Basic Books, 1959.

JENNINGS, HELEN HULL, *Leadership and Isolation, A Study in Personality in Interpersonal Relations*. New York: Longmans, Green, 1943.

_____, *Sociometry of Leadership*, Sociometry Monographs No. 14, 1947.

KENDALL, KATHERINE A., "New Dimensions in Casework and Group Work Practice: Implications for Professional Education," *Social Work*, 4, No. 4 (Oct. 1959), 49-56.

KONOPKA, GISELA, "Social Group Work: A Social Work Method," *Social Work*, 5, No. 4 (Oct. 1960), 53-61.

_____, *Therapeutic Group Work with Children*. Minneapolis: University of Minnesota Press, 1949.

LEWIN, KURT, *Resolving Social Conflicts*. New York: Harper & Row, Pub., 1948.

_____, "'Subjective' and 'Objective' Elements in the Social Field: The Three-Step Procedures," in Hare et al., eds., *Small Groups*, pp. 95-98.

LIPPITT, RONALD, "Applying New Knowledge about Group Behavior," *Selected Papers in Group Work and Community Organization*, pp. 7-17. Raleigh, NC: Health Publications Institute, 1951.

MERTON, ROBERT K., *Social Theory and Social Structure.* Glencoe, Il: The Free Press, 1949.

NEWSTETTER, WILBER I., "What is Social Group Work?" *Proceedings of the National Conference of Social Work,* 1935, pp. 291-299. New York: Columbia University Press, 1935.

REDL, FRITZ, "The Art of Group Composition" in *When We Deal with Children,* pp. 236-253. New York: Free Press, 1966.

SHALINSKY, WILLIAM, "Group Composition as an Element in Social Group Work Practice," *Social Service Review,* 43, No. 1 (Mar. 1969), 42-50.

SHERIF, MUZAFER, *The Psychology of Social Norms.* New York: Harper & Row, Pub., 1936.

SIMMEL, GEORG, "The Significance of Numbers for Social Life," in Hare et al., eds., *Small Groups,* pp. 9-15.

SOMERS, MARY LOUISE, "Four Small Group Theories: An Analysis and Frame of Reference for Use as Teaching Content in Social Group Work," D.S.W. Thesis, Western Reserve University, June 1957.

THOMAS, EDWIN J., "Effects of Group Size," *Psychological Bulletin,* 60 (1963), 371-384.

TYLER, RALPH W., "Implications of Research in the Behavioral Sciences for Group Life and Group Services," *Social Welfare Forum,* 1960, pp. 113-126. New York: Columbia University Press, 1960.

*What can I know?*
*What ought I to do?*
*What may I hope?* [1]
*I call the World a moral World in so far as it may be in*
*accordance with all the ethical laws—which, by virtue of the*
*freedom of reasonable beings, it can be, and according to the*
*necessary laws of morality it ought to be.* [2]

# FIVE
# THE VALUE BASE OF SOCIAL GROUP WORK

All intervention of a professional nature is goal-directed, regardless of whether it is dealing with inanimate objects or with human beings. An intervention that is called upon to deal with human relationships must consider ethical values in determining its purpose. The helping process of social work is strongly influenced by the profession's values and its view of the people with whom it is concerned. Social work has struggled through its history with its goal direction. It has gone through a period, which is not yet completely over, where it tried to take over the goal orientation of

---

[1] Immanuel Kant, *Critique of Pure Reason,* translated by Norman K. Smith (London, N.Y.: Wiley Book Co., 1933), p. 178.

[2] Ibid., p. 453.

medicine, whose key concept is "health," and which, when related to physical medicine, has a certain objectivity or tangibility. Yet the moment any profession is concerned with aspects other than the purely physical ones, the concept of health becomes more complicated and begins to include culturally determined ethical values. This value system—the "philosophy" of social work, as it is frequently designated—is the same for the whole profession:

> That philosophy ... is not different when the activity happens to be skillful leadership of groups, the casework method of helping troubled people, or a project in community organization. Indeed, the philosophy of social work cannot be separated from the prevailing philosophy of a nation as to how it values people, and what importance it sets upon their welfare.[3]

The key values of social work are ethical ones, since they concern themselves with interpersonal relations. They are "justice" and "responsibility" combined with a less defined, but somewhat different, value of "mental health." *Justice* means the basic acceptance of the dignity of each human being regardless of any specific attribute, such as race, sex, economic status, intellectual endowment, and physical prowess that might differentiate a person from others. Justice does not imply that all people are the same or require that all be treated the same; it implies only that all be accorded the same consideration, the same acceptance, the same love, and the same opportunity.

*Responsibility* includes the awareness of the interdependence of human beings, of the acceptance of the rights of others as well as of one's own, and of the concept of the brotherhood of all people.

*Mental health* signifies the understanding that the human being must have a sense of inner satisfaction and inner strength to be able to give to others.

These values are *a priori;* they are the axioms of professional practice. They are imbedded in the value systems of a large number of human cultures. Great religions, occidental and oriental, have incorporated them, and humanists have accepted them. They do not belong to one profession or to one discipline alone. They belong to all citizens in all human societies. The professions that work with individuals and their relations to each other must at every moment in practice come to terms with these questions of values, for they constantly deal, as Eduard C. Lindeman once said, with "facts infused with values." Social workers have hesitated at times to use such terms as "right" and "wrong" or "good" and "bad" when it comes to human behavior; they have wanted to avoid becoming too judgmental. Yet we must face the fact that we actually use these judgments in every aspect of our work with individual clients and groups.

[3]Bertha C. Reynolds, *Social Work and Social Living* (New York: Citadel Press, 1951).

Why should we help youngsters to learn not to steal cars? Only because we want them to avoid being caught? In that case perhaps someone can teach them to steal cars better. Why do we ask for humane treatment of patients in mental hospitals? So many are not yet curable, and the cheapest way to take care of them is to herd them into some large congregate institution and forget about them. The *dignity of each individual* as a value is the only answer to this. The idea of a "valueless" practice of social work hardly ever existed. When it was advocated it was more an attempt made to ward off arbitrary impositions of values. This idea had haunted social work practice from the beginning, especially in the field of public relief when people from comfortable middle-class backgrounds tried to impose their kind of living on others tortured by poverty and a life that could not conform to the totality of middle-class values.[4] The social worker had much to learn about understanding people and appreciating the cultural differences between them while, at the same time, maintaining clarity about ethical values. Eduard C. Lindeman, one of the few philosophers in social work, helped by his distinction between *primary* and *secondary* values. The first ones represent basic ethical demands, and the latter ones grow out of cultural mores that change in time and place. They are not easily separated or recognized in practice.[5]

Among social workers there is no common agreement as to the origin of the two primary values—the dignity of each individual human being and the responsibility of human beings for each other. Those social workers who come into the profession with strong religious backgrounds see them as values derived from a spiritual being, God; those who represent a more secular background see them as derived from ethical law. In spite of the difference of opinion in regard to their origin, there is general acceptance of these values as the basis of the profession. They are recognized as absolute values by the profession and axiomatic to its practice. Certain translations of these values into practice are commonly agreed upon by practitioners, regardless of the method they use.

1. Social work stands for the elimination of discrimination against anyone because of race, creed, national origin, sex, age, or social class. Beyond this it is one of the goals of group workers to enhance appreciation of people belonging to differing groups. This is a goal even where group work is practiced under sectarian auspices. A social work practitioner using the group work method in a Catholic, Protestant, or Jewish agency will always make an effort to help members to learn to appreciate and live with those of other religions. One of the basic tasks of the use of the social group work method is to help

---

[4]An illustration of this can be found in the bitter book, Caroline Slade, *Lilly Crackell* (New York: World Publishing, 1943).

[5]For a more intensive discussion of the philosophy of social work, see Gisela Konopka, *Eduard C. Lindeman and Social Work Philosophy* (Minneapolis: University of Minnesota Press, 1958), especially Chapter 5.

change the culture of racial discrimination through a learning of real appreciation of people of different backgrounds. (Application of the value of "dignity of each individual.")

2. All social group workers agree on the *value of cooperation.* In the framework of a highly competitive society the social group work method consciously includes provision for positive experience in cooperating with each other. (Man's healthy striving for individual recognition may destroy the value of "responsibility for others.")

3. The value system of the social group worker includes the importance of *individual initiative.* Social group work practice must enhance individual initiative in the framework of creative cooperation. (Application of both primary values.)

4. Another accepted value derived from the basic ones is *freedom of participation.* The dignity of individuals must be expressed through their freedom to express their thoughts and ideas and their right to participate in matters concerning themselves and their community. This concept is so basic to the group work method that it distinguishes its practitioner from the entertainer or authoritarian leader. Those roles are legitimate ones in other human endeavors, but they must be avoided in the helping process of social group work. This value also raises the demand for one of the most difficult processes of social group work, namely the encouragement of participation of each individual in decision-making. One of the greatest skills of the social group worker is to help individuals in different stages of development and with different capacities to participate in a given group situation. It is also one of the most gratifying accomplishments of the use of this method.

5. Agreement also lies in the value placed on high *individualization in the group.* One of the basic characteristics of the social group work method is individualization in the group. Although some activities can be conducted without it, they do not belong in the practice of social group work. The emotional satisfaction felt by people through mass events may have an important place in human society. However, such events do not use the social group method, for the social group work method always includes individualization.

There is certainly far less agreement in the area of *secondary values.* If they are values relating to cultural mores without major ethical implications, such as questions of taste and aesthetics, they usually do not present serious problems to the practitioner. The group worker should know him- or herself well enough to recognize quickly his or her own biases and to be capable of either letting members decide differently or to present to them reasons for such preferences. More difficult to handle are the secondary values that do include ethical considerations, for they are not as clearly outlined and not as commonly agreed upon as the previously named five primary values.

For instance: Should a delinquency institution be coeducational? Must every mother stay at home and not accept gainful employment? Must all women accept gainful employment? How compatible with good practice is the use of rewards? Answers to these questions differ, depending upon four factors influencing the practitioner: the group worker's own cultural and family background; the precepts and demands of given groups to which he or she belongs—such as religious, professional, or social groups, demands that sometimes create conflicts within the individual; personal experiences such as illness and experiences in groups at earlier times in life; and differing theories regarding human behavior.

A first step toward not arbitrarily using one's own values lies in the willingness to examine honestly and conscientiously the base of one's own values.

The profession of social work places upon the practitioner the stern demand to investigate constantly the source of his or her secondary values. It does not mean that these values should be rejected—on the contrary, to be an effective human being one must maintain standards. But a group worker must be willing to reject the secondary values if they are not compatible with professional demands, or be able to understand group members if their values are different.

Social workers should gain some knowledge of differing cultures in order to understand their own cultural and family backgrounds and to realize the way they influence their values. An anthropologist once remarked that people react to their own culture in the same way they react to their own drinking water. While they think their own has no flavor, they readily discern a peculiar taste in water from other regions. It is impossible for a person to understand and look objectively at his or her own cultural background without exposure to others. This exposure must include a real *experiencing* of other cultures, not just cold observation. It must become evident to the social group worker that others consider their particular values just as desirable as the group worker considers his or her own. This cannot easily be learned in the actual group work situation because of the helping role of the group worker. In this role the practitioner cannot experience another culture in the genuine way one can only truly experience it: by being an equal and a friend. The demand therefore for insight into other cultures is not an easy one to fulfill. It may be achieved before the start of professional education, either by belonging to organizations that offer experience with a wide variety of people of different cultural and social backgrounds, or by conscious effort in liberal education to let the student vicariously experience this through literature, theater, and the arts. It may be done in professional education by giving students opportunities to meet other students and to discuss openly and freely their differing values. Because of the importance of the value component in group interaction, social group work education places great emphasis on this. This will have to be done more than ever because of increasing stratification in present society.

Yet exposure to other groups alone does not lead to critical evaluation of one's own value system; it only provides the necessary prerequisite to do so. The social group worker must realize in order to be a responsible practitioner self-evaluation is necessary. A group worker can only fulfill his helping role if he, for example, understands that swearing does not have the same meaning to children from a certain neighborhood that it may have to him, coming from a different background. This group worker need not accept swearing in every case as "right," but he must learn to understand its meaning and not see it as a moral issue.

The same investigation must apply to values that are derived from the precepts of significant groups or personal experiences. Group demands can be very stringent, but the group worker must distinguish whether they are demands related to the basic ethical values of the profession or to a segment of the society in which the practitioner lives. To illustrate this: A professional group worker who belonged to a religious order accepted clearly the precepts of her religion, which demanded daily church attendance for herself. Yet in no way did she consider it right to make this same demand on the members of the groups in her charge. She had learned to distinguish between the demands and precepts of her group, which were binding on her, but which were not necessarily so for those with whom she worked—even if she considered them desirable for those people. Only if values are clearly understood can the worker distinguish between those which are indispensable to social work practice and those which may be desirable but must not be imposed.

The values growing out of specific personal experiences are often as deeply ingrained in a person as those originating in parental attitudes. A group worker argued vehemently with every reasoning available against a camping season that would last longer than two weeks. When she became aware of the rigidity of her rejection of longer camping periods she began to realize that it related to her own painful experience of a long separation from her parents. Only then did she understand that it might have a different meaning to others.

All forms of social interaction in a given culture are expressions of certain values. Some of these violate basic ethical demands, as previously discussed. Among these forms of social interaction are: discrimination; enforced segregation; and the withholding of opportunities from individuals because of their race, color, creed, nationality, sex, age, or social class. The social worker is obliged to work toward change in individuals as well as in the systems that foster such damaging practice. There are other forms of social interaction that also require active change, although they do not violate ethical values; rather they are harmful to the emotional or mental health of individuals. One example of these is presented here because the social group worker is especially concerned with it:[6] the threatening disappearance of friendship in our present culture.

In the post-World War II years, the United States has experienced an

---

[6]See also pp. 41–43.

increased growth of urban living combined with a general rise in the standard of living and an almost pervasive middle class. These changes have been accompanied by a loss of intimacy among people. Friendship in the sense of warm, giving relationships outside the family circle has become rare. People often have numerous group associations, but usually they are on a rather superficial emotional basis. Many suffer from the fact that they have no friends with whom they can openly discuss personal problems.

The fear of losing status prevents many persons from sharing their feelings of joy, anger, or distress with others. Association with others may serve professional or vocational purposes ("business contacts") or purely recreational or intellectual ones. A happy "front" is required, which prohibits discussion of any personal problem. The relationships among people are usually friendly but casual. In case of a major catastrophe, which is socially acceptable (e.g., a natural death of a family member or physical illness), colleagues or neighbors rally and help. But problems that involve feelings of unhappiness or inadequacy usually are avoided. The same applies to the genuine sharing of deep satisfactions—success may arouse envy. Thus the human being is deprived of the vital contribution friendship makes to life. People, however, cannot live without this support.

The loss of intimacy among adults outside the family circle has serious effects on young people. Some withdraw into serious emotional isolation; others develop only shallow relationships with people. Many of them can conceive of a comfortable and giving relationship only in marriage, hence they rush into marriage without ever having experienced a close and secure friendship with contemporaries previous to it.

The "youth revolt" of the late 1960s and 1970s was directly related to this loss of intimacy. Those needs have continued in spite of some movements of that period that almost exclusively stressed "feelings." Groups met for long weekends during which touching and feeling were promoted. Those methods provided satisfaction for a short time without providing continued support. Friendship groups are continuously needed. Young people found in their communes, their camps, their rock festivals, and sometimes in drugs this searched-for intimacy. Professional services, whether given individually or in groups, are only poor substitutes for real friendship. The social group worker may encourage friendship between group members and create an atmosphere of trust in the group. The group worker also works consciously on cultural change by drawing attention to the loss of a most valuable form of human relations.

## *SUMMARY*

The line between justified use of values in social work practice and of arbitrary imposition on others is fine. As usual, when human beings are confronted with such a dilemma they may fall into one extreme or the other. The fear of imposing one's own values has led at times to an unprincipled laissez-faire attitude in practice. On the other hand, the fear of becoming too permissive has led to an imposition of values and the creation of a dogmatic group climate. The clear acceptance of primary values and of the demand of honest investigation into the social worker's own value system are basic to social group work practice.

## BIBLIOGRAPHY

ADDAMS, JANE, *Democracy and Social Ethics.* New York: Macmillan, 1902.

COOKE, THE REVEREND TERENCE J., *Thomistic Philosophy in the Principles of Social Group Work.* Washington, DC: The Catholic University of America Press, 1951.

COYLE, GRACE L., *Group Experience and Democratic Values.* New York: The Woman's Press, 1947.

HALL, L. K., "Group Workers and Professional Ethics," *The Group,* XV, No. 1 (Oct. 1952), 3–8.

KAISER, CLARA A., "Social Group Work Practice and Social Responsibility," *Social Welfare Forum 1952,* pp. 161–167. New York: Columbia University Press, 1952.

KENDALL, KATHERINE, ed., *Social Work Values in an Age of Discontent.* New York: Council on Social Work Education, 1970.

KONOPKA, GISELA, *Eduard C. Lindeman and Social Work Philosophy.* Minneapolis: University of Minnesota Press, 1958.

—————, "Formation of Values in the Developing Person," in Dorothy Rogers, ed., *Issues in Child Psychology* (2nd. ed.). Monterey, CA: Brooks/Cole Publishing Co., 1977, pp. 292–297.

MURPHY, MARJORIE, *The Social Group Work Method in Social Work Education,* Vol. XI, *A Project Report of the Curriculum Study,* Werner W. Boehm, Director and Coordinator. New York: Council on Social Work Education, 1959.

PUMPHREY, MURIEL W., *The Teaching of Values and Ethics in Social Work Teaching,* Vol. XIII, *A Project Report of the Curriculum Study,* cited above.

REYNOLDS, BERTHA C., *Social Work and Social Living.* New York: Citadel Press, 1951.

TILLICH, PAUL, "The Philosophy of Social Work," *The Social Service Review,* XXXVI, No. 1 (Mar. 1962), 13–16.

WILSON, GERTRUDE and GLADYS RYLAND, "Social Classes: Implications for Social Group Work," *Social Welfare Forum 1954,* pp. 168–186. New York: Columbia University Press, 1954.

# SIX

# ASSESSING AND ESTABLISHING OBJECTIVES IN SOCIAL GROUP WORK
## *Diagnosis or Clarification*

After discussing the concepts of the individual and the group, and clarifying the value base of the group worker's approach, we can now develop the helping process of social group work as part of the general function of social work as discussed in Chapter 2. Let us return once more to the three points Marjorie Murphy presented in the *Curriculum Study,* on which there is agreement in regard to the group work method:

1.  Social group work is a method of rendering service to persons, through providing experience in groups. Development of the person towards his indi-

---

[1] Immanuel Kant, *Critique of Pure Reason,* translated by J. M. D. Meiklejohn (New York: John Wiley, 1943), p. 451.

vidual potential, improvement of relationship and social functioning competencies, and social action are recognized as purposes of social group work. The worker functions within a framework of ethical and social values.

2. Social group work is a generic method which can be used in different settings.

3. The method includes conscious use of worker-member relationships, relationships among members, and of group activity. The worker simultaneously uses relationships with individual members and with the group as a whole. He works as an enabler with both, helping members and the group to use their capacities and strengths. He uses himself differently in accordance with specific objectives and his assessment of members' needs, interests and capacities.[2]

Points 1 and 2 show the range of purposes for which group work help is needed and include a large range of agencies fulfilling such purposes. They fall clearly into two distinct categories:

1. Groups that serve the "development of the person toward his individual potential, improvement of relationship and social functioning competencies," as most youth groups and all groups with therapeutic intent, and

2. Groups that need help with "social action," frequently consisting of highly capable people in leadership positions in their communities who want to become effective combatants of social problems.

There has been and still is some controversy among social group workers as to whether these two categories fall within the province of social group work. Gertrude Wilson distinguished between growth oriented and task oriented groups, and was frequently attacked because she seemed to say that task oriented groups do not fall within the province of social group work.[3] To this writer the differentiation between growth oriented and social action oriented groups seems a clearer one, although perhaps some day a better and more refined classification can be found. Task orientation seems to be too large a classification, since this may include groups in a factory with the task of finishing a piece of machinery (obviously not in the orbit of social group work, although anyone working with such a group may gain from it a knowledge of group process and dynamics). It may include a group of severely handicapped people consciously working on the task of learning to move into normal society from which they may have been cut off for a long time—obviously falling within the orbit of social group work. If we distinguish between growth oriented and social action oriented groups, however, we stay clearly in the area of social group work

[2]Marjorie Murphy, "The Social Group Work Method in Social Work Education," *A Project Report of the Curriculum Study*, XI, Werner W. Boehm, Director and Coordinator, (New York: Council on Social Work Education, 1959), p. 78.

[3]Gertrude Wilson, "Social Group Work: Trends and Developments," *Social Work*, I, No. 4 (Oct. 1956), 66–75.

and we have a classification of different groups that is necessary for the determination of the differential use of social group work skills, although it may be a very rough and not highly differentiated classification. Both of these categories demand problem-solving; both relate to social problems; both demand group work skill through individualization in face-to-face groups; both need the understanding of individual and group dynamics; both require the same translation of values into action, which in this case is the helping process. Yet they are distinguished from each other by the fact that the individual in the growth oriented group needs direct help with personal development and problems, while the individual in the social action directed group needs help with becoming effective on behalf of problems not necessarily rooted within him- or herself or in relationships with others. Not every social action group needs a social group worker, but many do. This author also includes in this term staff committees of social agencies, which try to work on such things as the improvement of practice and adult committees in neighborhood houses. It must be understood, of course, that there may be individuals in such groups who need specific help for themselves and that it is part of the group worker's general responsibility for individualization to spot this. But individual treatment is not the purpose of social action groups, and turning them into therapy groups (i.e., growth-oriented groups) or constantly searching for "sick people" among the members is a misuse of the helping or enabling function in such groups.

It would be desirable if we had a more refined system of classifying groups, but this is not yet available.

In spite of the absence of a clear classification system in the total social work profession, the group worker must be able to assess individual members as well as the group as a whole so as to establish objectives for doing purposeful work. In working with individuals social workers have frequently used psychiatric classification systems, yet they become increasingly aware of the fact that these are not sufficient for the social work orientation of seeing the individual interact with others and the systems in which he or she moves. Much of what is called "diagnosis" in social work is not a diagnosis in the medical sense. It is more a summarized recognition of the individual and the group situation and it should entail a conscious clarification and ordering of observed facts. Social work diagnosis is an assessment of the group and the individuals who are in the group in the light of theory and a resulting establishment of goal-directed work. It often changes in the course of social work treatment because of changing conditions or the influence of new experiences and knowledge on the social worker and the client or members.

The absence of diagnostic categories lies in the nature of the phenomena with which the group worker works. This was early recognized by those who worked in child guidance clinics:

> We have little sympathy with the idea that an individual or his problem can be really known through 'an examination' and a labelling process—it requires, rather, an *examination into* what makes him what he is and makes him do what he does. It can only be lack of experience in studying life careers that leads anyone to believe otherwise. . . .
> . . . Important whole groups of facts are not taken account of in any ordinary investigation; for example, the powerful but formative influences of mental life that are always active in home and other associations beneath the surface of observable exteriors.[4]

Clarity of assessment and establishment of purposeful objectives is a prerequisite for competent help and for critical evaluation of goals reached. Without such assessment the work of the group worker either becomes vague ("I just work with this group," a young group worker in training said. "What is the purpose of your being there? What is it that you try to help with?" "I don't know; I am just there.") or it becomes sterile with a stereotyped kind of "recipe" approach ("I always use an observer and recorder. I always let the group be completely free to decide to do whatever it wants to do.")

Objectives are not determined by the group worker alone. They are determined by the group members' conscious needs, which bring them to the groups, the purpose of the agency or organization, and the group worker's understanding of the individual and the total group, including frequently a recognition of needs not conscious to the members. The latter does not mean that the group worker "always knows best," constantly searching for meaning that is in exact opposition to what members express. This tendency to never accept an expressed emotion or thought as real was an unfortunate byproduct of a misunderstood Freudian approach. It has seriously harmed the work of the human relations professions, because the knowledge of preconscious or unconscious motivation was used in an almost punishing, or omnipotent, way and allowed the group member or client no recourse when he or she disagreed with the professional. This was then chalked up as "resistance." It often distorted understanding into fanciful guesswork, instead of helping to determine what the person *really* wanted or felt. The group worker must know about the pre- and unconscious; it must be understood that many needs are not explicitly known to and often are not expressed by the group member even if known, hence the group worker must take seriously the *expressed* needs and consider them as strongly as those not expressed.

The three goal determinants—the member's expressed needs, the organization's purpose, and the group worker's understanding—may coincide, supplement, or contradict each other. Let us look at some examples of this:

[4]Judge Baker Foundation, *Case Studies*, Series 1, No. 1 (Sept. 1922), p. 3a.

### Example 1

Several adult patients in a mental hospital joined a group because they hoped that group discussions would help them get better.

The purpose of the mental hospital is to help the patient get better and the discussion group was formed for this purpose.

The social group worker, together with other members of the hospital team, had selected those patients whom he considered capable of involving themselves in group discussions that would help them get better.

In this example the goals of all three goal determinants coincide.

### Example 2

Youngsters in a delinquency institution participate in an activity group because they find it enjoyable. They want fun, stimulation, and satisfaction in accomplishing something with their hands.

The institution's goal is to help these youngsters to cease their delinquent behavior and to get satisfaction from "lawful activities."

The group worker also wants to help them enjoy non-delinquent activities. In addition he wants them to experience positive solutions to group conflict, which inevitably occurs in such groups; to experience a positive relationship with an adult; and to have an opportunity to speak frankly within the group about their problems, and to gain direct help with them through the instrumentality of the group worker and other group members.

In this example the goals of the three goal determinants partially coincide with each other and partially complement each other.

### Example 3

A gang of boys meets at the street corner to hang around and plan occasional thefts.

The agency in the neighborhood sends a group worker to work with the gang to prevent serious delinquent behavior.

The group worker has the same goal as the agency. Because of the situation of these particular boys a specific task is to help them feel more positively toward school.

In this example the goals of the agency and the group worker contradict those of the group members.

The last situation is the hardest one to work with. Since all group work is practiced in a reality situation, reflecting not only on past or future action, but also on present action, such divergence must be faced frankly from the beginning.

A helping relationship must be built on trust. The group worker therefore cannot manipulate a group for the purpose of working toward a specific goal, even if well-meant, without letting the members know about this and working it through with them. Not every step of the group worker's method must be consciously shared with them or explained, but the intent must be made known. A social worker once reported that his agency (a Department of Public Welfare) asked him to work with a group of men on relief who had shown little responsibility for their families or had deserted them, and who had made no effort to look for gainful employment. He felt embarrassed to share with them the concern of the agency and did not inform them of the actual purpose of the group, which was to help them take on more responsibility. He told them that he was working on a research project to find out what they were thinking. This is manipulation and not permissible in social group work. The group worker could have shared in an honest and yet respectful way the actual purpose of the agency by stating that the agency was concerned with the situation of the men and their families. To be helpful to both of them, the agency needed to understand the men's viewpoints and to work out, together with the men, a possible solution. This was the actual intent.

Social group work is the *application* of knowledge to *specific* situations. To help group members—young, middle-aged, old; some deeply troubled and incapable of reaching out; others highly aggressive and full of hostility; some unaware of inner pain, but inflicting it on others; others struggling with the daily tasks of growing up or with the limits imposed on them because of a racial difference—the group worker must first and above all try to *understand* and to feel deeply involved with each of them. He or she must realize that each member and each group is different from everyone else and from any other group, in the past, present, or future. *Individualization in the group*—individualization, not singling out—is one of the first and basic principles of social group work and the prerequisite for its particular helping function. No teen-ager can be "just another teen-ager," no Golden Age Club only "one of the many." Each person and each group must be seen in its uniqueness and work with them must be in accordance with this. The theories of individual and group dynamics offer a framework. They present *possibilities* of human behavior and its explanation; they present *averages,* but they never present actual human beings as they are. This must be underlined and fundamentally understood. Too often, theory is used rigidly with the assumption that it will give the explanation for every single person. Surely, being late to group meetings may indicate resistance (this possibility is indicated by the knowledge of dynamic Freudian theory) but it may also simply indicate that John always gets into a quarrel with his father whenever he gets ready to leave the house. Ella's wearing of a half moth-eaten coat may indicate rebellion against her mother, may express rejection of "middle-class" values, but may also just mean that she wants to look like others in her crowd. It is important to learn what it means to *Ella,* not to teen-agers "in general."

Theories are indispensable; they open practitioners' eyes to vistas they could not always see by themselves and could not find by pure intuition. They also help to order impressions and they often give meaning to seemingly unrelated observations. Yet group workers must know that theories are generalizations and that in practice they always must look for the *particular*.

How can one human being understand another one? What are the *media* the group worker can use to achieve this? A professional's toolbox does not include mental tests, X-rays, encephalograms, blood tests, and so forth—although results of such tests may be obtained from other professionals, if this is indicated. The tools are:

1.  The general theories of individual and group behavior, as discussed in Chapters 3 and 4, enlarged and intensified. When the practitioner works with disturbed people, additional psychiatric knowledge is needed. In community work knowledge is needed. In community work knowledge of the particular culture in which the practitioner works and from which the members of the group come must be added.
2.  Listening.
3.  Observation.
4.  Empathy.

The text will enlarge further on the last three tools.


## LISTENING

In general, people listen little to what others have to say. In a group of mothers on Aid to Dependent Children the most voiced complaint was that people did not listen to them, that they had made up their minds about what the mothers should do and how they should handle things before they themselves could say anything.

In a group discussion with delinquent girls the bitterness of the girls was directed mostly against adults who never listen to what "we have to say." A 10-year-old boy in a residential treatment center wrote, "Most important: The counselors must listen to us." This cry for being heard is the cry of the individual wanting to be understood. It is every individual's need and right. Effective help cannot be given without true listening. The group worker must listen carefully to *what* is said, to *how* it is said, and to *whom* it is said. All this has meaning and helps in better understanding:

### Example

It was visiting afternoon in camp. The children spoke eagerly about their parents' or other relatives' coming. John (12 years) said casually, turning to no one in particular, "There is too much to do in the fields these days. Nobody of my family will come, but it does not matter much." The casual way in which he spoke and his refusal to look at anyone revealed clearly his fear, his longing, his fierce wish "not to be found out"—his desire to be a "man." The group worker felt he must respect this boy's struggle and yet let him know that he was understood. He said, almost casually and to the whole group of boys: "Yes, I think some will have no visitors. It is harvest time. I guess that is a bit tough on the parents. Why don't we write to those who could not come?" John looked up eagerly, some others crowded around.

We see how sensitive the group worker was, not only to the content of the words, but also to the way in which they were spoken and to the feeling behind them. He then used his understanding to help John—not sentimentally by commiserating with him, but by respecting his effort to be "grown-up" and by giving him at the same time an outlet in action; this helped others in the group too.

In "I Am Lazarus," a short story describing the feelings of a young mental patient, Anna Kavan sensitively describes non-listening and what it does to a person:

### Example

The young man stood still and picked one of the grasses and brushed it against his cheek. It touched his skin lightly, prickingly, like the electrified fur of a cat in a thunderstorm. He picked several more grasses.

Suddenly he was aware of a presence. The gym mistress cycling along the path had approached noiselessly . . .

"Why, Mr. Bow, what are you doing with those?"

The young man laboriously assembled words in his head. He wished to explain that the grasses turned into a soft furred cat and arched its back under his hands.

The gym mistress did not listen to what he was trying to say. It was not the fashion at the clinic to listen to what patients said. There was not enough time. Instead, she put out her hand . . . and took the grasses away from Thomas Bow and threw them down on the path. . . .

"You don't want those," she said. "Nobody picks grass. We could pick some flowers though, if you like." She reached down for a handful of moon daisies and offered them to him. "There, aren't they pretty?" She was very good-natured about it.

Mr. Bow unwillingly accepted the flowers. . . .

. . . When the gym mistress was not looking he dropped them and trod on them with his brown shoes.[5]

Mr. Bow was not helped—he only felt misunderstood—and the person who had no time to listen missed a golden opportunity to find out more about the mysteries of thinking and feeling in this particular patient: Perhaps just hearing about his love and delight with the soft, furry things might have given some insight into his state of mind and his fears.

The listening a social group worker must learn is different from the listening we usually do in our daily lives. We are used to listening through the screen of our own preoccupations, our own thinking. For instance, observe group discussions on a social evening: most of the time each person

---

[5] Anna Kavan, *I Am Lazarus* (London: Jonathan Cape, 1945), p. 11.

presents only his own ideas with a disregard for what anyone else has said. More often, then, these are interrupted monologues rather than true dialogues, which require an interchange of ideas and a building upon one another's thoughts. Listening is an art involving conscious self-discipline to consider truly the *other one*, not just oneself. If one seriously does this, the unexpected will sometimes be found, as in an incident reported by Helen Padula that occurred in a mental hospital:

### Example

An old man complained persistently to his wife although he received the ice cream she ordered for him, he had to eat it in the bathtub. His wife apologetically brought the complaint to the social worker's attention. She didn't think there was anything to it—but her husband was so emphatic! The social worker agreed it sounded too absurd to be true, but she would inquire. It *was* true. The man's ice cream happened to be delivered at the same time his bath was scheduled. No one had thought to rearrange the one or the other![6]

Aside from the almost incredible bureaucracy seen in this illustration, we must also realize the frustration of the patient to whom no one had listened: even his wife did not take his words seriously! It is to the social worker's credit that she did not simply dismiss what he said as a figment of the imagination of a sick mind; she listened and she investigated, and she found that the patient's complaint was valid. *All social workers must listen to what their clients say;* otherwise they may miss the salient clue to a purposeful, goal-directed solution.

Let me cite one more example to illustrate the many facets of this capacity to listen:

### Example

In one of the group meetings Susan argued vehemently for legalization of marijuana. She boasted of her pot smoking. When the talk turned to something else she always brought it back to this theme. The other group members became enraged with this and tried to ignore her remarks. The group worker said earnestly, "Just hold it a minute. Susan is trying to tell us something, but we don't listen—really." Susan looked up, startled. Tears began to flow. She said, "I feel . . . so" and, sobbing, told of her fears, good, bad trips, her desperate sense of loneliness.

The group worker had listened with sensitivity and perceived the concern behind the boasting.

[6]Helen Padula, "Releasing the Human Potential in Chronic Mental Patients through Social Work Services," paper presented at the Workshop conducted by Ontario Department of Health, May 25-26, 1961, mimeographed; published in *The Social Worker*, 29, No. 4, Canadian Assn. of Social Workers (Oct. 1961), p. 3.

## OBSERVATION

Observation is similar to listening, but it includes awareness of nonverbal expressions of feelings and thoughts. Much of the action and communication in groups is of such nonverbal nature. This is one of the reasons why the group work method is so appropriate in working with people who are not highly intellectual or introspective (e.g., young children or adolescents and adults who come from cultures that are not given to much discussion). Many such persons cannot discuss their individual problems within the confines of an office or put into words their anguish or sufferings, but they can act them out. Thus the unique value of observation. Consider the following:

### Example

There were only three boys in a group at a newly established child guidance clinic. All three had been referred because of low achievement and other difficulties in school. John, at the age of 10, was considered "hopeless." He hardly spoke and, when questioned, answered only in monosyllables and with great reluctance. He lived with a grandmother to whom he clung fiercely at the slightest indication by authorities that he might be better off in another environment. He absented himself from the home whenever he pleased; he slept in parks; he truanted. All attempts at the clinic to involve him in some friendly discussion had failed.

One day the group worker prepared paper, pencils, water colors, crayons, and clay for the boys to work with, whatever their preference. Erik quickly reached for the water colors and worked rapidly with broad strokes and somber colors; aggression and fear practically stared out from the paper. Jim drew tiny, timid lines with pencil on white paper; they bespoke aimlessness. He did not need to speak; the way in which he worked and used the materials spoke as clearly as words of his guard against intrusion and his feelings of defeat and inadequacy. John just sat there, sullenness all over his face. When Erik reached for a fresh sheet of paper, John glanced at his design, guardedly, almost furtively—the first clue to the group worker that John was aware of the others. John's hand opened, then closed—a sign of a wish to do something and yet not wanting to give in to this wish. The group worker reached for the clay, rolled it in her hands to form a ball, and then, smiling at John, rolled it casually over to him. John caught the clay ball, rolled it back and forth, and then made a dent in it here and there. When the group worker stopped looking at him, he began to work with it intensely and without looking up. In this hour John suddenly bloomed forth, producing little works of art—miniature cars and animals and houses and trees, exquisite in all details. Nobody had ever known of this gift before.

We see in this example the power of observation and the way that facial expression, choice of material, and the movement of hands all became meaningful to the sensitive observer. And we can see how the group worker reacted quickly and appropriately to these signs to help all three youngsters, but especially John, on the road toward a more satisfying life.

Just as important as the observation of individual behavior in the group is the observation of relationships: Who chooses whom as friend? What members usually arrive together for a meeting? (Note that the group worker must always be in the meeting place before the members arrive.) What members leave together?

### Example

Elmer was considered the boy who started every mischief in the classroom. "He is the instigator. When he appears the class becomes unruly." The group worker's observations found that Elmer was always alone at recess. He was the first to leave. He was passive, quiet. Yet when he re-entered the classroom one of the boys winked at him and the unrest in the class started. Elmer was really not the "instigator," the "leader."

He was an isolate, so hungry for any kind of acceptance that the class used him and made him the scapegoat.

Observation of body language can give a clue to a better understanding of emotional relationships.

### Example

Mr. and Mrs. Smith had come for marriage counseling. They maintained that they deeply respected each other, but for some unexplainable reason they were unable to talk to each other. In individual interviews they expressed affection and admiration for each other. In a group session, the group worker observed that every time Mrs. Smith talked, her husband started to drum with his fingers on the table or on his knees. His facial expression though was one of an eager listener. The group worker asked, "I may be wrong, but are you annoyed by what your wife is saying?" First there was surprised denial. The group worker did not persist, but said that the repeated impatient drumming seemed to indicate something. Mr. Smith stared down at his hands and then exclaimed, "She drives me nuts!" And only then was he able to express his anger. Observation, shared respectfully with the person involved, had broken the ice.

## EMPATHY

The Minnesota Indians have a proverb that says, "Never judge a man until you have walked a moon in his moccasins." No picture can express more beautifully the need for empathy in understanding another person. One has to "walk in his shoes," and not just for a short time, but "for a moon." Nor is it sufficient to try them on while sitting down. One must do the "walking."

Students living in the vicinity of college campuses are usually poor— they experience poverty. Yet they still do not live through the same kind of poverty that the person on relief experiences. The college student's poverty exists for a limited time; there are expectations of employment once he or she receives a degree, which will amply compensate him or her for this period. The person on relief, however, has no definite limit on the duration of poverty. There is less hope for this person.

We cannot—as social workers—walk in the moccasins of all our clients. We cannot live through all the desperate pains of abandonment by parents or spouses, of unemployment, of discrimination, of mental or emotional sickness, of imprisonment, of crippling physical handicaps, or of utter hopelessness. Yet somehow we must learn to understand and to feel these things. Bertha Reynolds once said, "It is the sensitivity of the socially vital layman raised to the nth power which makes the difference between amateur and professional skill in working with social relationships."[7]

There was a time in social work when the idea was advanced that only students with happy family backgrounds should be accepted in schools of social work. Some even went so far as to suggest that any applicant motivated by some strong personal experience of suffering, be it physical, emotional, or social, should not be accepted for fear that this might indicate a neurotic identification. This, of course, is nonsense. There is always the possibility of neurotic use of human experience, but this may relate to happy experiences, too. In fact, a too shallow, undemanding life will not usually produce a good social worker.

Saroyan spoke of a man who came to see him and ask whether he could become a great writer:

> As he read I felt that there was a good man, and yet I could not help wondering what would come of his writing of poems. For he was very faraway from the dirt and anxiety of the world.[8]

This again does not mean that every social worker must have lived through great tragedy or that he or she must have been inflicted with pain during the educational process. It does mean that a social worker must be open-minded about the many anxieties people encounter and not shy away from a closer look into the problems of life. A comfortable withdrawal into the four walls of an office cannot keep empathy alive. A practitioner who works with the bitter teen-ager who is out to "make money quickly" cannot help the person if she does not learn to *feel* what it means to live in a crowded tenement, to see no beauty, to hear day and night the noise of quarrels, to be chided in school for not having worked the lesson when the needed book is not available in the home. This understanding of the teen-ager's lot may help the group worker to better appreciate his need to "make money quickly," and enable her to work with him on the basis of understanding and empathy. The group worker may even come to question the

[7]Bertha C. Reynolds, *Learning and Teaching in the Practice of Social Work* (New York: Farrar, Straus & Giroux, 1945), p. 51.

[8]William Saroyan, *The Bicycle Rider in Beverly Hills* (New York: Scribner's, 1952), p. 5.

textbook theories of differing values between lower and upper class when this teen-ager, and others like him, begins to trust her and to talk shyly about his "sissy" dreams of a clean home, of love, even of learning. He may also learn to look behind the facade of middle- and upper-class homes in search for the same naked hunger for things and the drive to "make money quickly."

And most important of all the group worker must feel what *injustice* means to a person, whether it is belonging to a minority group, or not having as much intelligence as someone else, or not being as physically attractive as others, or whatever. Injustice, whether it be really inflicted or only felt as such by an individual or an entire group, leads to many different forms of behavior—teen-agers, for instance, as a group frequently feel they are unfairly treated. Some forms of this behavior may be constructive—a determination to break through the barrier by participating in community life or by becoming more understanding and tolerant of others. Some forms may be destructive and manifest themselves in delinquency, the creation of hate groups, or withdrawal. The group worker cannot be effective if he or she is only a cold onlooker. And yet, while trying to feel and understand the problems of those in need of help, the group worker should not, like the actor, become completely identified with these persons while fulfilling the professional role. The social worker must feel simultaneously like the group members, and yet feel differently—like the *helper*. The objectives of the group members as well as those of the agency must be clear to the group worker. The group worker cannot join the gang as a delinquent. He cannot help the prisoners defy authority in prison, although the practitioner must understand why they feel like doing so. A group worker may feel deeply the pain of the growing adolescent who must postpone fulfillment of his mature physical urges, but she must help him to counteract them in a meaningful way and thus help the adolescent acquire a consideration for others.

Empathy—identification with clients and members—has sometimes been looked upon by members of the social work profession as dangerous to good social work practice. On the contrary, it is indispensable if it is combined with the discipline of the *helping role*.

The three media of understanding—listening, observation, and empathy—are centered in the personality of the social group worker; they are not "objective" tools. Group workers, then, must realize that they see others through the screen of their own personalities and life experiences. *Phenomenology,* a psychological system widely accepted in Europe, stresses this fact. Without placing it into a total system, social work practice has taken this into account. This is the reason why social workers must develop enough insight into their own personalities to be conscious of at least the makeup of their own particular screens. This helps them to come closer to understanding the members and groups they work with and to take account of their own biases even though they cannot completely eliminate them.

A combination of an innate capacity for empathy with heightened awareness of oneself and one's value system, and constant patient exercise in sharpening the powers of observation and listening are needed for the particular fact-finding process of social group work. The knowledge of individual and group dynamics then contributes to the ordering of the facts and their proper assessment. The group worker's fact-finding tools are not always sufficient for all the group situations that are encountered. Professional integrity then demands consultation and help from others in such related professions as psychology, psychiatry and education.

Let us look at the fact-finding, assessment, and objective-setting processes in practice, by presenting a few examples:

### Example 1

A neighborhood friendship group of 15- and 16-year-old girls who had met in each other's homes had asked to come to the agency. They had accepted the agency's policy of having an adult worker meeting with them. None of the girls had previously participated in any activities at the Neighborhood House, but the families were known, because of participation by younger brothers and sisters, and because the agency had been asked to help in some instances with brothers who had been on probation or parole.

At the first meeting Judy came early and alone. She looked unusually mature, physically, but seemed to get much pleasure from going around the room with the group worker, touching everything and keeping close to her in the manner of a younger child. Four other group members came together; two others followed, also together. During the meeting there appeared little difference between the two latter groups. Judy remained an isolate although she was outspoken in her comments in the group discussion. Her comments remained usually "in the air" and were not picked up by the others. On the surface she seemed not to notice this.

The girls expressed dissatisfaction with their club's activities. They did not know exactly what to do. When the group worker asked whether this was the reason they had decided to come to the agency, there was first a quick "yes," then much giggling and finally an outburst of hostility against "those kids in school" who had given them a "bad name." They wanted to do something about this. "Those kids" had accused them of letting themselves be picked up by boys at any time and of being "easy." They expressed hurt and anger at being "maligned." The group worker wondered whether they knew how such rumors may have started. There was immediate sensitivity as to any possible implication that there may have been any truth in this (although the group worker had tried to avoid this) and sharp denial of the slightest interest in boys. The group worker let them know that such an interest was quite normal and acceptable at their age. This opened a flood of virtuous accusations against other girls, none of whom were present. Joan and Violet vehemently denounced all men as being "no good." Judy, Sue, and Violet, too, discussed their brothers, who were then in training schools, and expressed bitter feelings against them, saying that they were the cause of their "bad reputation." They seemed almost forlorn. They spoke, sometimes angrily, sometimes almost tearfully.

They hated school and spoke with distaste of teachers and classes. Some complaints seemed genuine; some were said with an eye on the group worker, obviously to provoke her.

At one point, Sue said to the group worker: "You don't say much. Do you think you can stand us?" The group worker said that she would like to get to know them, that she knew it was important for girls to talk about things that concerned them, and that she was looking forward to working with them. Sue turned around saying, "News that someone cares." It was said flippantly, yet somewhat wistfully. . . . With hope?

The girls talked about clothes, again expressing dissatisfaction with and some envy of others. The group worker suggested that at another meeting they could make colorful felt cut-outs to decorate their simple skirts (a teen-age favorite at that time), while continuing to talk. This aroused excitement, a lively discussion, and some random planning, interspersed with laughter and much running around the room.

The group worker asked whether it was all right for her to visit each one of them before the next meeting so that she could get to know them and their families. This was accepted—to the group worker's surprise—with actual enthusiasm, and the girls suggested several times when it would be best for her to come.

What were the facts the group worker gained from this meeting alone that would help her to determine the objective of her role with this particular group?

This was an adolescent girls' group with many of the normal interests of such groups: boys, clothes, activities. Yet they felt they had to deny one of these basic interests.

They were, or they felt themselves to be, deprived and rejected by other girls. They had the same aspirations as the "good" girls, but felt hampered by their family reputations—at least three of them expressed this.

The remarks of two of the girls seemed to point toward poor relationships with their fathers, although this was not certain.

They disliked school.

They seemed to have an eager wish to be accepted by an adult (see the reaction to the offer of the home visit), but Sue's remark, "News that someone cares," and the apparent acceptance of it by the others showed that they did not expect much from adults.

As a group they seemed to be closely knit, with one person a neglected isolate. Reasons for this were not yet obvious in this meeting.

The group worker had not yet many facts pertaining to individual girls. Judy's isolation and the discrepancy between her physical development and her social maturity pointed toward her need for special attention. Sue might be the spokesperson for the group and the most aggressive, and yet she might prove to be the girl with the greatest need for closeness to an adult.

First meetings usually yield only impressions of individuals and they must be cautiously interpreted. Only when a more trusting and close relationship is established can one expect members to be free to reveal themselves.

The understanding derived from this first meeting is far from complete, but it is considerable. By knowing the neighborhood where the girls come from, by visiting them and their families in their homes (a very important and indispensable part of group work in neighborhood work), and by using the information known to the agency, the group worker can acquire valuable knowledge pertaining to each individual girl and to the entire group.

Her group's summary, the diagnosis and establishment of purpose, read:

> This is a group of teen-age girls from low-middle class backgrounds in a neighborhood and school district which includes high income families. School activities involve at times a considerable amount of money.
>
> Five out of the seven girls come from home backgrounds with family difficulties (desertion, alcoholic fathers, brothers in delinquency institutions), two girls come from fairly stable families, but with money worries.
>
> All of the girls have truanted at one time or another and all have poor scholastic records. None of them tested below average. All of the girls date, some of them have been sexually promiscuous with boys. All of the girls are hungry for acceptance by adults and yearn to be "like others," have the same status as other girls. They have a "fighting spirit" and revolt against what they see as injustice, the higher economic status of others, their own low acceptance.
>
> Though the group looks like one with a close bond, each girl is actually preoccupied with herself, and uses the others as a crutch. This is also the reason why they cannot be "bothered" by Judy.
>
> *Objectives:* to help the girls gain satisfactions for themselves so that their bitterness diminishes and they can begin to relate to each other. To help them talk out their concerns with the aim of finding acceptable ways to change some of the situations (for instance discuss with the school the problem of too expensive activities) and to help them see their own part in their problems and motivate toward change (as school attendance).
>
> To provide the girls with a warm and accepting and understanding adult so that they feel wanted and important as individuals and learn that such a relationship is possible. This should hopefully be transferred then to other adults too.
>
> To help the girls have experiences of achievement and carry through responsibilities to raise their self-confidence and to strengthen them to live with certain home situations that cannot be changed. Enlist community resources for those with family problems who have not received enough attention.

The preceding is only a summary of the goals for this group. The way of carrying them through is the next step of the group work process.

Only one individual diagnostic summary is given to show the specific way in which the group worker pulled together her knowledge of an individual and established objectives in working with her. They are never established for the individual, but always are worked through *with* the individual:

### Example

Judy, 15 years, 9 months, is the second of four children. All the other children are boys. The oldest one is in a training school. Judy's father is an alcoholic; he is frequently abusive to his wife and the boys but he shies away from Judy when he is drunk and tries to make her his "ally" on the rare occasions when he is sober. Judy detests him and is ashamed of him, but fears him less than the rest of the family. She is aware of her power over him, especially when he is drunk. She is the adult in the family and has often shielded the younger boys and her mother. She is protective of them, but hates the older brother, whom she identifies with the father.

The mother is a tired, frightened woman, prematurely old, who gladly lets Judy take over.

The family lives on the sporadic earnings of the father, who is a window washer, and has some additional support from a brother of the mother. Judy does occasional baby-sitting in the neighborhood. Judy is one of the girls in the group who had occasional sex relations with boys. "I don't care much for them," she confided to the group worker. "It was just something different. I have not done it for a long time."

Judy's isolated position in the group seems to be caused by her surface affectation of indifference. She participates, but without any emotional involvement. She avoids close contact with any particular girl. Teachers report that her indifference is "maddening."

Two signs point toward much more inner involvement than Judy wants to admit: her tenacious and regular attendance in the group, in spite of group rejection, and her habit of coming early and discussing her situation with the group worker.

Many of Judy's needs are the same as those of the other girls. The group worker must be available to Judy for those individual interviews she seeks out. Judy can accept this relationship only because it is not a highly formalized one, because she can "withdraw" into the group when the meetings begin. This must be allowed her until she asks for more help. Later she may either accept more intensive individual help, or, if the other girls are ready too, she may be encouraged to bring her concerns to the group. Judy also must be helped to be a "younger child" in the group to allow for all the child-needs she could never fulfill and the too adult role she continues to carry at home.

The group worker can be of help to Judy by presenting a strong mother person, whom she misses. If possible—also for the sake of other group members—a male worker should later join the group. Judy must be helped to allow herself to show emotions, positive and negative ones. She needs warmer relationships with other girls, and this involves work with the total group as well as with Judy. If possible, help should be given to the whole family, using the group work approach to overcome suspicion among family members.

### Example 2

The long-range objective for this group of men who were for many years in a mental hospital, was set by the staff—release from the hospital. Yet little was known about these men and so the immediate targets of the group had to be changed according to the best understanding of the social worker. The "group" consisted of 37 men at Hilltop, a mental hospital.

This was their community and these were the members:[9]

The men slept in three long narrow wards, none with an outside door, on unpainted cots with broken springs. The single bathroom boasted barely enough equipment for a medium-sized family, and not a single facility was enclosed. There was only one six by nine inch mirror. In place of towels, a sheet was thrown across the door. In the dining room were wooden tables and benches. There was no kitchen. No cooking was done in Hilltop; food was brought over in open pails from the kitchen in nearby Hillcrest.

Privacy was an unknown commodity. A few shelves in a small closet served the needs of all. Any patient fortunate enough to own personal belongings stuffed them into his pants pockets, or hid them under his mattress.

A single attendant ran the building, into which other hospital personnel seldom penetrated. The physician assigned to it made rounds sporadically. The only "luxuries" were a small television set and a water cooler, donated by a volunteer group from nearby Catonsville, who in very recent years visited the men and served refreshments one evening a month.

Hilltop, like its tenants, was neglected, rejected and withdrawn. But its tenants are harder to describe. My first impression was of a faceless mass of mechanized robots. As I gradually became better acquainted with them, they became 37 individual men, each with his unique share of physical and emotional ingredients. I want no more convincing evidence of the resilience of the human personality. The Hilltop men wore, in a fashion all their own, the shabby, faded, wrinkled, often soiled, uniformly gray hospital clothes. Many wore long winter underwear, vests, sweaters, jackets, and heavy trousers throughout the year, regardless of Maryland's famous summer temperatures. Since belts were traditionally not issued to them, they held up their pants with rope, or with suspenders tied by string to the belt-loops on their pants. They tucked their shirts into their underwear, and many didn't bother to put even the most essential buttons into buttonholes. The clothes were not their own in any personal sense. They went from Hilltop to the hospital laundry, came back to Hilltop, and were distributed without regard to individual size or preference. The men cared for themselves in a crude way. They worked, ate, slept, needed little attention, rarely got into difficulty. They were stoic, mute nonentities, known only to the attendant in charge—and not even he knew all by name. The majority, like sheep, followed the few who knew when to get up in the morning, when to wash, when to come to meals, and go to and from work. Those who could not shave were shaved. Those who did not know how to bathe were bathed, or went dirty.

They did not talk to each other. Some had not spoken a word for years; a few could not speak English. Though they spent their lives side by side, at meals, in bed, in the showers, in the fields, they hardly knew one another. This was no group, but an indistinguishable mass. They didn't live; the tide of bare existence had ebbed for them as they moved to Hilltop, and never risen again.

Their faces were as institutionally anonymous as their baggy hospital pants . . .

How to get started? The obvious point of departure was the men's hospital records. They weren't much help, beyond the barest facts of admissions dating from the days when everyone admitted to a mental hospital was expected to spend the rest of his natural life behind locked doors. (Much later I learned

[9]Pansy K. Schmidt, "Assignment: Democracy's Scrap Heap," *Journal of Social Work Process,* 12 (1961), 73–93.

that not even these "barest facts" were to be trusted; one man, hospitalized for 23 years, had been "ashamed" to tell his name to the police bringing him to the hospital, and had been admitted under a pseudonym he selected on the spur of the moment!)

Fairly typical was Abel Monou's record:

"1905: Committed to Spring Grove. 1923: The *first* "progress" note. "He is well adjusted, cleans attendants' quarters in the criminal building, delivers papers to various employees in and near Hilltop." 1955: After half a century in the hospital, Mr. Monou was performing the same tasks, but the note adds, "he has become somewhat sloppy about his work and person."

More helpful than the records was a series of meetings to "staff" all 37 patients. Dr. Ward, Mrs. Padula, Hilltop's attendant, and I—what a sad, sorry parade of men sat down with us, one by one, for discussions to evaluate the potentialities of each. We talked about leaving the hospital—but of all 37, only five could be tempted into any expression of a desire to leave.

The members refused, but the objective stood. It seemed best to separate the group, to interview each man alone:

My next step, it seemed to me, was to find an office—just space enough for a desk and two chairs—where I could arrange weekly individual interviews with my new clients. The contrast between that peaceful, conventional mental picture of my operations, and the way I actually operated, is ludicrous. Fortunately my search for an office, though frantic, was futile. There certainly was no space in Hilltop. An attempt to use Hillcrest was doomed to failure, because the men went into panic as four grim barred doors were locked behind them on their way to the office Dr. Ward found for me there.

Weeks later I came to know that an office, which to me was not only familiar, but essential, would have been a foreign object to these patients. I am quite sure that many of them would have adamantly refused to sit across a desk from me. My search for an office had a happy, though unexpected ending, as I held my individual sessions with the men hunched over a familiar wooden table in their own dining room. And by then I knew that most of my preliminary work would have to be done, not with individuals, but with the group—also in familiar surroundings, their own dingy day-room.

And the first group meetings?

In spite of my years of experience of working with the mentally ill, I became anxious, even panic-stricken, when my calling of their names echoed back from a wall of silence. It was a sad silence: many had forgotten the sound of their names; others had not heard themselves addressed by name for many years. They knew, as did the attendant, that they would never leave the hospital; and as I reminded them that I was here to discuss plans for leaving, they didn't even hear me, let alone understand my words.

The "sound of silence" mounted until it thundered in my ears, and I could see in their eyes the fear of cornered animals, defenseless against their fate.

Beating a hasty retreat from the discussion I had planned, I started talking about things they could understand: the broken bedsprings, the need for a paint job to spruce up the drab walls and furniture. Wouldn't they like to have towels to dry their hands on, instead of that sheet? Didn't they sometimes wish there was more than one mirror? Wouldn't some pictures on the wall look pretty?

I was encouraged as a quarter of my audience gradually joined me in discussion. One asked for plastic glasses instead of heavy cups from which to drink their milk or water. Another, bolder, spoke up for transportation to and from the movies held weekly in the hospital auditorium—the four-mile round-trip was too far to walk after a day on the farm.

Seven men agreed that if I invited the doctor to our next meeting they would request his help in winning some reforms. Though timid and fearful at first, these patients heard themselves criticize the authorities at the meeting. The right to complain—inalienable even though it's *not* included in the Bill of Rights—gave them some sense of their individuality. At a later meeting, they reached the more advanced point of criticizing me and my function. . . .

The objective had to be changed—at least for the time being. Before the patients could be prepared for release from the hospital they had to learn to be *people* again with the capacity to have opinions, to contradict, to make suggestions, to participate with others. Only the exercise of such capacity, carried out over a long period of time, could help the patients, or at least some of them, to become ready to leave. The original assessment of this situation was not easy because of the wish to fulfill the agency's request and the human resistance in everyone at taking small steps when one had expected to take big ones.

## SUMMARY

The assessment of the group and the establishment of objectives (group diagnosis) is one of the first steps in the group work process, parallel to the assessment of and establishment of objectives for each and with each individual member in the group (individual diagnosis).

The social group worker works with two large categories of groups: *growth oriented* and *social action* groups.

Each group is unique and must be treated as a unique entity.

The tools of assessment the social group worker uses are: (1) knowledge of individual and group dynamics; (2) knowledge of social environment and its meaning; (3) listening; (4) observation; (5) empathy.

The group worker must enlist the help of other professionals wherever indicated. The major source of assessment and setting of objectives is the group members themselves.

Three of these assessment tools—listening, observation, and empathy—are part of the group worker's self. They therefore are not wholly objective. To diminish the element of subjectivity, the group worker must combine self-awareness with sensitivity toward others.

## BIBLIOGRAPHY

COHEN, NATHAN E., "Services to Groups and Individuals in Groups," *Social Welfare Forum 1957*, pp. 15-20. New York: Columbia University Press, 1957.
JUDGE BAKER FOUNDATION, *Case Studies*, Series 1, No. 1 (Sept. 1922).
KLEIN, ALAN F., "Individual Change through Group Experience," *Social Welfare Forum 1959*, pp. 136-155. New York: Columbia University Press, 1959.

KOLODNY, RALPH L.,   "A Group Work Approach to the Isolated Child," *Social Work*, 6, No. 3 (July 1961), 76-84.

KONOPKA, GISELA,   "Group Therapy in Overcoming Racial and Cultural Tensions," *American Journal of Orthopsychiatry*, XVII, No. 4 (Oct. 1947), 694-699.

——————, *Group Work in the Institution, A Modern Challenge*. New York: Whiteside, Inc., 1954.

——————, "Resistance and Hostility in Group Members," *The Group*, XVI, No. 1 (Oct. 1953), 3-10.

——————, "The Method of Social Group Work," in Walter A. Friedlander, ed., *Concepts and Methods of Social Work*, pp. 116-200. Englewood Cliffs, NJ: Prentice-Hall, 1958.

LIFTON, WALTER M.,   *Working with Groups; Group Process and Individual Growth*. New York: John Wiley, 1961.

OSBORN, HAZEL,   "Some Factors of Resistance which Affect Group Participation," *The Group*, XI, No. 2 (Jan. 1949), 3-11 (with discussion by Harriet Young, 12-18).

PHILIPS, HELEN U., ed.,   *Achievement of Responsible Behavior Through Group Work Process*. Philadelphia: University of Pennsylvania School of Social Work, 1950.

——————, "Social Group Work, a Functional Approach," *The Group*, X, No. 3 (Mar. 1948), 3-7.

POLANSKY, NORMAN A.,   "On the Dynamics of Behavioral Contagion," *The Group*, XIV, No. 3 (Apr. 1952), 3-8; 21; 25.

REYNOLDS, BERTHA C.,   *Learning and Teaching in the Practice of Social Work*. New York: Farrar, Straus & Giroux, 1945.

REYNOLDS, ROSEMARY,   "Services to Individuals within a Group Work Setting," *Selected Papers in Group Work and Community Organization*, pp. 32-42. Raleigh, NC: Health Publications Institute, 1951.

SARRI, R. C. and M. GALINSKY,   "Diagnosis in Social Group Work," in R. D. Vinter, ed., *Readings in Group Work Practice*, pp. 39-71. Ann Arbor: Campus Publishers, 1967.

SCHWARTZ, WILLIAM,   "The Social Worker in the Group," *New Perspectives on Services to Groups: Theory, Organization, Practice*. New York: National Conference on Social Welfare, 1961.

SHERIF, MUZAFER and CAROLYN SHERIF,   "Psychological Harmony and Conflict in Minority Group Ties," *The American Catholic Sociological Review*, XXII, No. 3 (Fall 1961), 207-222.

SHIFFMAN, BERNARD M.,   "Effecting Change through Social Group Work," *Social Welfare Forum 1958*, pp. 190-202. New York: Columbia University Press, 1958.

SLOAN, MARION B.,   "Factors in Forming Treatment Groups," *Use of Groups in the Psychiatric Setting*, pp. 74-86. New York: National Conference on Social Welfare, 1960.

SULLIVAN, DOROTHEA F., ed.,   *Readings in Group Work*. New York: Association Press, 1952.

——————, *The Practice of Group Work*. New York: Association Press, 1941.

TRECKER, HARLEIGH B., ed.,   *Social Group Work: Principles and Practices* (rev. ed.). New York: Whiteside, Inc., 1955.

WEINER, HYMAN J.,   "Group Work and the Interdisciplinary Approach," *Social Work*, 3, No. 3 (July 1958), 76-82.

WILSON, GERTRUDE,   *Group Work and Case Work*. New York: Family Welfare Association of America, 1941.

——————, "Social Group Work: Trends and Developments," *Social Work*, 1, No. 4 (Oct. 1956), 66-75.

WILSON, GERTRUDE, and GLADYS RYLAND,    *Social Group Work Practice.* Boston: Houghton Mifflin, 1949.
WITTENBERG, RUDOLPH M.,    *So You Want to Help People.* New York: Association Press, 1947.
——————, *The Art of Group Discipline.* New York: Association Press, 1951.

# SEVEN

# THE HELPING PROCESS OF SOCIAL GROUP WORK
## *Practice*

The term "treatment" was taken over from medicine into the social work vocabulary, as was the term "diagnosis." Mary Richmond, whose famous *Social Diagnosis* heralded the beginning of professional casework, had worked closely with physicians in Baltimore and had learned from their systematic approach to problems. With the influence of psychiatry on social work, the term treatment became more and more associated with the idea of treatment of emotional personality problems, something Mary Richmond had not intended. Social group workers often shy away from the term because of this connotation. It is an appropriate term, though, if understood as "the act, mode or process of treating anything, as a raw

[1]Thornton Niven Wilder, *The Woman of Andros* (New York: Albert Boni and Charles Boni, 1930), p. 128.

material, substance or product;" that means a conscious and purposeful way of acting. It means also for social group work, in certain agencies at least, the "management of illness by the use of drugs, dieting or other means designed to bring relief or effect a cure," with an emphasis on "other means."[2] We must remember that the general goal of social group work is help with the basic needs of individuals to be important and to participate and the basic need of the total human society—expressed in the small group—for interdependence. The term practice is more inclusive.

According to the function of the particular agency or organization in which the social group worker works and the specific individuals and groups he or she is called upon to serve, the helping process must be modified according to the degree of health or sickness present or objective to be fulfilled. It must be modified, but the major processes used are the same because of the given frame of reference (see Chapters 3 and 4) and the underlying philosophy (see Chapter 5). No single profession can encompass *all* helping media. In a group of inmates, for instance, a certain member needs not only the experiences that can be provided in the group, but dental care as well; his decayed teeth, besides being physically damaging, have a negative emotional impact on him. The group worker recognizes "dental care" as part of the treatment. It is the responsibility of the social worker to use all available resources to provide the care that cannot be provided in the group meeting.

The major helping media available to the social group worker are:

1. The purposeful, warm, understanding, professional relationship between the group worker and the group member.
2. The relationship among group members—the group process.
3. Verbal communication—discussions, "talking."
4. Nonverbal communication—program, play, experience.
5. Purposeful choice and creation of environment.

In the following sections the group worker's use of these helping media will be illustrated through case material.

## 1. RELATIONSHIP BETWEEN GROUP WORKER AND GROUP MEMBERS

Rudolph Wittenberg called relationship a "transmission belt" between human beings.[3] A good relationship makes honest communication possible and its quality determines whether treatment is effective or not.

Help can be given only in a relationship of trust and mutual respect.

[2]Definitions taken from *Britannica Dictionary*, Vol. 2, Part I (New York: Funk & Wagnalls, 1956), p. 1389.

[3]See Rudolf Wittenberg, *So You Want to Help People* (New York: Association Press, 1947).

Yet this frequently does not exist from the beginning. The group worker is always the "outsider" in the group. Nothing significant can happen until the members have learned to trust the person. The relationship between group worker and members is characterized by the group worker's attempt to understand—the empathy that was discussed previously—combined with a professional responsibility to help in whatever way necessary. The group worker must find the strength in the members and add his or her strength to theirs. Social action groups, for instance, or professional committees, frequently feel discouraged when they do not see immediate success. To help them continue their work, the group worker recognizes the discouragement, its explicit cause or, at times, its irrational source. The practitioner's responsibility is to appraise the probable capabilities of the members so that they can move toward better solutions. While not playing Pollyanna, pretending that everything is well, he or she cannot become part of their despair. The group worker's helping role demands the mobilization of their strength. In the growth oriented group this means a serious working through of the forces that prevent the members from using their strength, a talking-out or an acting-out, and a testing of new-found capacities. Relationship means that the *intent* of the group worker is not only present within, but that it is felt and accepted by the group members. This individual must be able to *communicate* his or her genuine concern with the members. The establishment of such a relationship is a difficult task. Many people try to help others and mean well, but the recipients of their efforts do not feel served and do not really accept their help.

### Example

The new gym teacher in the training school complained, "I do everything possible—I even bought new balls. The boys need more exercise, need to get out, but they don't budge.

He had to learn that it took time to establish a relationship of trust between himself and the boys before they would involve themselves in anything he thought was "good for them." Yes, they liked to play ball, but they also distrusted anything offered to them by an adult; they assumed a trap and constantly tried to preserve their shield of hatred that allowed them to continue feeling bitter about the adult world in general.

### Example

The girls were incredulous. It was just not possible. The "mean" police women had collected money and bought a TV set for the cottage. Although they refused to write a "Thank you" note, they could not explain why.

It was obvious to the group worker that any admission of recognizing this gift meant to them that they could no longer blame those "mean police women" for everything, and that they would have to look into themselves for possible answers.

We see here how emotions block the acceptance of help, of relationships, because of the fear of introspection—yet change can come only when this is possible.

Helen Perlman wrote that "the identifying mark of a professional relationship is its conscious purposiveness growing out of the knowledge of what must go into achieving the goal."[4] Diagnosis and treatment are closely related. Relationship in group work is uniquely characterized by the fact that it is not a one-to-one relationship between the helping person and one client, but a relationship between the helper and individuals in a group and with the group as a whole. This has significant meaning. The group worker does not establish relationships with individuals one by one; an atmosphere of trust and give-and-take with the whole group must be created. This often means slow development and the acceptance of the fact that, as a group, members can be far more resistant than as individuals. In a group members support each other; they are not alone in the face of authority.

Social workers, psychologists, and psychiatrists, who are accustomed to working with individuals in a face-to-face relationship, always marvel at the greater temerity people exert when they are in a group.

Relationships in group work also cannot be as formalized as in the individual interview. This greater informality is especially obvious in activity groups, but it is also part of discussion groups, even therapy groups. A psychoanalyst describes this when talking about the group sessions he conducts:

> Functioning hour after hour as a shadowy figure in a dimly lit room with one patient at a time shuts out a lot of living; that is one of the occupational disabilities of the psychoanalyst. In the group, I felt much more of a human being—a more sociable and lively one. The situation was more challenging. It required qualities of leadership as well as technical skill and the ability to keep track of several lines of communication at a time. Yet the brighter atmosphere and more spontaneous emotional processes were at one and the same time more relaxing and more invigorating. The dramatic spirit of the interaction, the repartee and the intensity of the feelings coming to the fore made more of me come alive in the group sessions.[5]

In the reality of group interaction group workers can never be aloof. They are not detached observers, although they must be capable of sharp observation. Group workers are active in a way appropriate to the group situation or to an individual member's needs. Their helping role includes support and demand, often at the same time. Their basic respect for each individual demands acceptance of each person, even if group workers do not agree with an individual's views or actions. The responsibility of prac-

---

[4]Helen Harris Perlman, *Social Casework* (Chicago: University of Chicago Press, 1957), p. 68.

[5]Hyman Spotnitz, *The Couch and the Circle* (New York: Knopf, 1961), p. 19.

titioners demands intervention in damaging actions or feelings while still accepting each member. This means that group workers are neither *permissive* nor *authoritarian-directive*. Acceptance and limit setting are not considered contradictory in the use of the group work method, but are used according to the assessment of the group members' needs and the situation in which they find themselves. The concept that acceptance and limit setting are not contradictory is such an important insight that group workers should be very aware of this. The widespread myth that *acceptance* means total permissiveness has harmed many programs in education, social welfare, and therapy. Those who insist on harsh treatment in an authoritarian vein try to keep such myths alive so as to justify rigid and punishing procedures.

In groups that are highly emotional—therapy groups, for example, or parent discussion groups—or in work with youth groups, the social group worker encounters the phenomenon of *transference,* so well-known in individual treatment.[6] In the group, transference is directed not only from the group member to the group worker, but also from one group member to another. It is not part of the group work method (as in psychoanalysis) to provoke transference. The reality situation in the group partially counteracts this. However, the group worker must be able to recognize transference and work through it, if it occurs.

In the last decade a great deal of debunking of Freudian theory has occurred and there is—as so often occurs in history—a total reversal: For a while much of social work, especially casework, accepted Freudian insights unquestioningly, but it now completely rejects Freud's theory. Most group work theoreticians and practitioners—including this author—have never totally accepted theory without trying to look at it critically. To me, transference is not a Freudian invention, but an observable phenomenon. All of us experience occasionally a certain reaction to a person, a name, or even a landscape that is not related to its present reality, but to something in the past. (Seeing heather in bloom is not just an aesthetic experience with me. I feel like crying and embracing the world with love. Why? It was in the time of blooming heather that I fell in love.) When we react to people in that manner—and especially when we are so unaware of it that it colors our actual relationships with them—this is transference. A graduate student experienced this with one professor: "For a whole year I could not stand this instructor—I did not want to talk to her. Only recently, when I went home, I realized that she talks like one of my aunts whom I thoroughly dislike."

### Example

Mr. Bell was one of the members of a group of former mental patients, young men and women. Mr. Bell had needed only short hospitalization, but was still unable to work. He was married and had two children. His mother was living

---

[6]Transference is understood as the unconscious displacement to the therapist of emotional attachment and reactions to a person in the client's past.

with the family. Mr. Bell participated lively in the group, but only on an intellectual level. After the third meeting he told some of the members angrily that the group worker seemed to pick on him and he did not like to be chided because he had not yet accepted employment. Actually the group had discussed employment problems with little reference to Mr. Bell.

In the course of the next meeting, Mr. Bell said, for the first time showing more emotion than usual, "I can just see what you think, Mrs. Hare (the group worker). I resent the way you look at me. I am no bum." Another member tried to reassure him. The group worker held back, realizing that Mr. Bell finally showed emotion and needed to work through this.

During the fourth meeting, Mr. Bell avoided any direct addressing of the group worker. He was back in his role of the intellectual, trying to "explain" some of the feelings of others and getting much hostility from other members. At the end of the meeting he said angrily, but with some control, "You people have no spine. You always side with her, just because she is in the driver's seat."

In the fifth meeting, Mr. Bell blew up. He gave the group worker a good "dressing down." She was just like all those females, always feeling superior, always "knowing better." But she was not so "hot" herself. Had she not forgotten to bring the book for Miss Chandler she had promised? (She really had forgotten it and apologized.) She was not doing her job.

Mr. Bell seemed elated when he came to the eighth meeting. He said that he had discussed with his wife the problem of having his mother stay with them. He then was able to talk this over with his mother and make reasonable plans for another arrangement. It felt like a weight off his shoulders. Then he added sheepishly, "And I could have never spoken up to her (the mother), if I had not told you off first, Mrs. Hare."

Mr. Bell had worked through his transference without being forced to do so. The group worker's skill lay in recognizing and accepting the hostility as a transference phenomenon. This helped Mr. Bell to work through his problem. It also helped him that the group listened to him, that he could complain to others "in the same boat" without being forced to directly attack the group worker who stood for the person he resented and feared. The group situation allowed him to practice before he could attack directly. He also was allowed to take his time: He was not forced too early into working through the transference. He needed a "pause" of several meetings without his continuing the attacks, when he took again the "adequate" intellectual role instead of the child desperately trying to grow up.

### Example

Tilly, 4 years old, was referred to the Child Guidance Clinic and accepted on an emergency basis, rather unusual for a child that young. She had made several attempts to kill her newborn baby-sister. The parents were afraid to leave her or the baby alone for even a minute.

Tilly was tiny for her age, beautiful, and very bright. In spite of her unusual verbal capacity she did not talk with anyone at the Clinic. Her play in the psychiatrist's office was guarded, covering up feelings. Tilly was referred to a small preschool group of four children at the Clinic. In the beginning of the group meetings, there was little interaction, only parallel activities. The children were drawing. Susan was starting to draw on a light blue square of paper. Tilly had chosen a red one. Suddenly Tilly jumped up, tore Susan's paper away from her, and pushed her hard. It was significant that she chose Susan, the smallest and youngest child in the group. The "guard" Tilly had kept up when meeting adults broke through when confronted with another child who stood for the hated new sister.

When Tilly was offered the same kind of drawing paper as Susan, she violently refused it. Nothing would do for her except Susan's own paper. Yet Susan was not the baby for which she stood; she was not helpless. She resisted. The group process—left alone—would have led to a violent fight with both children being hurt, not only physically, but also psychologically. Tilly probably would have won, triumphing over the "sister" and taking it for granted that this must always be the outcome. Susan probably would have lost and learned that "the strongest wins," thus making her stand up less for her rights than she was already capable of.

The group worker recognized the needs of *both* children; she also recognized Tilly's reaction to Susan as one of transference. She put her arms around both girls and held them closely and warmly. Tilly needed to feel that being confronted with a "new baby" meant no loss of tenderness. The group worker told them in a soft voice that it was tough to have sisters; she used simple words for Tilly's feelings. She did not force Tilly to give up the paper, but neither did she let Susan feel that she *had* to give it up. She reached for the whole stack of blue drawing paper and placed it before the girls. "There is enough for all of us (the *Us* is important!); just use it." Susan reached for another paper; Tilly tore three sheets apart (the inner rage was now directed toward a "thing") and then began to draw. The big stack of paper had symbolized love—a love large enough to be shared without loss. Some weeks later Tilly's mother told the caseworker, with whom she had interviews, with tears in her eyes, "Look in the waiting room where Tilly is waiting for the group to start. Just look!" There was Tilly placing a baby doll carefully into a doll carriage, cooing over her—Tilly, who had not touched a doll since the birth of her baby sister!

## 2. RELATIONSHIP AMONG GROUP MEMBERS

This latter example has moved us already from the discussion of the relationship of the group worker to the individual member, to the constant involvement of the group worker with the relations of members with each other—the group worker is not only aware of the group process but of the responsibility to work with it. Group work is not work with an individual against the background of a group. It is *individualized work with group members in and through* the group. The group worker's role is to forward the relationships of its separate members and to make this relationship the most significant one. This is one of the most important attributes of the group work skill. It is also one of the frequent sources of frustration to the beginning group worker who complains, "I can't always say I have helped with this or that—the group members do so much for each other!" This becomes in the long run the greatest source of pride and satisfaction for all group workers: to have helped members to help each other instead of becoming dependent on the group members.

There have been frequent discussions as to whether the group approach or the individual interview is the more helpful method to people who need assistance with their social functioning. This kind of discussion is senseless, just as senseless as the indiscriminate use of the group approach simply because it has become a fad. Most people need at certain times help through either one or the other method or both together. Neither one is auxiliary to the other. Each is to be used when it is appropriate. Both methods in social work—casework and group work—have many media in common. Purposeful and voluntary relationship is the major tool of both methods, but each method has certain unique characteristics with different meanings to the individual client or group member. What, for instance, is unique in the casework situation, that does not exist in the group work situation? It is the complete attention that the helping person gives to a specific individual at a given time. The client may know that there are others who also receive the caseworker's attention—this might even cause resentment at times—but at the given time the person receives full and undivided attention. One can also rely completely on the confidentiality of whatever is discussed because of the caseworker's being professionally bound to this. These are two important and unique aspects of the casework situation (or any other individual-to-individual treatment situation).

What, then, is unique in the group work situation that is not found in the casework situation? It is being surrounded by others "in the same boat," by equals, by being not a client, but a "member." It allows for a feeling of identification that is impossible to achieve on an individual basis with even the most accepting social caseworker, because of his or her role—known to the client—as the helping person. Group work allows for reassurance, but it also confronts the group member with people who are not bound by the professional principle of "acceptance." They will therefore express themselves and relate themselves to others on the level of equals; they will express hostility, anger, or disgust as well as love and tenderness, and express it on a personal level. This they experience as in life outside the group meetings, but with the help of the group worker.

The relationship with the group worker must always be shared with others in the group, hence it is not surprising that sibling rivalry is frequently relived and worked through in groups.

Confidentiality, important in certain groups with which the practitioner works, is not a matter of certainty as it is in the casework process. It must be established by a special and voluntary effort on the part of group members; they must each be involved in the responsible action demanded of them through a specific act.

Awareness of the unique aspects of each method will help ease the tension of rivalry and will permit the approach to be employed that is best suited to the needs of the particular people who come for help in a given situation.

The relationship among members becomes important in the group for both diagnostic and treatment purposes. Tilly could not work through her sibling rivalry without meeting a real Susan, but she had to meet her under the protection of the group worker.

### Example

The freshman student group had met several times discussing students' responsibilities in regard to racism in our society. Discussion had moved from the intellectual level to insight into their own and other people's feelings. George, who wore his hair long, always appeared in an open shirt, and usually talked in a very emancipated way, had been very quiet that day. When questioned about what happened, he hung his head and said in a low voice, "I want to be so independent, so myself, but—I am afraid. I cannot really contradict anyone."

Janet: "Odd, I always thought I was the only coward in our generation." There was laughter and then Ernest spoke up quietly, "It is really not being a coward. I guess being afraid is being human. Next time you are really scared, George—or I am—let's at least tell each other!" The whole group drew together with a warm feeling.

We see the comfort derived by the admission and sharing of what was for one member a painful feeling of inadequacy. This is possible only if the group has experienced this kind of sharing as a part of its work together. We see how group members help each other: Janet helped George to feel that he is not so alone in being afraid and Ernest helped by promising active support and by allowing for the feeling that this is not as serious a defect as George thinks. Laughter is one of the greatest human assets, if it is well-meaning and not derisive. It occurs frequently in groups, because of the informal situation and the interaction with equals.

But group members also can pose demands; they do not allow for easy withdrawals from problems. Here is the excerpt from a record of a group of female patients in a mental hospital.

### Example

The group had been talking about crying. Bertha said, "I can cry, but what's the use?" W. said, "Crying is certainly an acceptable way of telling someone that you're angry, isn't it?" Again Bertha said, "What's the use?" She began going over her life story with the other patients. They commented, asked questions, and tried to help her understand more clearly what she was saying. Miriam said, "But don't you see? These are only the problems you are facing now, but they're not the cause?" It was interesting to note the patience and understanding that Gert demonstrated in trying to lead Bertha into some kind of acceptance of the fact that these were the effects rather than the causes. At one point Bertha ran out of the room to get her Bible, and said, "See, I just want to show you I'm trying to get better by reading helpful Bible passages." Ina said, "Reading the Bible may help, but it is no substitute for dealing with your problems yourself."

Bertha is not allowed to run away from responsibility in relation to her problems. Gently, but firmly, other group members let her know this. It will be harder for her to shrug this off than the remarks of a person in authority whom she regards as the "healthy one" who might not understand. Her own co-sufferers hold her to the need to work on her problems.

There is always a blending of the group worker's efforts with those of the members. And there is nothing more therapeutic, satisfying, or growth-producing than to experience the knowledge that one can help another person. The *mutual* helping process of members is possible in the group, while it is not possible in the worker-client relationship. It is a vital part of the group work to enhance opportunities for this.

### Example

A group worker recorded: Although the men went as a group, we split up on reaching the shopping center (to reduce the conspicuous aspect). We gathered again as a group later and returned to the hospital as a group. But each had had an individual experience. And each had also had a sharing experience. Mr. Kidd was wrapped up in his problem when we started out. As the group split up, he and Mr. Eisen went with me.

We passed a book shop. I noticed a new book with a huge swastika on the cover. Knowing that Mr. Eisen had spent years in a concentration camp, I watched him as he approached the book. He stood for a long time in front of it, then shuddered and uttered a disgusted sound. He said, "It's awful." Mr. Kidd had become fascinated by a lighted globe and was twirling it on its stand. I walked over to him with Mr. Eisen and asked Mr. Eisen where he had come from. He said, "Berlin." Finding this on the globe, I also found Baltimore, and showed, with spread fingers, how far he had come. He looked up and smiled broadly. Mr. Kidd stood at his side and muttered, "Gee . . ." Later, in the coffee shop, Mr. Eisen began to shake violently. Other people in the restaurant were looking in our direction. Mr. Kidd reached over and placed his hand lightly on Mr. Eisen's arm and the tremors subsided. When Mr. Eisen began shaking again, Mr. Kidd repeated his remedy, with the comment, "It works," and then smiled softly at Mr. Eisen who smiled back.[7]

What deep satisfaction for Mr. Kidd to discover that "it works" and that the "it" is he; what a powerful way of pulling him out of his self-concern! And what comfort to Mr. Eisen to experience this human kindness, spontaneously given, after he had just relived the horrors of his past.

[7]Robert Neubauer, "Agency Function as a Dynamic of the Social Group Work Process for the Realization and Enhancement of Change in the Long Hospitalized Patients in a State Mental Hospital," unpublished thesis, University of Pennsylvania, School of Social Work, 1961.

Sometimes group members need much support to be able to respond to others, and it must come first from the group worker. The following example presents work with a group of Bluebirds (9-year-old girls), as recorded by the group worker:

### Example

Everyone was very busy and I had a little time to talk with Katie. I realized that Katie had so little relationship with anyone in the group that it would be necessary for me to develop a strong relationship with her to make her feel that she had support in me. The opportunity for talking with an individual youngster is, of course, really difficult in such an active group, but since everyone was so busy and occupied right now, I sat down near where Katie was threading beads and started a conversation. I asked her what we had here that she liked best.

"Beads," she said laconically. She showed me her chain. Beading was fun, I agreed. What else did she think was fun? She stared down at her work.

I told Katie that the reason I was here was so that I could help the girls have fun. That didn't mean you had to do something all the time. It was all right to do nothing, if you liked this. But I was here so that whenever anyone needed me, they could come to me. Katie looked at me seriously, said nothing, but did not move away. I went on to say that I was wondering if it was a little hard when you come into a new club and meet new people. She looked at me very gravely. Still she did not speak. I said that it was always that way when we met new people and came to a new place. After awhile when you get used to people, it's easier. At this Katie nodded and smiled a bit. Apparently this little talk had helped. Not ten minutes later, Katie engaged in conversation with other children, something which she had not done so far in this meeting or in the last.

The group worker showed Katie that she understood the difficulty of being a newcomer and an isolate. She responded to the tangible interests of a little girl, but helped her to feel free to move toward others. Her concern was more on relationships with other members, although she foresaw the possibility of involving herself more with Katie than with the others. And she also helped Katie to feel free to drop an activity, if she so desired. Apparently this made it possible for her to move toward the other children.

Yet member-to-member relationships are not always helpful. Human beings have the capacity to love and support each other, but they have just as strong a capacity to hurt each other cruelly, either in deeds or words. Group relations in themselves are not always helpful. Those who completely rely on the natural course of the group process and advocate a complete non-interference, as some theorists have done, are not really aware of the strength of this process that can destroy people. I remember vividly one such group that I observed conducted under this theory:

### Example

One boy, the leader in his group, used the others to torture one of the group who apparently was selected as his victim. They jeered at him and taunted him when he began to tremble with rage, frustration, and fear. They chased him and poked him. When one of the boys refused to follow the order of the leader in this cruel game, the leader threw him down, sat on him and thumped this boy's head against the floor. During all this time the person who conducted the group made no move.

The children not only harmed one another physically, but they carried with them the conviction that this kind of acting-out was all right since it was done under the eyes of an adult. This is not group work. It is part of the social group work method to combine the use of *limitation* with acceptance. The judicious use of limitations can be guaranteed only through the process of understanding and diagnosis, and must never rely on dogmatic attitudes. At times, many outbursts of hostility must be accepted—even provoked, if this is the only way for the group member to work through those feelings. Yet the person must be helped to do this in a way that is not harmful to anyone. Personal needs are always balanced by the needs and rights of others.

Let us look at an example that occurred among a group of delinquent boys in an institution:

### Example

... It was a hot day, and the wind was blowing without relief. This weather seemed to make itself felt with everyone, and the boys were restless. Things went all right, however, until Ned and Larry got into a fight. Neither boy had any self-control, but Larry had a real fit and was dangerous. He threw stones and took up the scissors and a large pole. Fortunately, he is not very quick, so W. could get hold of him. W. held both his arms, talking in a soothing voice until he relaxed under her hands. The difficulty was that Ned did not let him alone, but again provoked him. Larry's rage mounted once more, and besides physical force he used terrible language. Again he reacted to the holding and the soothing words like somebody coming out of a trance. He then lay down on the ground, completely exhausted, sweat standing on his forehead. When he had rested a little, W. asked him if he wanted to draw and write out all his anger. He was perfectly willing to do this, and Ned immediately asked for paper too.[8]

The group worker understands the rivalry between the two boys, she knows of their backgrounds and of Larry's constant frustration because of his comparatively low intelligence. She realizes the influence of the environment, the weather. This understanding dictates the nonpunitive attitude of the group worker, but it also demands her active interference in the fight: she knows that these boys can physically harm each other. She then tries to allow the anger to continue coming out, but through a less dangerous channel, thus not overstressing the pressure and helping the boys to experience less destructive ways of expressing their feelings.

---

[8]Gisela Konopka, *Therapeutic Group Work with Children* (Minneapolis: University of Minnesota Press, 1949), pp. 56–57.

Another example of necessary limitation, because of possible psychological damage, is seen in the following excerpt:

### Example

Phyllis, 6 years old, had a tragic history. Her father had died before the child was born. Her mother had been hospitalized for a long sickness over several years, beginning when Phyllis was 2 years old. She was left with a woman who "took care" of her by strapping her into a chair for the whole day, taking her up only when she was too soiled. No one had known about this or interfered until the mother returned to the home. By that time Phyllis was almost mute. She began to learn to walk quite rapidly, but was extremely hostile toward her mother and let her touch her only reluctantly; she kicked and bit her whenever possible.

Phyllis was placed in a group at the child guidance clinic because any undiluted contact with an adult alone provoked violent outbursts that lasted for hours, during which Phyllis could not be handled.

When Phyllis saw the other children, she stood still, then glanced around and walked slowly up to them. She saw the table covered with pencils, drawing paper, clay, and dolls. With one sweeping movement everything was thrown to the floor. The group worker said quietly, "You can play with all those things, Phyllis. You can use them, no one will take them away from you." Phyllis looked surprised at this unexpected reaction and bent down to collect the dolls. But the fear of "losing" was again overwhelming. She lifted her skirt like an apron and dropped everything into it. Then, straightening up, she began to run around the room holding on to as many of the things she carried as was possible. She screamed like a wounded animal. At this time the group worker could feel that "acting out" was no longer a release, but an increase of pain, and also frightening to the other children. She opened her arms and caught Phyllis almost playfully. Phyllis began to sob. The group worker comforted her, but released her quickly since she knew about Phyllis's fear of women. She turned to the other children and said that Phyllis had never had many toys and had had a hard time. Would they like to bring her some of the dolls that had fallen down? With the compassion so common to children who have suffered, Ellen and Rachel quickly picked up some dolls for Phyllis and then offered her some of the cookies prepared for a snack. Phyllis was in this way relieved of the adult presence and could get used to it with the help of the other children.

The group worker had set a limit to strong acting-out behavior. The way it was done was dictated by her understanding of the individual and the group situation, using herself, interaction among the children, and "objects" (e.g., the dolls, etc.).

In adult action or educational groups the role of the group worker is mostly to open up resources but also keep in mind that the aim is mutual help and that this can be achieved only by fostering enduring relationships.

### Example

Mr. and Mrs. G. and Mrs. M., all American Indians, had asked for some help with a program to assist newcomers to the city from the reservation. They suggested a training course for ten to 15 women who already lived in the cities to become the teachers to the newcomers. Such a course in problems of everyday living was started. It soon developed that more and more women attended—up to 30—and the meetings moved into many other areas of concern. The group worker records about one of the sessions:

"There were eight people present at this session. The reason for the low attendance was that many were up North harvesting wild rice.

"We had no outside speaker. We looked over the *Indian Resources Directory*. We had previously decided that we would go over it and update it. However, this was not possible at this meeting because those who were present were not very familiar with the various agencies. It was more a new learning of resources available for them.

"Because there were so few present and because most of the women who came were usually the silent ones, I found that in this small group there was much more interaction. When 20 people had been present these women were fearful of speaking out. Now, in this small group they felt comfortable.

"We talked about discrimination and the Chicago riots. It was impressive to hear how well-informed several of the women were. They had never before indicated that they knew so much about current events.

"Mrs. N. said that her son is at a school he does not like. He would prefer Meadow High. What can be done about this? I will check into it and bring the information back to the whole group.

"Mrs. A. told us with great satisfaction that Ella Smith—the social worker from a public agency who had previously talked with the group—had really been helpful in a recent contact about her daughter. Her daughter had been ill, the doctor she called was out of town and she just did not know what to do. She had been most worried about how to pay another doctor's bill. She had called Ella. The person from the Medical Assistance Department came immediately and her daughter got a doctor right away. Others commented that it helped to hear what really worked."[9]

## 3. VERBAL COMMUNICATION

We saw in the previous discussion the importance of guided group interaction as a helping tool in social group work. Relationships among human beings—their feelings and their thoughts—are expressed in many different ways. One of the major ways of expression is words. Just as in individual interviews, the group worker also uses this form of communication purposefully and skillfully. Encouragement of interaction in discussion groups is a significant quality of social group work. A discussion group where the person in charge questions one member after the other and where each responds in turn is not group work. The group worker always tries to increase the interaction and mutual help among the members.

Here is an excerpt from a meeting of parents of mentally retarded children who met regularly with a group worker to help them think through possible plans for the children. The excerpt presents a second meeting with this group:

[9]Recording done by Diane Hedin, Center for Youth Development and Research, University of Minnesota, 1968.

**Example**

We started out talking of the feelings of disappointment that we have in the children. Mr. Lowry brought up the fact that he had felt disappointed and there was a general feeling of denial in the air. Mr. Jones, upon encouragement from the worker, commented that he was concerned about the things that his child was being cheated of, mentioning the educational and peer relationship problems. There was a defensive feeling when W. suggested that everybody had feelings of disappointment and noted the naturalness of these feelings. Mrs. Sims brought up her feelings of disappointment that Susan could not be "the oldest sister" and be a leader to the other kids. She stated some of her desires. Mrs. Jewel suggested that perhaps the fact that her oldest child was the satisfactory child made it more reasonable for her to accept John. The group did not really tolerate her denial. Mr. Vetter picked up and stated that he felt that it was something different from feelings, and described his fear of the future. Mrs. Jewel could understand that better. She said she, too, was very much afraid of what would happen if anything happened to her or her sister, for who would be interested in her son?

From the beginning the group worker had created a climate that allowed the parents to speak freely about their children and their own reaction to them. This is not easy—and we see the forms of denial, of trying to present the problems as comparatively small. Yet when they talk to one another they begin identifying with one another and become freer with others, and especially more honest with themselves. A mother of a very disturbed youngster said after such a meeting, "It helps me so much to hear what someone else thinks and lives through. It is a comfort to see that I am not the only one who has these problems. It is even more important that I begin to think, 'Well, this is perhaps the same with me—or with Herb,' and I learn."

Group work allows for the "anonymity of insight." A person may gain insight without necessarily having to admit it or to pronounce it. At times this saves the person's self-esteem and allows for the privacy of discovery of his or her innermost drives, without having to admit them to someone else. Sometimes free and open sharing of feelings is most important and necessary; at other times, the knowledge is beneficial to the individual alone. When I hear of great pressure exerted on group members to say whatever they feel, I can't help thinking of the beautiful passage in Steinbeck's *Grapes of Wrath:*

... Uncle John's eyes were tired and sad. "I been secret all my days," he said. "I done things I never tol' about."

Ma turned from the fire. "Don' go tellin', John," she said. "Tell 'em to God. Don' go burdenin' other people with your sins. That ain't decent."

"They're a-eatin' on me," said John.

"Well, don't tell 'em. Go down the river an' stick your head under an' whisper 'em in the stream."

Pa nodded his head slowly at Ma's words. "She's right," he said. "It gives a fella relief to tell, but it jus' spreads out his sin."[10]

"Talking out" may mean relief to the troubled person, but it may also increase the disturbance or guilt feelings that the person is experiencing.

Because of the high value group work places on participation, group discussion is used for many purposes other than those of the therapeutic or social action variety. The capacities to listen to different points of view, to work through conflict, to argue rationally, and to allow for rationality in those with whom one does not agree, are necessary for a living democracy and are not inborn.

### Example

A group of teen-agers in a settlement house complained violently about the restrictions imposed on them by the city curfew law. It was too stringent and completely unreasonable. John said, "We just won't obey it." Pat said, "I am scared to be picked up, but I'll come along." Ernest stabbed viciously at the table; Jim said that this was the way it always was, "You can't do a thing. They just do this to spite us."

The group worker wondered whether they knew how it happened that this ordinance had been passed. No, they did not. He explained, often interrupted by the angry youngsters. He then asked them again to give all the reasons they had against the curfew law. Jim said, "Why? We just talk about it." The group worker said that people can do something about ordinances or laws, if they care enough, find good enough reasons, and join together to present them to the ones who make those laws. Slowly a less emotional discussion started.

The meeting ended with a resolution to work further on this.

In the course of the next weeks a project started, with the young people taking responsibility for writing out their reasons against the curfew law, discussing this with others and their parents, and bringing the pros and cons to the group meeting. They visited their alderman with the group worker, and were surprised to find him interested. He suggested that they attend a meeting at the city council to see how business was conducted. They were especially pleased when the mayor invited them after the meeting to visit him in his office.

They drafted a new suggestion for a different curfew law—a far cry from their original rejection of everything the law stood for.

We see here how help is given with learning of action in a democracy and how, at the same time, this means an inner growing-up process, which is frequently left uncompleted even in adults (one need only observe actions in legislatures or the United Nations). The group worker's responsibility and skill lay in the creation of an atmosphere free enough to allow the

---

[10]John Steinbeck. *Grapes of Wrath,* copyright 1939 by John Steinbeck. Reprinted with permission of The Viking Press, Inc.

youngsters to express their spontaneous resentment, and then in helping them with rational approaches to the problems and allowing an outlet for their disagreement in the form of responsible action as opposed to simple rebellion.

It is part of the skill in leading group discussions to bring in everybody, and yet not force anyone to participate in a way that makes the group worker conspicuous or very uncomfortable. And it is also necessary to know when *not* to use group discussions, when a simple statement of facts, for instance, is far more appropriate. Discussion leading is of such importance in the use of the group work method that it is often taught as a separate course in the education of group workers.[11]

## 4. NONVERBAL COMMUNICATION

Verbal interaction is only one way in which human beings relate to each other. Group work, because of its origin in informal education and recreation, has always been especially attuned to the many other media through which help with interrelations can be given. The "use of program" was looked upon disdainfully at one time by those who considered activities superficial, but it is increasingly recognized as a significant helping tool.

Play for children is their most important expression; it is their occupation, not something done "on the side." In play they express feelings, thoughts, anger and love, fear and the conquering of fear. In play they begin to feel their strength, and learn the despair of defeat. Adults need play in forms different from those of children, but it is necessary to both. The word "recreation" is a very beautiful one. It includes the idea of creative work, of re-creating capacities. A student once said, "I think my mother never played." When he was asked what she did in the evenings when the family relaxed, he replied, "She was always doing embroidery." Then he realized that this was her play—not an active one but a quiet enjoyment of the lovely colorful strands of yarn. This was her recreation.

Activities, doing things together (or alone, when one needs this), allow for much expression, for identification with people whom one admires and needs, for a feeling of accomplishment, for "telling" without words. Peter taught me that, when as a new group worker I tried to bring him to tell me about his worries. Peter was 11 years old and had already been in an institution for delinquents and was on parole. He was drawing and I tried to talk with him. He looked up, "Oh Gisa, I am not much of a talker." But he continued to draw intensely. And I learned that, by glancing on that

---

[11]See Gisela Konopka, "A Brief Note on the Differential Use of Group Discussion," *The Social Service Review*, XXXII, No. 3 (Sept. 1958), 287–289.

paper, I could learn more about Peter than he could ever tell anyone, since he really "was not much of a talker." The wild lines, the red and the deep black, the burning airplanes crashing down and the little boy running from a huge fiery rocket—in his drawing Peter had "said" all there was to say about his inner turmoil. When Peter leaned back against me when we sat in a circle on the floor, throwing a ball around, I knew he was yearning for a mother—but he never could say it in words.

Work with delinquents has shown frequently that they cannot be reached by interviews. Yet sometimes hours spent without a word with an adult—cutting wood or fishing, for example—have made the first identification with a probation officer possible. Many young people are not as verbal as university students and are not as introspective. Changes in their feelings and attitudes come more from *experiencing* than through talking out and interpretation. The purposeful and skilled use of program is, in my opinion, the most hopeful tool in working with the large number of young delinquents who act out. Since most delinquent acts are committed in small groups, it is important to keep the members together to allow them the feeling of security they gain from each other while helping them with a change of values.

A young probation officer in Germany reported about his group work with 17- and 18-year-olds under his supervision:

### Example

These were boys difficult to reach. They had been small children during the hungry war years and were reared by parents who had not stood up for human values—many of them had quickly changed from Nazism to a sullen neutrality. The boys were quite cynical and had a "chip on the shoulder." They trusted no adult and complained that they were not trusted. To them, words were only shields hiding other meanings—this applied to themselves as well as to others. The probation officer was just another hated and rather despised adult.

The probation officer had started weekly group meetings with the boys. He had suggested a bicycle tour of about ten days in the summer. During those meetings they prepared for the tour, fixed up the bicycles, studied maps of where to go. The trip appealed to the boys, since they did not have enough money to go by themselves and they had to report anyhow to the probation officer. It was a "convenience." The probation officer knew that he took a risk. He knew that bicycling meant riding on narrow paths, one after another. Any boy could disappear easily. Nevertheless, he made up his mind not to ride as the last, so as not to give the boys the impression that they were being watched.

Already during the first days of the trip he felt a different atmosphere in the group. Somehow the informal contact, the removal from the "office," seemed to change the relationship. The boys were less sullen. There was joking. Evenings in youth hostels brought them together on an equal footing with adolescents from universities, some of whom were foreign students, something they had not experienced previously.

On the fifth day they took quarters overnight in a barn of a convent. When the probation officer woke up, the boys had disappeared. He was frightened and deeply disappointed. Then he looked out of the window and saw:

In the farmyard stood the convent's truck. His boys were helping the sisters load the sacks of grain on the truck. They went back and forth with the heavy sacks on their backs following with obvious pleasure the directions of the sisters.

"I was ashamed of myself," the probation officer reported. "The boys' chip on the shoulder was not so irrational. I who had worked with them for quite a period of time, too, had doubted them."

The sisters prepared a wonderful breakfast for the boys. The probation officer had never seen the boys so glowing, so satisfied. He never let on about his doubts; he asked only why they had not awakened him too. One of the boys said a bit sheepishly, "We just liked to do this all by ourselves." And another one added, "You have enough work with us!" There were no more words, but a bond, a special positive one, had started between the boys and their probation officer.

I found that in European countries the group work method is frequently used in probation and parole work. It may have to do with a general recognition of the fact that many people are not very verbal and have a strong need to overcome remnants of an authoritarian culture. The group lends itself especially to this. An Italian social worker suggested that fear of group work in her country is related to remnants of fascism, that the social worker wants to be totally in control of the situation and is afraid of the strength that comes from group associations. She considered group work a method, indispensable in overcoming the old authoritarian patterns.

In the United States the use of the group work method in correctional services in the institutions as well as probation and parole services has vastly increased.

The use of nonverbal material is also important in working with adults. Family life education has been predominantly directed to middle-class parents who can communicate, and its importance must not be underestimated. Yet too often persons with less verbal capacity miss this help. Group work's tool of "program" allows for entrance into families who need help with rearing children, but who cannot easily participate in groups that use the discussion method exclusively.

### Example

A neighborhood center in a low-income area in a highly industrial city offered a day camp for first-grade children. The mothers of the children were invited to come one evening a week to make games or toys for the children. The purpose was threefold: to make these things, since little money was available for the program; to help the mothers learn more about the needs of their children; and to help the mothers raise their own self-confidence in dealing with their children—something that they seemed to lack.

While the hands were occupied, the talk was lively and unselfconscious.

The following is an excerpt from one of the meetings; it shows the interplay between "doing" and "thinking," "feeling," "learning":

Mrs. Shaw worked on making a jigsaw puzzle. She exclaimed, half-angrily, half-laughingly, "Now look! My lines look as crooked as if Sheila had made them." Sheila was her 6-year-old daughter, the fifth of seven children. She was excessively shy and always had a beaten look. She seemed to wake up only when stories were told. One day she had surprised everyone by spinning her own story in front of the whole group, showing much imagination and actual command of language. This had happened when the children had sat quietly around the group worker who sat with Sheila huddled on her lap.

Mrs. Shaw continued, while erasing and redrawing her lines: "That kid drives me crazy. She is so clumsy; she can't do a thing!"

Mrs. Aaron, next to her, said, "Oh, I was just such a kid! My mother always gave me so many whippings, I didn't dare to try anything. But today I'm a pretty good cook, and when Sam (her husband) was out of a job, I got myself some work in the factory and I was no worse than the other women."

Mrs. Shaw said, "I just get so mad at her!" And then, with a little laugh, "But just look at my lines! They're no better than Sheila's."

The group worker told Mrs. Shaw about Sheila's lovely storytelling. Mrs. Shaw looked surprised.

We see here a mother who is beginning to see her daughter in a less negative light. It started with her realization that she, too, could not do everything right. She then received some more understanding through another woman who identified with Sheila and could show that she had become quite an adequate adult. The group worker added an observation of Sheila's strength. There was no "interpretation," no drawing of attention to what Mrs. Shaw experienced—this would have been inappropriate in helping Mrs. Shaw. Yet she *felt* a change in her understanding of Sheila, as seen in her comparing herself again with Sheila.

The group worker continued to work with both Sheila and her mother through the rest of that summer. Sheila gradually lost her beaten dog air. Her warm realtionship with the group worker, the experience of doing some things well, the relationship with the other children who did not make many demands on her, and especially her mother's new attitude all contributed to this change.

Appropriate use of program involves knowledge of the specific psychological impact of materials or games, and much imagination. No group worker can be adequate in the use of all kinds of activities. Group workers either use resources outside the group or involve group members as helpers. They use their self-awareness so as not to impose their own interests, but to consider the needs of the group members. They also are aware of cultural differences in the use of program. The members of a Golden Age Club, for example, told a group worker that they would like to discontinue the meetings where they sang with a young enthusiastic volunteer. The group worker was surprised since this club had asked especially for someone who could lead them in singing. He learned, however, that the young man had listened rather disdainfully to the kind of songs the group wanted to sing and then had proceeded to teach them Bach cantatas.

The psychological impact of many materials still needs research. Group workers have learned by experience and from educators, especially from preschool and kindergarten teachers, and more recently from occupational therapists. There are materials such as wood, paints, and clay that lend themselves particularly to more solitary activities in a group—necessary sometimes at the initial meetings of groups. Some materials allow for more working out of feelings than others. Wood is stubborn, resistant, and needs an orderly state of mind if one wants to accomplish something. Yet scrapwood that can be wasted may be helpful to children who have to work out anger. They can hammer, cut, or nail at will. Clay is soft and yielding, and can be shaped and reshaped—wonderful for the very insecure person since it permits hesitation, dreaming. Yet clay can be used differently; a very aggressive boy wedged the clay with vengeance, threw it hard to get out the air bubbles, and almost boxed with it. Weaving demands calm and helps the withdrawn person to accomplish something. It surely was a misplaced activity in an institution for delinquent girls where the girls—full of conflicts, drives, suffering, and resentment—were supposed to weave lovely smooth cloth out of fine yarn. And some materials can lead to surprises! Elmer, tiny, undernourished, and "tough," with a string of thefts behind him, reached constantly for the lively colored felt and sewed (!) with strong bright colored yarn, obviously working out all his yearning to get out of his drab surroundings and allowing himself to be the soft, playful child hidden behind the tough exterior.

There are also the materials and activities that allow for more interaction: the cookout, the making of a fire, storytelling, the cardboard boxes to be made into a puppet theatre, dramatics. This last is almost indispensable in good group work for a variety of purposes: Dramatics allow for expression of feelings. Many people cannot express themselves openly. They can do it though, when allowed to take part in a play.

### Example

Ella was always polite, always doing everything asked of her. She was a "prim little old lady" and the girls in her camp cabin misused her by letting her do the disagreeable work, but gave her little recognition in return. The group worker discussed with the camp counselor how important it was to let Ella come out of her shell—she was a very unhappy girl.

The occasion came when the cabin members suggested they put on a play for a camp fire. They wanted to write it themselves. It should be about parents and kids and school and camping. Sylvia tried to "cast" the girls, assigning Ella the role of an older sister. The counselor, sensitive to the opportunity for Ella, suggested that no casting be done in the beginning. Each girl should just speak up spontaneously whenever she felt she wanted to enter. Thus they could work out the story. They began this in the evening with the lights out.

Out of the dark came Ella's voice, angry, obstreperous, resistant. She took on the role of the youngster who did not want to go to camp, who talked back to her parents, who finally went, but who instigated all kinds of practical jokes against the girls in her tent. She played out all her resentment. The girls were amazed and impressed.

Ella's behavior outside the play did not change overnight. Yet during rehearsals she became more and more alive. The girls began to treat her less like a doormat.

The final presentation of the play brought huge applause. A sparkling Ella danced around the fire and, for the rest of the camp season, she was a pleasant, and no longer a submissive, camper.

Ethel Waters, the great actress, wrote beautifully about what the acting out of a dramatic part meant to her emotionally and how it changed her behavior toward others:

> I could not convince them that the role gave me the sort of release I'd long needed. Being Hagar softened me, and I was able to make more allowance for the shortcomings of others. Before that I'd always been cursing outside and crying inside. Playing in *Mamba's Daughters* enabled me to rid myself of the terrible inward pressure, the flood of tears I'd been storing up ever since my childhood.[12]

For some people even the personal presentation of a role in a drama is too threatening, too revealing. Yet they yearn to have the feeling of release Ethel Waters talks about. Puppets are a good medium for them because they present a mask. Ella found her courage first in the dark; others need the little dolls to hide behind.

Moreno has developed dramatics into a treatment medium for mentally sick people.[13] The use of this technique requires special training and is not usually part of the equipment of the social group worker. Moreno's method is helpful to certain patients and under certain conditions, but—as is true of all techniques—it must not be used without diagnostic thinking. Social group workers use dramatics like any other tool in relation to their understanding of the individual and his or her situation. Jack Simos describes such diagnostic thinking in his stimulating book *Social Growth Through Play Production*.[14] In the following excerpt he presents the impact of participation in dramatics on one boy in a treatment institution. The boy is named by the character he portrayed in the play.

### Example

Moody was a rather wiry, dark-complexioned, black-haired boy, who had been at the institution for about four years, although during this time, on one occasion, he had been tried in a foster home where his demanding attitude and his fidgety restlessness could not be tolerated, and from which he was, therefore, returned to the institution. He was 16 years old and the only full

---

[12]From *His Eye Is on the Sparrow* by Ethel Waters. Copyright 1950, 1951 by Ethel Waters and Charles Samuels. Reprinted by permission of Doubleday and Company, Inc.

[13]See Jacob L. Moreno, *Psychodrama* (Beacon, NY: Beacon House, 1946–1959).

[14]Jack Simos, *Social Growth Through Play Production* (New York: Association Press, 1957).

orphan residing at the treatment center, his adoptive parents having been killed in an accident when he was eight years old. Although electroencephalograms did not yield positive evidence, there was suspicion of brain damage deduced from his behavior and from psychological testing. At any rate, he had been dealt with as such. His overall IQ was 85 and he functioned on a dull, normal level. He had suffered temper tantrums and outbursts of rage which were so severe that he frothed at the mouth. He was so completely out of control that it required three adults, on one occasion, to contain him.

... He was a boy who suffered failure after failure; in his four years at the institution he could not point to one successful achievement. Yet he was selected not only for the play but for the prominent part of Moody....

... Because he was so fidgety and easily distracted, he was often a disciplinary problem during rehearsals but not to the extent anticipated. The trauma of the first run-through, ... was too much for him, however. He was so frustrated at missing some lines that he almost had a temper tantrum but managed to control himself, at least to the extent of running outside to let off steam. After calming himself, he returned and objectively studied the script to determine where he had slipped.

His portrayal was the most colorful and imaginative achievement in the group.... But he had no real difficulty with lines and thoroughly understood their meanings and the whole play. The one exception was a scene which called for resignation but which he insisted on interpreting as defiance. He could not seem to humble himself even in a play.

Needless to say, he received a great deal of praise for his performance and was looked upon with a new respect. His feeling of accomplishment could be literally observed in his bearing. His shoulders straightened: he carried himself more erect, and his whole demeanor took on a new look of confidence.

He also developed a greater self-control. Although he subsequently became involved in a few incidents where he overturned chairs and destroyed property, these never attained the degree of violence and uncontrollable rage which had characterized his temper tantrums heretofore.

In a psychological retesting shortly after his performance in the play it was discovered that his IQ was 101.[15]

The group worker had observed Moody's dramatic way of expressing himself (this was omitted in the excerpt quoted) and saw his possibility as an actor. Dramatics allowed Moody to express some of his own feelings (to see, for instance, that he could not portray resignation), but it also made demands of self-control on him through a medium he wanted, not through the hated adult authority alone. It also gave him the feeling of success, of being appreciated by others—a feeling so desperately needed by every human being and usually increasingly denied to those who need it most. And, as we find so frequently, the removal of emotional blocks allowed intelligence to function more freely.

Dramatic activities are an especially valuable program tool in group work, because they combine uniquely the opportunity for diagnostic study, release of feelings, demand for a certain inner discipline, use of imagina-

[15] Ibid., pp. 99–102.

tion, reliving of painful or joyful experiences, verbal and nonverbal expression, and feelings of accomplishment and appreciation by others.

Children's play and games have many characteristics of dramatics. The doll family play and the fierce-pretended soaring into space of little boys and girls fulfill similar needs. In an experiment with regressive shock therapy with highly disturbed psychotic patients, the social group worker and occupational therapist together made use of this knowledge. They considered normal play activities of the age group to which the patients were regressed and offered outlets for them in a more adult form. In case the patient should remember later, he should not feel embarrassed by having acted on a childish level. For example, women at a certain stage of regression were offered play with dolls, which they accepted with eagerness, and were told that they could sew and dress them for the children on the children's ward. They did use the dolls like children, but they were thus protected against any future embarrassment. They felt free to use the toys only when they were in a group. In the evaluation of the experiment it was acknowledged that patients seemed to make better progress when treatment was accompanied by this social experience. The results were not conclusive, however, and need further study.

*Experiencing* is one of the key words in social group work—experiencing of relationships with a helping person, with equals, with things, with one's own feelings, thoughts, emotions, skills, and interests. Group association always involves experiencing and learning. The group work skill enhances or corrects this experiencing through the conscious use of the media we have discussed. In the previous examples we saw their being used to help individuals in their normal growth problems, to help mentally or emotionally disturbed children or adults, or those who have become delinquent. We saw the application of group work skill to social action. Because of this quality of realistic experiencing of oneself in relation to others, social group work is also well-suited to help with the difficult problem of race relations and other intergroup tensions.

Legislation makes justice possible. Yet beyond this, true appreciation of people who are different is necessary. Discrimination harms the one discriminated against as well as the one who discriminates. The group work approach allows for experiencing of differences and similarities and the working through of feelings about them. Once, belief in the ameliorative power of the group process was so great that it was assumed people would appreciate each other if they only met. This is true sometimes, but not always. It may also intensify each person's prejudices. Group work adds to the mere encounter of people the help and skill of a person who uses all of his or her understanding, acceptance, knowledge of how to work through conflicts, and appreciation of nonverbal media to guide the group.

In the post-World War II period neighborhood and settlement houses, YMCAs and YWCAs, and other youth serving agencies had been in the forefront in using social group work to break through distrust between racial and religious groups.[16] In the 1960s minority groups had to stress the enhancement of the self-esteem of members of their own ethnic groups. Caucasians needed to probe into their own racist attitudes. Yet the need to increase mutual respect among all human beings persists and with it the need for the continued skill of the social group worker. In working with adults the group worker must help members to accept and work through expressions and feelings of hurt and hostility. "Telling it like it is" and going from there to "changing it like it is" becomes the major task.

To illustrate the helping process of social group work through the use of program, relationship, and verbal interaction, case material of group work is reproduced here as it was presented at the Annual Meeting of the American Orthopsychiatric Association in 1947. This case material is also presented to indicate the continuing relevance of group work. In rereading the material the only basic change that needed to be made was in terminology.

### Example

We usually think of the preschool child as least affected by racial or cultural tensions. Yet the four- and five-year-old early learns the attitudes of his environment. A small preschool group consisted of: Bert, a Jewish boy, age 4; George, a black boy, 4; Chris, 3½, and Jim, 4, two white boys of Irish-English parentage. Greatest anxiety in this group was seen in Bert, who was referred because of extreme aggressiveness with other children. He was removed from nursery school because he could not adjust to regulations. Bert was the youngest of three siblings with strict parents who had little understanding of and patience for the needs of a young child. They lived in one of the most dilapidated districts of the city with little playground space. In the neighborhood lived mostly people of Jewish and Italian background and blacks. In the home were also the grandparents, orthodox Jews. It is clear that many other factors were involved to produce disturbance in Bert than his cultural background alone. In play interviews he showed much anxiety toward adults and a great need to release active energies. In the group he showed reluctance at first in playing with George, the black child. Apparently helped by George's outgoing and warm-hearted behavior he soon teamed up with him. His conflict about being Jewish came into the open around Christmas time. The children listened intently to the *Night Before Christmas* when Bert suddenly pointed to Santa Claus saying, "Bad Santa Claus, I don't like him," and slapped the book shut.

Two weeks later, without any provocation, he suddenly shouted profanities, among them, "Dirty Jew, dirty Jew." Each time he said this he looked provokingly at the worker. Through the caseworker's contact with the mother

---

[16]See Galen M. Fisher, *Citadel of Democracy* (Berkeley, CA: Howell-North Press, 1955); Dorothy I. Height, *Step by Step with Interracial Groups* (New York: Publication Services, National Board, Y.W.C.A., 1955); Eleanor L. Ryder, "Some Principles of Intergroup Relations as Applied to Group Work," *Social Work with Groups*, 1960 (New York: N.A.S.W. 1960), pp. 52–61; and Jack Weiner, "Reducing Racial and Religious Discrimination," *Social Work with Groups*, 1960, pp. 62–73.

we knew that Bert had only recently received a severe beating because he had said "Dirty Jew" at home. It was clear that the child was struggling with his own status in being Jewish.

It was planned to use the Christmas party the following week to show him that being Jewish was as good as belonging to any other religion. Bert was delighted with the Christmas tree. His mother had said that he felt deprived in not having one at home. He and his sister had rigged up an umbrella with cotton and twigs pretending this to be a Christmas tree, and hid it so the grandparents would not see it. At the Clinic he touched the twigs and the ornaments of the tree, exclaiming over them. When the children sang, the worker asked Bert whether they did not light candles at home too, and whether he did not want to sing his song for all of them. He hesitated, but when the worker herself started the Chanukkah Song, a very surprised and happy look came over his face. He sang while the other three boys admired the unusual language. Encouraged by the admiration of his little friends and the first recognition of his being Jewish by children who were not, he asked whether he might hold a candle. With the Christmas tree in the background, ice cream cone in one hand, and the candle in the other, Bert proudly said the Hebrew benediction. The importance of the event became clear when an excited and happy Bert ran downstairs at the end of the party and told his mother "I lit the Christmas tree and I lit a candle and I sang a Chanukkah Song and she (pointing to the worker) knows it, too." Through this experience Bert got a feeling of acceptance from the adult and from the other children who admired and enjoyed his performance. He was able to accept himself as a Jew among non-Jews.

The second group consists of four adolescent girls. Betty, age 13, was referred by Juvenile Court because of loitering, staying out nights, and conflict with her parents. She was a lively girl of Hungarian parentage, and Hungarian was spoken in the home. There were many family conflicts.

Harriet, age 16, an attractive, serious girl, who had been a recluse for three years, showed compulsive symptoms. Her movements were extremely slow. Psychiatric interviews helped to find the causal basis of the problems and some interpretations given by the psychiatrist helped her considerably. She expressed the desire to join a group at the Clinic to "get used to people." Harriet's father was dead and she lived with her mother and sister. Both parents had come from Germany.

Edith, 14, a tall and attractive black girl, had been referred by Juvenile Court because of conflict with her parents. At the age of 11 she had given birth to a child. Edith was an ambitious girl who was intent on making good in school. She had insisted that she be allowed some social outlet and therefore was invited to join the group.

Dinah, a 15-year-old black girl, was referred for severe psychosomatic symptoms, intense conflict with her mother, and strong sibling rivalry with two younger, more attractive sisters. Dinah's family lived in a housing project.

Expressions of tension in the racial and cultural area were innumerable. Betty, as member of a comparatively recent immigrant family, showed her insecurity when the girls talked about learning languages. She said, "I know another language, I know Hung... , I mean Latin, the way they sing in church." She was not able at this point to admit her Hungarian background. Two meetings later the girls played records. One of them was the Hungarian Rhapsody. Harriet said she loved classical music, that she thought this record beautiful. The worker said, "It is the Hungarian Rhapsody, it has the fire of Hungarian music." Betty looked pleased and said that she knew a little Hungarian, even spoke some words when the girls encouraged her to do so. Her language background had not only become acceptable but had even given her some status in the group. At this point Harriet mentioned that she knew a few German words, thus revealing her own background. Harriet's difficulty, closely related to her fear of contact with people, was in contact with the black girls. She was much too gentle and polite to express these feelings in the presence of the girls, but at home she mentioned that it worried her when a black girl hung her coat over her own coat. Because of the many contacts under various conditions offered by the group, Harriet found, much to her surprise, that she and Edith, one of the black girls, had many interests in common. Both loved history, cooking and singing, and both heartily disliked arithmetic. Harriet exclaimed, "Why, I never thought we could like exactly the same things." Edith felt free to talk about her being black. After feeling the acceptance of the worker, she could even ask about her worries over discrimination of the schools.

Dinah had a harder time. She was very conscious of her dark color and repeated that she liked Edith's light brown color and how pretty Harriet was. It helped a great deal when Edith and Harriet started commenting on some of Dinah's pretty dresses. At this time the worker brought a magazine to the group. While looking it over Dinah pointed to a blouse similar to her own and asked whether it was all right for her to wear a blouse with such a low-cut neckline. The worker answered (and she could do so genuinely) that this was especially suitable because she had such lovely smooth skin. The surprised look said more than words. From then on, Dinah took more care of her appearance, apparently accepting herself with more ease, and also began to discuss discrimination. The girls discussed the lynching of a Negro and compared it with Fascism in Germany. Dinah said, "I would never want to live there." Edith replied, "But we are not always treated right here either." The worker encouraged their conversation. Harriet agreed that things should be changed in race relationships.

Proof of Harriet's change in this respect was seen in the way she herself piled coats and jackets together without regard to whom they belonged. At the time of Harriet's referral to a neighborhood group the worker discussed with her whether it made any difference to her to be in a group with black girls. Harriet said that she hardly knew the difference anymore, and added, "I was afraid of all girls a year ago, now I sometimes wonder why—and so I was even more afraid of them—but now I am no longer afraid, and it makes no difference."

In a group of 12-year-old boys there was apparent conflict between Aaron and Ralph. Aaron, a severely disturbed, 12-year-old Jewish boy, had a great need to point out his being Jewish, apparently testing whether others would accept him. Ralph, referred because of difficulties in school, was a very light black boy, who appeared almost white. The father had deserted the home, and Ralph lived with an indulgent mother in poor economic circumstances.

In one of the meetings Ralph constantly taunted Aaron, who had said that he could not eat cookies because of the Passover holiday. Ralph said he would not like being Jewish, and when asked what he would like to be he quickly said, "Italian—because there are so many of them." Later he called Aaron "Moses." Aaron retaliated by saying that Jesus had not lived. Ralph turned to the worker and asked, "Did Jesus live?" And then, "Did Moses live?" Aaron insisted that his mother had told him Jesus never lived. Ralph said with great pride that Jesus had died on the cross. Seeing Aaron's unhappy face, the worker added that Moses died on a mountain seeing the Promised Land. Aaron added happily, "Yes, it was the Mount Sinai." A few minutes later Ralph asked Joe whether there were black boys in his school. Joe said casually, "Only a few, but I like them." Ralph nodded his head "Yes?" The worker asked whether the color of people made any difference. Ralph, full of relief, said loudly, "It sure doesn't." Then he asked Aaron if he might use the jigsaw and when Aaron gave permission, he said, "Thank you, Aaron, thank you so much."

We see how these two boys, each insecure as members of two minority groups, attack the other minority group because of their own insecurity. Ralph showed his conflict with his own group when he expressed the wish to be Italian, this being a majority group in his neighborhood. The group situation allowed these two boys not only to express their feelings, but to do it without being hampered by an adult or forced into a serious fight as is often observed in unprotected situations. Aware of the conflicts of both boys, the worker was not interfering in their fight, nor was she so passive that they were left helpless and frustrated. Some time later Ralph brought a dark black boy to the group introducing him as his friend, thus indicating his own acceptance of his race.

The above records bring forth the apprehension of the child belonging to the discriminated group. We will now illustrate the fears of a group of six- and seven-year-old girls belonging to the majority group. Dolly was referred because of moodiness. Her brother's removal to an institution by court order had left her fearful. The two children, of English parentage, had lived with their mother (the father was dead) in a housing project. We knew of recurring quarrels with black children in the neighborhood.

Dolly first refused to sit beside a black girl; she said she was afraid of her. A similar reaction was seen in her 11-year-old brother. When he first came to the group and saw the black boy, he recoiled saying, "Oh God, is he in our group?" In the course of only a few meetings this boy had learned through the close contact with a gentle black youngster that there was nothing to fear and soon the two were seen walking home together.

The sister showed the same initial fear. This time the black child she met was not as gentle as the one her brother had met and she had to face the reality of this girl's aggression. She tried to avoid conflicts. The worker encouraged her to fight back. When Dolly learned that the black girl could be both aggressive and amiable, and that she could play and fight with her as with anybody else, she seemed to relax.

Dolly had a hard time working through prejudices fostered in her home and neighborhood. It was the freedom she felt in contact with the worker and the knowledge of complete acceptance by her that made it possible for her to work through some of the prejudices in quite a mature way. The following incident was recorded at a time when mothers often brought their children to the group and stayed for the first few minutes. Dolly said in a loud voice to the worker, "You know, my cousin does not like you because you are Jewish." Her mother, embarrassed, said "Hush, hush, don't say that." The worker smiled at Dolly and said that they could talk about this later, that she need not be worried. She was worried though, and in a serious way screwed up her face and said, "But I like you, and she just doesn't like you because you are Jewish." Since many mothers were around and very embarrassed, the worker put her arm around Dolly and said that they certainly would talk it over later in the day. At the swimming pool Dolly cornered the worker again and said, "I do like you, I told her, I did not care, I like you better than I like her." The worker said she liked Dolly too, and that people have to know each other to learn to like each other. Later in the day, Dolly asked, "Are you really Jewish?" and then anxiously, "Do Jews believe in God?" When she was reassured, she seemed to feel better.

Some weeks later the girls looked through the book, *One God.* Dolly proudly said, "I know now that Jews do not believe in Jesus, but they believe in God and that is good too." She wanted to take the book home to show her family. It was around this time that Dolly, who had previously refused to sit beside Eva, a black girl, said, "I want to be friends with Eva." She had learned to overcome her fear of the unknown through acceptance from the worker and contact with people of other groups. In a less frank and accepting environment this child would never have dared utter her thoughts and therefore would never have worked through her feelings regarding Jews and blacks. She had learned to individualize people as people and not as races.[17]

The problems of these children stem from a racist system that places a higher value on one race than on another. Group workers, in their professional and citizen capacity, must work toward basic change of such a system. At the same time their responsibility for individuals, their lives, their feelings, and their relationships continue.

## 5. PURPOSEFUL CHOICE AND CREATION OF ENVIRONMENT

Concern with a healthy environment, human and other, is a general social work obligation. The conscious use or creation of environment will be discussed here only where it falls into its more narrow concept as a part of the group work process.

The office, with walls that allow for privacy and furniture that lets the client feel that he or she is considered a person with dignity, was found to be helpful to the casework process. The long, hard benches for relief recipients, the questioning in large rooms where everyone could overhear everybody else's problems, the brown, cheerless walls, were symbols of a welfare approach lacking the basic philosophy of modern casework and group work. There is no question that excellent practice can be done in a most desolate environment, but then it is done *in spite* of it.

Since a sense of intimacy and individualization is inherent in the group work approach, the group needs for its meetings a place to allow for closeness and mutual attention.

[17]Gisela Konopka, "Group Therapy in Overcoming Racial and Cultural Tensions," *The American Journal of Orthopsychiatry,* XVII, No. 4 (Oct. 1947), 694–699.

The group worker met her group of 10-year-old boys after school in the gym of the nearby neighborhood house. They needed a physical outlet after sitting still at school. They ran and jumped and shouted.

After about half an hour of this, the group worker called them together to move into a small clubroom where they could make plans for their next meetings. The boys were delighted. "Will this be our very own, every week?" Roger asked.

Roger seemed to express the feelings of the others too. Physical surroundings are consciously planned.

**Example**

A group worker planned to meet with an out-patient group of adult epileptics who needed help with social relations. They were not able to hold onto jobs because several of them had been kept at home for a large part of their lives and did not know how to meet strangers. Only one in this group had ever dated. It was important to have the group meetings in the hospital to symbolize their being part of treatment. The meeting room should not be an office, but a comfortable living room so that the patients could get used to a social, informal situation. The nurses offered their nicely furnished dayroom for the use of the group. Before the meeting the group worker arranged the chairs so that people could see each other, but not in a rigid circle. A few chairs were left at the side with small tables full of magazines next to them. This would allow the shyer members to withdraw when they needed to, without being too obvious.

She also arranged for refreshments. Food and coffee per se were not so important but it was important to have something for their hands to do; hands can feel like awkward lumps when one is in a new social situation, and the group worker realized this.

For a committee meeting of a community planning group the room can be arranged quite differently—often a round table is an appropriate setup for such a group, while it can be a retardation to a group that consists of shy members whose purpose is to discuss emotional problems.

It has been frequently advocated that classrooms be used during after-school hours for recreational and informal educational purposes. This is appropriate for certain kinds of groups, yet others should not be placed in this environment. Acting-out adolescents, for instance, with school problems, cannot feel that the classroom has another purpose besides the one they are familiar with, and will be provoked into destructiveness if they meet in school rooms.

Turner describes an experiment with "unclubbable boys," in London (in the United States they would be called gangs). These boys met with their club leader on a river barge. The program gave outlets for adventure, spirit, achievement, and physical labor. The environment itself had meaningful impact; the old barge was like a home but, with the open river surrounding it, was not too confining. On the one hand, it was a house that had to be kept in order and that provided for pride in a form of ownership, and, on the other, it was a moving vehicle that carried the boys from one place to another and demanded their skill in handling it.[18]

Every social worker knows the impact of housing on people. Slums threaten more than the physical health of people. The famous German caricaturist of the 1920s, Heinrich Zille, used as a caption under one of his biting sketches, "You can kill a man with an ax, but also with housing." Lack of privacy, ugliness, and dreariness weigh as heavily on the soul as on the body. The concern for decent housing belongs to many professions. There is one specific form of "housing"—or environment—that is of direct concern to the social worker, and especially to the social group worker: this is the environment in institutions where children and adults who have been removed from the general, regular stream of community life live for twenty-four hours every day. Institutions are group-living agencies with the total impact of such, only intensified by the fact that the individual cannot leave at will. This applies equally to mental hospitals, treatment centers for children, delinquency institutions, and prisons. Even today many of these places are dull, ugly boxes built for mass living, without privacy. Instead of rebuilding healthy human beings they seem like slums, or worse, and contribute to the "mangling of the soul," as Fritz Redl once called it. I have seen mentally disturbed children kept in a large cage where they could only feel inhuman and like criminals. I have seen in a modern mental hospital a children's unit that consisted exclusively of wards with hospital beds, that provided no playroom, no comfortable chairs, no place to keep a piece of private belongings; toys—essential for the normal child to grow on and so much more essential for the sick one—simply were not available.

I have seen dayrooms totally devoid of furnishings in institutions for mentally retarded preschool children; I have seen the children locked in them, with nothing available to stimulate whatever spark of interest or creativity they might have had, with nothing but emptiness that would destroy it further. I have seen children do nothing all day long but crawl around on the floor, like little animals.

I have visited an institution for the blind with cheerless, gray walls and long lines of beds, without a single sign of beauty. The excuse was, "The children can't see anyhow." My reply was, "Can't they feel? Can't they feel the smoothness of a beautifully shaped piece of wood, the strength of a stone sculpture, the manifold forms of ceramics, the textures of materials for bedspreads, tablecloths, curtains? What about staff working with them. Don't they react differently to color in the rooms instead of the deadly 'institutional gray or brown?'"

---

[18]See M. Lloyd Turner, *Ship Without Sails* (London: University of London Press, 1953).

I have visited training schools where the youngsters ate on long tables from ugly metal dishes. The noise made it impossible to hold any kind of conversation—something a youngster should learn to make mealtimes more enjoyable—and the ugliness of the eating utensils gave the boys a feeling of being inferior, of being "prisoners," and they acted accordingly.

I have seen modern prisons built with tiled walls to make cleaning easy, but they gave the feeling of coldness, of being a bathroom instead of a living unit. I could go on . . . .

There are small things in the living environment that count heavily when one is separated from home and feels inferior: no mirrors in hospitals for mentally sick women; steel mirrors in detention homes for girls (safety is supposed to make this necessary, yet in a place where regular mirrors were installed, not a single girl had broken them in years); drab clothes that do not belong to a specific person; naked light bulbs. Once I visited a children's unit in a mental hospital and had breakfast with the children. The room was attractive, and so were the trays brought in for breakfast. I happened to sit at a table with four withdrawn, mute, teen-age girls. Nobody touched the food. On each girl's tray was a whole orange. I began to peel one, divided it and gave it to the girl next to me who ate it with pleasure. Then I felt a finger poking me. One of the girls silently pointed at her orange. I peeled all three of them and the girls ate. The kitchen help came to take away the trays from all the tables. I looked around—almost all of them were half full. The fresh orange was a fine idea, but nobody had considered that these slow patients did not know how to get it ready to eat. Nobody considered their slowness in general. The schedule was made according to hospital routine.

These humanizing attributes of the environment are the business of the social worker. Not every institution can start to build new units, although this becomes increasingly necessary. But intense and imaginative attention to environment can vastly improve existing facilities and make a therapeutic group life possible. One of the large, old institutions for delinquent girls changed the environment by arranging for separate apartments in the different stories of the old house, dividing the large sleeping quarters into smaller units, building a private closet for each girl, and adding dressers.

New institutions have often accepted the basic concept of an institution as a group-living community that must allow for individualism. Large mass institutions—for years not allowed in the Scandinavian countries—are beginning to disappear. Planners are now giving attention to beauty as well as to utility in designing new buildings. This does not require precious or expensive materials. The physical environment must differ according to the specific purpose of the particular institution and the particular population that it accommodates; a treatment center for emotionally disturbed children should not look like a prison for adult offenders. Planning for both must be directed toward the kind of guidance that is necessary to help human beings find themselves and to restore their capacity to live with others. A primitive forestry camp can provide as helpful an environment to a prisoner—assuming it is not exploitative—as the most highly civilized, cheerful, and comfortable cottage of a modern hospital to a mental patient.

### Example

In one correctional institution morale was low and every attempt at rehabilitation seemed to fall flat. Then the new superintendent began to change the physical environment. The men had always taken their meals at long benches facing the wall or the back of the men in front of them. He arranged a normal table situation, and replaced the tin food utensils with plastic ware. Food was brought in on hot steam tables where once it had been served half-cold. He made other changes. Sheets were changed once a week instead of once a month—this meant an increase in the number of laundry workers, which meant, in turn, fewer idle hands. In the past, when the men were out of their cells, they usually stood around in the corridors or sat on the floors. The superintendent had the prison workshop make chairs, which were placed in the corridors so that the men, if they wished, could sit like other human beings. In the past, the men had had to speak to their visitors through wire screening so heavy that they could hardly see to whom they were talking. The superintendent had these torn out and the security of the wire replaced by a human guard. And he added a homey touch: prison-gardeners were commissioned to see that a vase of fresh flowers was placed in the room during visiting hours, thus creating a more pleasant atmosphere. These changes came about slowly and began to open up possibilities for real treatment. The men no longer talked to each other only in secret, but began to enter into open discussions. They talked about and appreciated the changes, and began to take an interest in themselves. This made it possible to establish a prison council and to begin involving the men in concern with their own fate as a community.[19] And this opened the door to the use of other therapeutic and educational methods.

Such changes in the environment make it more possible to work with the people who live in the institution and it shows them respect as human beings. Only thus can a healthy group process, conducive to rehabilitation, start.

But the described examples of improvement of institutional living are only makeshift, although necessary. Knowledge of group process has increasingly shown the disaster of forced mass associations. The concern for a healthy environment dictates the group worker's fight against mass institutions and for smaller community-based facilities for delinquents or for young or old in any form of distress who cannot or do not want to stay with their families. The physical setup can and should be related to the people who live in them. Young people will want bright colors, pillows to sit on,

---

[19]Maxwell Jones has enlarged on this in his book, *Therapeutic Community*, published in London in 1952 by Tavistock Publications.

and an opportunity to rearrange their rooms. Other people may want more traditional furniture. Flexibility needs to be guarded in all environmental planning.

In the community, social group workers can help citizen groups to be increasingly concerned with their own environment and form effective group action to be heard.

### SUMMARY

The helping process of social group work is carried out through:

1. The purposeful, warm, understanding, concerned relationship between group worker and group members.
2. The relationship among group members (the guided group process).
3. Verbal communication.
4. Nonverbal communication.
5. Purposeful choice and creation of environment.

No one of these media can be used dogmatically and indiscriminately. Their use must vary according to the group worker's understanding of the individuals and the group, according to a particular agency's purpose, and according to the needs and purposes of the group and its individual members. They are used by the group worker—*a person*—and hence they must be used with care, for they may take on exclusively the qualities of the group worker's personality. The social group work process has the aspects of an art based on science.

### BIBLIOGRAPHY

COYLE, GRACE L., "Definition of the Group Worker," in Harleigh B. Trecker, ed., *Group Work—Foundations and Frontiers.* New York: Whiteside, Inc., 1955.
——————, *Group Work with American Youth.* New York: Harper & Row, Pub., 1948.
GUZIE, FRANCES P., "Emerging Patterns in the Use of Program in Social Group Work," *Group Work Papers 1957*, pp. 38–49. New York: N.A.S.W., 1958.
KONOPKA, GISELA, "A Healthy Group Life—Social Group Work's Contribution to Mental Health," *Mental Hygiene*, 45, No. 3 (July 1961).
——————, "Discipline in Youth Groups," *The American Journal of Catholic Youth Work*, I, No. 1 (Winter 1960), 21–28.
——————, *Group Work in the Institution* (rev. ed.). New York: Association Press, 1970.
——————, "The Application of Social Work Principles to International Relations," *The Social Welfare Forum, 1953*, pp. 279–289. New York: Columbia University Press, 1953.
——————, "The Method of Social Group Work," in Walter A. Friedlander,

ed., *Concepts and Methods of Social Work,* pp. 116–200. Englewood Cliffs, NJ: Prentice-Hall, 1958.

——————, "Social Group Work: A Social Work Method," *Social Work,* 5, No. 4 (Oct. 1960), 53–61.

——————, *Therapeutic Group Work With Children.* Minneapolis: University of Minnesota Press, 2nd printing 1965.

MIDDLEMAN, RUTH R., *The Non-Verbal Method in Working With Groups.* New York: Association Press, 1968.

NORTHEN, HELEN, "Interrelated Functions of the Social Group Worker," *Social Work,* 2, No. 2 (Apr. 1957).

PAPELL, CATHERINE B. and BEULAH ROTHMAN, "Social Group Work Models: Possession and Heritage," *Journal of Education for Social Work,* 2, No. 2 (Fall 1966), 66–78.

PARADISE, ROBERT, "The Factor of Timing in the Addition of New Members to Established Groups," *Child Welfare,* XLVII, No. 9 (Nov. 1968), 524–529.

PERLMAN, BERNICE, "Group Work with Psychotic Veterans," *American Journal of Orthopsychiatry,* XIX, No. 1 (Jan. 1949) 69–78.

PHILLIPS, HELEN U., *Essentials of Social Group Work Skill.* New York: Association Press, 1957.

REDL, FRITZ and DAVID WINEMAN, *Children Who Hate—Controls from Within.* Glencoe, Il: The Free Press, 1951.

——————, *The Aggressive Child.* New York: Free Press, 1957.

SCHWARTZ, WILLIAM, "Group Work and the Social Scene," in Alfred J. Kahn, *Issues in American Social Work,* pp. 110–137. New York: Columbia University Press, 1959.

——————, "The Social Worker in the Group," *New Perspectives on Services to Groups: Theory, Organization, Practice,* pp. 7–29 (with discussion by Ruth E. Smalley, pp. 30–34). New York: N.A.S.W.

SIMOS, JACK, *Social Growth Through Play Production.* New York: Association Press, 1957.

TRECKER, HARLEIGH B., *Social Group Work: Principles and Practices* (rev. ed.). New York: Whiteside, Inc., 1955.

VINTER, ROBERT D., ed., *Readings in Social Group Work Practice.* Ann Arbor: Campus Publishers, 1967.

WEINER, JACK, "Reducing Racial and Religious Discrimination," *Social Work with Groups 1960,* pp. 62–73. New York: N.A.S.W., 1960.

WILSON, GERTRUDE and GLADYS RYLAND, *Social Group Work Practice: The Creative Use of the Social Process.* Boston: Houghton Mifflin, 1949.

WITTENBERG, RUDOLPH M., *So You Want to Help People.* New York: Association Press, 1947.

*Man is born a pre-destined idealist for he is born to act. . . . To act is to affirm the worth of an end and to persist in affirming the worth of an end is to make an idea.*[1]

# EIGHT

# PRINCIPLES OF SOCIAL GROUP WORK IN PRACTICE

"There is nothing we can do with him," was the general attitude of the neighborhood, adults and children alike, in regard to John. "He is born mean." Parents forbade their children to associate with him. On the playground children called him tauntingly, "the killer." At the age of 9 he indeed had an impressive record of misdeeds: he stole with skill; he tripped smaller children. Yet he himself was one of the thinnest, smallest 9-year-olds that one could imagine. He flew into a rage at the slightest provocation and had hit a girl so hard with a piece of wood that she had had to be hospitalized with a broken arm. He was one of the few children who man-

[1]Harry C. Schriver, editor and annotator, *Justice Oliver Wendell Holmes, His Book Notices and Uncollected Letters and Papers* (New York: Central Book Co., 1936), p. 143.

aged to escape from the juvenile detention home. He seemed to be of average or better intelligence, but testing was almost impossible because of his hostile sullenness in the testing situation—to him, adults were the ultimate enemies. His school achievement was very low and he could not read. His mother was unhappy about his behavior, but was also convinced that he was "born that way, just like his father who deserted us." She was an unhappy woman, incapable of giving warmth to her children. John was the second of three children. All of them showed difficult behavior, but his was the most destructive.

Give up? Accept the fact that this 9-year-old is destined for a "life of crime"? Here were difficult forces to overcome—in the child, in his human environment. The basic attitude of the social group worker is one of optimism. He is the idealist of whom Holmes speaks so beautifully. It is not an idealism that disregards reality with its limitations, but one that makes action possible. It is a stubborn belief in the capacity of the human being to grow and change if given help. This optimism is part of a general trait of American culture. But it is not the kind that Jacques Maritain rightfully designated as an illusion:

> In some respects the American conception of life appears as a continuation of the eighteenth-century optimistic views on Man and Nature.
> ... belief in the goodness of Nature, the natural goodness of Men, in the Rousseauist sense.[2]

I am aware of the fact that the last ten years have brought a change in this. There has been a debunking of idealism in the American culture. In some ways that has led to greater realism, but it has also brought about a certain cynicism that prevents action. This author welcomes the loss of illusions, but hopes for a continuation of a view of life that demands of everyone active involvement in the shaping of our destiny.

It is an action-idealism with consideration of all the facts without sentimentality, but with the conviction that often the feeling of genuine hope conveyed to individuals or groups can help them to move out of situations that would otherwise seem to drag them deeper into difficulties. A philosopher, Leonard Nelson, a follower of Kant and Freud and a creative thinker in his own right, wrote a philosophical treatise on this in which he developed clearly and logically the necessary and *possible* "alliance of Idealism with Realism."[3] In the treatise, he separated the realistic idealist from the purely sentimental enthusiast or the pessimist who uses a pretended realism to avoid action:

---

[2]Jacques Maritain, *Reflections on America* (New York: Scribner's, 1958), p. 131.

[3]Leonard Nelson, *Politics and Education*, trans. W. Lansdell (London: Allen & Unwin, 1928), p. 186.

The Idealist is neither a dreamer nor a doubter, but he looks at the world as it is, with the eyes of the Realist, and from such realism his energy and his courage spring. . . .
Realism teaches the Idealist to know the means which are necessary for the attainment of his aim. It teaches him that pious wishes have no power to move things in the world of space, and that we must get our hands busy if we want to make this world better.[4]

With such an attitude of thoughtful weighting of facts (realism) and hope for possible change (idealism) the group worker approaches a child like John, a group concerned with a slum clearance project, or a bleak mental hospital ward. This basic attitude not only prompts the social group worker to take action, but usually activates the individual or group that he or she is working with, too. This latter phenomenon is seen increasingly in all educational and healing arts.

John, for instance, was not seen as a "hopeless case," but rather as someone in need of the efforts of several members of a child guidance team. (Such a team consisted traditionally of a psychiatrist, a psychologist, and social workers, mostly case workers, but occasionally also group workers.) It was agreed that the first approach could be made only through group work, because of his deep suspicion and hostility toward adults. He needed to be a little boy among other children in a group that was small enough so that he could feel important. The group worker had to be prepared for much hostile behavior and to protect the others from him but, at the same time, without rejecting him. John needed to experience some tangible success in something, either in things he did with his hands or in the simple—and for him, not so simple—experience of having spent an hour with other children without insults and fights. He needed to be "left alone" inside a group without being neglected. He had always known only the role of the outcast or the one who got attention because of misbehavior. He needed to feel that an adult believed in his capacity to change without making him say so in words, without his promising to be "good," without his being asked to make a return in exchange for the attention, affection (only cautiously shown) or quiet, helpful restraint extended to him.

These were things John needed; they explain why he started first in a group conducted by a social group worker. At first he tried to live up to his reputation as "the killer." But how could one keep this up, even a "hardened" 9-year-old, when limitations always included a message that he could act differently, when he saw that those other kids "had their problems" too and that the group worker met them with the same kind of respect? Then there were activities that were fun, things John would have liked to do, but from which he persistently had been excluded—like doing woodwork. In the beginning he did rip apart pieces of lumber or made sharp swords, but he was not the only one to do this; others did it too. What would the group worker do? She admired his skill when he stopped just cutting things apart; she commented on the sharpness of the edge, "Well done, John. What would you like to do with it?" "Kill someone." "Whom?" "You." "Really?" And John suddenly felt something he would have liked to have pushed far away from him. He turned quickly. Tears welled up— tears! Such a silly thing! Sure he hated her; she made him cry, did she not? But he had never cried before. He felt anger and yet. . . . He did not understand.

The group worker realized John's struggle with himself, the first softness beginning in him, even if John himself could not admit it, and she wisely neither forced an answer nor "explained."

Layers of hate cannot be torn away. They must come off slowly, be lifted with infinite care, like those layers of earth the archaeologist lifts off a precious piece of art he has found covered and encrusted with the dirt of centuries.

The group worker purposely let John alone in this precious minute and turned to another child, thus not making him feel that she had abandoned him. John was relieved; he was neither the center of attention nor was he forced to express hate or to apologize. He could watch what other children did: Jim, who also had made a sharp sword, cut paper with it and seemed to enjoy this; Simon used his to make patterns in the sandbox— "like a baby," thought John. Without realizing it, he moved closer and closer to the sandbox. Suddenly his sword touched the soft sand, swirled it around, stabbed it. For twenty minutes John was blissfully a baby, partially an aggressive one, playing with sand. The group worker made no comment. She knew that a most important process had started: John had allowed himself to be the baby he never had been and yet had yearned to be. Part of the baby was aggression, but part of it was also the need for love.

John had many more experiences: flare-ups, relapses into open anger, sudden feelings of tenderness. He even began to join in discussions with other boys. These happened usually when they were eating and when Owen started talking about school—Owen was the talker in the group. They all hated school, and mostly reading. It was John who blurted out one day that it was awful, that he hated all the other children because they could read street signs and he could not. The group worker asked, "Would you like Mr. Dennis (the psychologist) to help you learn to read? You know, I think you can catch on pretty fast. Remember when we did the woodburning the other day? You knew the letters we used right away." "She really likes me," thought John—or better, *felt* it. "She really believes I can do things."

Weeks had passed and since those first meetings, John had begun to trust and believe in his counselor—he had certainly tested her, over and over, by kicking others, and even by kicking her, but now there was a new conflict within him: He wanted her all for himself; the other kids should not be there. "Can't *you* teach me?" said John.

The group worker understood. When the layers of hate begin to fall away, the skin under them is tender. The child had returned to an earlier stage—that of an infant—and the adult he had learned to trust should be all his own, his mother. The sharing that was so helpful in the beginning because it allowed distance from the adult now had become irksome. The child was ready for a more intensive one-to-one relationship, but, at the same time, he had to learn to accept the sharing of beloved people—of mothers, fathers, teacher.

John still needed the group, but he also had to be helped to accept a relationship with another adult. The group worker could not simply refuse John. To him that would mean that he was again rebuffed, as he had been so often in his early life. And yet she had to help him transfer his good relationship to others too.

The group worker explained to John that she was not as capable as Mr. Dennis of helping him with his reading but that she would gladly sit in at the first session if this would make him feel a bit more comfortable. She also told him more about Mr. Dennis and his way of doing things. John was not yet ready for this step: He did not want to go—but, at least, he was not hurt.

The words TIME and PATIENCE must be written in capitalized letters in social group work.

A few weeks later Owen told John that he was a "dope" for not having gone to get help with reading. He, Owen, had now gone through the primer, and "Boy, it is much easier now!" No one in authority could have called John a "dope," even at that time, without arousing old resentment. A few months earlier, no child could have called him that. But now he was so much more a child among children! "Dope yourself," he shouted at Owen, but he did not hit him. The group worker knew she too could be more direct now. "Why not try it, John?" No answer yet. . . .

It was around Easter, and the boys had gone with the group worker into town to buy "surprises" for their party. In the department store John passed a counter with furry toy rabbits; he returned to it again and again. The group worker wondered what he wanted. "Could I have one of those?" This was said shyly and a bit ashamedly. "Surely, if they are not too expensive." Again the miracle to John; here was an adult who did not think it unusual that a 10-year-old wanted a toy rabbit. In the bus John held the paper bag with the rabbit. From time to time his hands reached into it and stroked it. Once he caught the group worker looking at him. He stiffened. Would she laugh? But she did not; she just nodded agreement.

The group worker realized that this was a very crucial moment for John. For the first time he had allowed himself, consciously, to be a little boy with a need for tenderness. It was important that no one make fun of him at home, especially not his mother. Here was a moment where the judgment of the social worker had to be fast, clear, and—if necessary—unconventional. Usually the caseworker had interviews with the mother; the group worker had only a few contacts. This time, however, she decided to stop with John at his home to enlist his mother's support. Before reaching his home she asked John whether he wanted to show his mother the rabbit. He said he would like to but wondered whether she would make fun of him.

At home all three talked together about the trip. John kept the rabbit hidden in the paper bag. His mother finally inquired what he had there, and John shyly produced the toy. The group worker turned quietly toward his mother, "It is lovely, is it not. It means much to John." She had not taken from John the responsibility of showing his purchase to his mother, but she supported him and, at the same time, enlisted his mother's help, making her feel that *her* actions were important to John. The mother, who had learned much about herself and John in her interviews with the caseworkers, smiled and admired the beauty of the rabbit. And John went to bed with the rabbit cuddled in his arm.

The next week at the Easter party, Jim, another group member, brought young, fluffy chickens to the group. He held them tightly—so tightly he almost suffocated them. The group worker showed him how the little chickens suffered by this, even if he wanted only to prove his love. John, for the first time, found words for feelings: "Loving is soft, isn't it?" The group worker's arms went around both boys, then Owen and Gary joined them. They talked about their fears, of needing big people to protect them, of former hates, of anger.

A warm bond had given them courage to let down the hard barriers against each other and the adult.

They asked to make Easter cards for their mothers (it was not the group worker's suggestion; it came from them).

They began to retransfer their love to the person who was the real power in their lives. They could do it only because they had worked it through and out on the group worker. They also could like each other, in spite of vying with each other for the love of the adult. They became 10-year-olds, but only after they had been allowed to be very little boys without having to be ashamed of it.

They asked for spelling lessons. John asked Owen (and the group worker chalked down a silent "progress," because he asked another boy and not her) whether Owen *really* thought Mr. Dennis could teach him reading, whether he was mean, whether he liked "kids." And John began reading lessons. . . .

It was some weeks later that John brought a neighborhood friend to the group. He "showed off" in the healthy and delightful way in which any

10-year-old introduces his friends and "his" group. The friend was duly impressed by the things they made, by the boys, by the whole place.

John had taken another step—he had gained status with a neighbor.

We have followed this one child through his experiences with group work treatment to show the use of the different media in social group work; the integration of the underlying attitude of respect and optimism with the reality of understanding the child in his changing feelings and relationships on the part of the group worker; the diagnostic decisions made in relation to the existing needs of the individual child and other group members; and the use of relationship, of transference, of group interaction, of verbal and nonverbal program activities—all this to help the child recover a sense of worthwhile self. Thus he gradually became able to relate to others in a giving way, whereas, initially, his relationship to others was mainly destructive. We see from this illustration how closely intellectual understanding of individual and group dynamics is intertwined with sensitive empathy and infinite patience, and how they both help the child to grow by making demands that are not overwhelming.

We see this general sequence of the group work process: (1) "getting to know each other" (and in hostile people this includes much testing of the person they consider responsible or in authority); (2) holding affection (and sometimes dependency and jealousy of the sharing with other members); (3) the working through of one's problems or handicaps on a verbal or nonverbal level; (4) renewed testing of the authority figure (but on a level different from in the beginning); and (5) a moving out to healthy and normal relationships with adults and children and the need for and the beginning to actively reach out for achievement.

Although in this example I purposely chose to focus on one child to present the helping process, the example also shows the interaction of several children, the way they influence one another, and the way the skilled social group worker uses group process either to relieve an individual from too much attention or to help the person gain it.

It also illustrates the slow development and importance of group bond, and its freeing force when the individual group member feels true acceptance. In many forms of therapy the freeing of one's inhibitions to express hostility is stressed. This is frequently needed in many people, especially when people are too frightened (or too constricted) to show negative feelings. Even warmth and love are often carefully and successfully hidden—either because they seem like something to be ashamed of or because those feelings have been rebuffed so often that the individual has put on too many protective layers and is no longer aware of them. To develop a group climate that allows for the expression of genuine positive feelings while allowing also for the working through of conflict, anxiety, and other negatives is one of the skills of social group work.

Let us return to theory.

The previous chapters have evolved the following scheme of the group work method:

> Social group work is a method of social work that helps persons to enhance their social functioning through purposeful group experiences and to cope more effectively with their personal, group, or community problems.

> Premise 1.  Social work as a profession is concerned with enhancement of persons' social functioning.
> Premise 2.  There is significant correlation between social functioning and group experience.
> Premise 3.  People need help—at times, professional help—to enhance social functioning.
> Premise 1 is a matter of agreement, tradition, social sanction, and definition.
> Premise 2 is proved by clinical and laboratory research.
> Premise 3 is proved mainly by observation and clinical experience.

There are many ways, lay and professional, to enhance social functioning. Social group work is one of them. Its specific effectiveness lies in the psychological makeup of human beings: Two basic needs—*the need to belong* and *the need to have self-respect*—are dependent on fulfillment of positive group experiences. A third need is located in the totality of human society, namely, *the need to cooperate with each other*. For the individual it means taking responsibility for one another, and this includes—and requires—group interaction.

The problems that social group work addresses itself to range from healthy developmental social needs of individuals to severe disturbances in them. Group work also directs itself to social problems, especially in the area of group relationships, such as class and race prejudices.

The *point of entry* is generally a request for help, sometimes openly expressed, sometimes not.

Group work skills are *procedural and interactional.*[5]

Procedural skills mean the use of the scientific method: the process of collecting facts, of assessing them, and of establishing objectives for individuals and groups. They are based on knowledge (dynamics of the individual, group process, and the social systems in which they move); and on the individual capacities of group workers (listening, observation, empathy). Ruby Pernell describes them as:

---

[5]These terms are taken from Ruby B. Pernell, "Identifying and Teaching the Skill Components of Social Group Work," a paper presented at the Annual Meeting of the Council on Social Work Education, St. Louis, 1962.

the steps in a methodological, knowledgeable procedure of giving help: the identification of the Professional Purpose, Study, Diagnosis, Selection of Goals, Treatment and Reporting.[6]

The interactional skills are the means through which group workers become effective. They are based on their own and on the profession's ethical convictions and on their sensitive use of self (art). Pernell summarized the interactional skills as:

> Those behavior responses appropriate to individual and group need, within the purposes of the social group work service. These we identify according to the scheme . . . as Accepting, Relating, Enabling and Supporting, Limiting, Guiding, Alleviating and Interpreting.[7]

Any practice theory consists of:

1. An abstract scheme of knowledge.
2. A value system.
3. Selected specific aims of a given practice.
4. Action principles derived from the above three items.

The first three items have been discussed in previous chapters.

Out of knowledge, philosophy, and skill evolve basic principles for the practice of group work. The word "principles" is used here in a dual sense: as "the essence" of the group work method, determining and describing its nature; and as a rule of conduct, as "guidelines" for the social group worker.

There have been several attempts to delineate such "essentials" or principles. My own first attempt was worked out in 1955 and was used also in the Curriculum Study. It consisted of the following ten points:

1. The function of the social group worker is a helping or enabling function: this means that his goal is to help the members of the group and the group as a whole to move toward greater independence and capacity for self-help.
2. In determining his way of helping, the group worker uses the scientific method: fact-finding (observation), analyzing, diagnosis in relation to the individual, the group, and the social environment.
3. The group work method includes the worker forming purposeful relationships with group members and the group: this includes a conscious focusing on the needs of the members, on the purpose of the group as expressed by

---

[6]Ruby B. Pernell, "Identifying and Teaching the Skill Components of Social Group Work," a paper presented at the Annual Meeting of the Council on Social Work Education, St. Louis, 1962; mimeographed, Graduate School of Social Work, University of Pittsburgh, No. 4366, p. 5.

[7]Ibid.

the members, as expected by the sponsoring agency or the organization to which the group belongs, and as implied in the members' behavior. It is differentiated from a casual, unfocused relationship.

4. One of the main tools in achieving such a relationship is the conscious use of self. This includes self-knowledge and discipline in relationships without the loss of warmth and spontaneity. The group worker is not a shadow. He must be a real person.

5. There should be acceptance of people without accepting all their behavior: this involves the capacity for "empathy" as well as the incorporation of societal demands. It is the part of the method that is most closely intertwined with a high flexibility and abundance of warmth in the social group worker as well as identification with values and knowledge.

6. Starting where the group is: the capacity to let groups develop from their own point of departure without immediately imposing exacting demands.

7. The constructive use of limitations: limitations must be used judiciously in relation to individual and group needs and agency function. The forms will vary greatly. The group worker will use mainly himself, program materials, interaction of the group, and awakening of self-criticism in the group members.

8. Individualization: it is one of the specifics of the group work method that the individual is not lost in the whole, but that he is helped to feel as a unique person who can contribute to the whole.

9. Use of the interacting process: the capacity to help balance the group, to allow for conflict when necessary and to prevent it when harmful; the help given to the isolate not only through individual attention by the group worker alone but also by relating him to other members.

10. The understanding and conscious use of nonverbal as well as verbal material: I especially put nonverbal material first, since the group worker deals to a large extent with this, especially in work with children. His capacity to use program materials, which do not demand verbal expression and yet are helpful, should be very wide.[8]

This statement is not completely satisfactory because it includes too great a variety of concepts and it does not strictly present principles. The following is a new attempt:

1. *Recognition and subsequent action in relation to the unique difference of each individual* (Individualization in the group).

Group workers must never see the group as an anonymous mass. Their responsibility is to understand each individual and to help each individual in regard to his or her own specific needs as well as in regard to the needs of the total group and the society in which it exists. This principle

[8]Grisela Konopka, "The Generic and Specific in Group Work Practice in the Psychiatric Setting," *Group Work in the Psychiatric Setting* New York: Whiteside, Inc., 1956), pp. 21–22. See also Marjorie Murphy, "The Social Group Work Method in Social Work Education," *A Project Report of the Curriculum Study*, XI, Werner W. Boehm, Director and Coordinator (New York: Council on Social Work Education, 1959), pp. 125–126.

includes skill in assessing a situation and the complicated skill of focusing on and working with individuals in the group context.

2. *Recognition and subsequent action in relation to the wide variety of groups as groups* (Individualization of groups).

Group workers realize that a group is more than the sum of its individuals. It is an organic whole with specific characteristics of its own, expressed in its form of bond, its particular interaction between members, its subgroupings, its form or lack of leadership, etc. Its characteristics are related to the group's goal and composition. This principle includes the skill in diagnosing a group and in acting according to this diagnosis as well as the understanding of the individual as expressed in principle 1.

3. *Genuine acceptance of individuals with their unique strengths and weaknesses.*

Group workers do not only *understand* the individual. They act toward each individual in a way prescribed by the profession of social work. (This certainly will apply also to other professions). Acceptance includes the profession's value orientation, the respect for each individual. Group workers do not necessarily *approve* of each individual's actions or qualities; in fact they do use some value system to assess the acts as being "strengths" or "weaknesses." The individual is accepted in his or her totality.

4. *Establishment of a purposeful helping relationship between group worker and group members.*

Group work practice is based on the assumption that change in an individual can occur only through interaction with others. To accomplish change in a beneficial direction, people need help, and in certain instances, professional help.

5. *Encouragement and enabling of helpful and cooperative relationships between group members.*

This principle is based on the same assumption as principle 4. It is recognized in group work that relationships between equals—between the members of the group—have as much importance as individual relationship to the group worker. These relationships can move in a negative or positive direction. (The determination of whether the change is "negative" or "positive," "healthy" or "sick," "good" or "bad" includes an assessment of the individuals and the group and the use of the professional value system). It is the role of group workers to aid in the development of relationships between members, which become beneficial to them.

6. *Appropriate modification of the group process.*

The group process is expressed in interrelations between group members, the formation of subgroups, the establishment of bond, the development of leadership, the creation of isolates. Group workers must see these constellations and assess them, and know when to work with them, strengthen them, or help to change them.

7. *Encouragement of each member to participate according to the stage of his or her capacity, enabling each individual to become more capable.*

*Participation* is a key word in the use of the group work method. It means that each member must be helped to independently become part of the group effort. This capacity to participate varies from individual to individual. Group workers must accept the stage of the individual's capacity to participate (this is often expressed as "starting where the member is"), help the member participate on his or her own level without feeling pushed or embarrassed, and guide this person into a healthier or more capable stage.

8. *Enabling members to involve themselves in the process of problem-solving.*

Group workers do not solve problems *for* the group. They must not be overbearing, always knowing what is "best" for individual members or for the group as a whole. They help members to become part of the problem-solving and to find their own solutions in interaction with others and with the group workers.

9. *Enabling group members to experience increasingly satisfactory forms of working through of conflicts.*

This principle relates to forms of conflict-solving in group interaction and in the individual. The group as a whole may be enabled by the group worker to move from "slugging out" a difference of opinion to solving conflicts by talking them out, learning to compromise or to use different democratic methods. The individual, for example, may be helped to stop running away when a conflict situation arises and to face the situation and gather the strength to work it through. Significant for the group work method is the fact that this can be *experienced*—as well as talked through—in the presence of a helping person, the social group worker.

10. *Provision of opportunities for new and differing experiences in relationships and accomplishments.*

Here again the key word is *experience*. It is characteristic of the group work method that it lends itself to living through problem situations with the help of the group worker, instead of reflecting on them. Working through new relationships is part of daily human life. Group workers assist those with this problem when special help is needed, as, for instance, when people move from rural to urban communities; when racial groups meet that have never met before or have met only with distrust, not as equals or as friends or neighbors; when a child moves into adolescence and must find new ways to act towards the opposite sex; when a youth group has only seen authority as an enemy and now is challenged to revise attitudes and feelings by meeting adults who work with it.

*Accomplishment* is assumed to be one of the major ingredients of general mental health. It is often denied to people. It is the group worker's responsibility to allow for this vital experience by providing opportunities for accomplishment to individual members as well as the whole group.

11. *Judicious use of limitations related to the diagnostic assessment of each individual and the total situation.*

The principle of acceptance, which is explained under principle 3, is frequently misunderstood as meaning total permissiveness. This is not considered helpful, since it would include permission to harm each other or to harm oneself, physically or emotionally. Limitations are therefore an important part of the intelligent and purposeful work with individuals and the group. This principle includes diagnostic thinking and skillful use of all the media available to the group worker, such as relationships, use of the group process, and program.

12. *Purposeful and differential use of program or action according to diagnostic evaluation of individual members, group purpose, and appropriate social goals.*

By *program* is meant any activity that the group does in the presence of the group worker during the course of group meetings. These activities must not be planned according to the particular needs or interests of group workers themselves, but only with reference to the group members.

13. *Ongoing evaluation of individual and group progress.*

Periodic evaluations or assessments are part of the group work method; they help to keep the group worker's efforts purposeful and flexible. They are shared with the members of the group and help them to move toward individual or group goals.

14. *Warm, human, and disciplined use of self on the part of the group worker.*

This principle is part of all previously named principles, but especially of principle 4. It is presented separately to underline the importance of the quality of the group worker's approach to individuals and groups. This principle demands of group workers a discipline that prevents them from using the group for their own personal satisfaction (this does not exclude their satisfaction in doing a good, professional job), yet it also requires them to be real people, not just cold, impersonal, or shadowy observers.

In terms of characteristics of group workers, these principles presuppose practitioners with (1) a high capacity for empathy; (2) flexibility; (3) keen perception and intelligence to analyze and assess not only individuals, but also highly complex situations; (4) capacity to relate warmly to people; and (5) creativity or imagination.

Since the group worker's self is the major tool of the group work method, and since the method does not include "neutrality" or a "shadow" relationship, but a disciplined, warm use of this self, the principles come to life only if used by a person who has and who increases the above potential qualities in him- or herself.

In addition to this it must be stressed that these principles implicitly include the values of respect for every human being and of responsibility for each other. Without them, as mentioned earlier, the method becomes an empty technique.

The last part of this chapter will present and analyze record material. Each record will illustrate a wide variety of principles followed in the reality of group work practice. The incidents are taken from practices in different settings.

The reader is reminded again of the fact that social group work is an art based on science and, therefore, the personality of the group worker enters into its practice. These recordings were made by the social group worker immediately following the meetings.

The first two examples present first meetings of a group worker with members of the group, the *beginning* of the group work process.

### Example 1

This example demonstrates the *beginning* of the group work process in a *natural* group. This is a group of five 13-14 year-old boys who hang around the neighborhood. They had come by themselves to the community center and had asked for a place to meet. They were told that they were very welcome and that it was the custom to assign a social group worker to each group. They had accepted this. The only thing known about them was that all five were low school achievers and that they were known to annoy merchants in the neighborhood by hanging around in their establishments, but they were not openly delinquent.

The group met at 7 P.M. at the Center. Present were five boys: John, Herb, Mort, Sam, and Chuck. The group had no definite program in mind for this evening. Instead, they wanted to just "go riding" in the station wagon. The group worker agreed to this.

*Adolescent need for adventure. Car as a status symbol, but out of reach at that age. Group worker accepts these needs as legitimate; car also offers an intimate "meeting room." Allows members to start where they are.*

During the evening, the boys displayed quite uncontrolled and impulsive behavior. They opened the car door, threatened to jump out, and, at one point, fooled around with the football and dropped it out of the window, losing it. At the first disagreement, they began their impulsive and testing-out behavior.

The group worker stopped the car and they all got out, picked up dried cattails, and began throwing them, primarily at the group worker and at the station wagon.

*Judicious use of limitations. (Limitation is achieved here simply by changing the situation).*

The group worker joined in with them and allowed them first to take out many of their feelings on him, while returning some of their "fire," making it a real give-and-take situation, keeping it on a friendly basis.

*Group worker accepts members' needs to "test" a new adult—confronts them with a non-punishing, but not "passive" adult.*

Later he was able to help them choose sides and make a kind of game out of it. This worked fairly well and the group was able to get back in the wagon after spending much of their energy and to drive back to the city.

*Creates outlet for hostility through games (creative use of program).*

Their acting-out behavior again started as they arrived in the neighborhood. They rejected at first all attempts of the group worker to set limits.

*Interesting example of "role" behavior of a total group. Outside of the neighborhood, the boys allow themselves to "mellow" and shed the "tough" shell. In their neighborhood they must again live up to the role they think will give them status.*

They had planned to ride to a drive-in. After talking it over with the group worker, they all agreed that they would behave themselves at the drive-in; otherwise, as one of them put it, "They won't give us anything to eat."

This they were able to do and they returned to the neighborhood about 9:30 with the group worker dropping the boys off at their homes.

*Group worker chooses an opportunity to know the boys individually.*

As he did so, John said to him that he hoped the group worker wasn't mad at the group. He said, "We were just trying to find out what kind of a guy you are." They discussed this for a while and the group members were able to see that much of their behavior was directed at "testing" the group worker.

---

*A sign of beginning relationship, and some help for insight.*

---

They assured him that they would not create this many problems at future meetings. They planned to meet every week.


## COMMENT

We see here a beginning relationship between group worker and members, but still a very tenuous one. The group was an entity before the group worker entered. He was the "stranger in the group." The testing process is a natural one in the beginning, but was obviously intensified here by the fact that the group had not asked for a group worker and had only accepted agency policy.

The group worker began to get some knowledge about the group as a whole, but very little as yet about each individual in it. However, he acted according to the principles of acceptance, judicious use of limitations, individualization of the group, and use of program based on an assessment of the needs of the members as he saw them.

### Example 2

This example demonstrates the *beginning* of group process in a *formed* group. This is a group of 15-16 year-old girls in an institution for delinquents. The purpose of the group is to help the girls to discuss freely their problems, to work through some of their feelings about their placement and about themselves. The group worker is originally from India, and has no difficulty with the English language. This account is taken from the recording made by the group worker after her first meeting with the girls.

Norma and Jean offered the group worker a chair, and sat down close to her. Norma is a pretty girl, with a cheerful expression and a friendly smile. She seemed easily excited and very demonstrative of her feelings. She tried to learn the spelling of the group worker's name. The group worker said that she had made name tags for herself and the girls, which would help "us to learn each other's names quicker."

---

*Technique of individualizing and helping girls to learn a "social custom."*

---

When the group worker took out the tags and the pins from her bag, Norma said that she had come fully prepared to meet them. She seemed very happy with her name tag and pinned it on quickly.

---

*Being prepared indicates that the group worker cares.*

---

She complimented the group worker on her attire, heaved a sigh, and said she wished she had a similar dress.

---

*Beginning identification, because of a shared value.*

---

Jean offered to show the group worker their dorm. The group worker told her that she had taken a tour on her first visit, but that she thought it would be more interesting today, since she now knew some of the girls.

---

*Group worker understands the girls' need to show "their" place, to give. She accepts this with warmth.*

---

Both Norma and Jean led the way through the dormitory and gave explanations of the living arrangements. The group worker complimented them on their dorm. Norma and Jean pointed out their own beds and the little stuffed animals that decorated the room.

When they returned to the meeting room they were joined by Ida and Sue. Ida gave the group worker a weak smile in reply to her greeting and sat down next to Norma. Sue stood smiling, slightly on the edge of the group; she seemed to be appraising the group worker. She finally sat down next to her.

---

*Group worker observes carefully, noting appearance and speech, in order to get to know each girl.*

---

Sue was an attractive girl, seemingly sophisticated, but when she began to speak, she kept fumbling for words and had difficulty in expressing herself. The worker introduced herself, asked their names, and gave each of them a name tag. Sue liked this idea, and tried to pronounce the group worker's name. Ida remained quiet. The group was joined by Peg and Ann, who came in running and said hello to the group worker and the others. They went through the same introduction procedure.

Liz walked in very slowly and took a seat at the far end of the table, facing the group worker. After the introduction, she reminded the group worker that she had been the girl who was lying in bed sick when the worker was shown around the dormitory some days earlier.

Ella, Jane, and Mae came in next. They seemed more hesitant than the others.

The girls asked the group worker various questions about herself, ranging from her age and family to the significance of the red mark on her forehead and the political situation in India. Peg and Sue were especially interested in comparing rates and types of juvenile delinquency in India and the United States, the system of dating, the age of marriage and the restrictions imposed on young people by their families and schools.

*The group worker's foreign origin allows adolescent girls some vicarious enjoyment of adventure. It is significant that they move immediately into an area that relates to their own problems.*

The worker realized that this was a beginning for discussion of their own feelings about all these things, but she did not pursue this lead at this time because the girls showed great impatience in raising their questions.

*In a later meeting the group worker should move here into the helping role with the girls. The first meeting allows the girls to completely determine the content. The group worker listens, observes, and notices.*

Norma tended to be more patient than the others; Ida was rather quiet; Mae said nothing, even when encouraged by the group worker. Yet all of them seemed to be listening. Ann wanted to know where India was, and tried to find a map. When she could not find it, the girls laughed at her. The group worker assured Ann that she would bring one and show it to her at the next meeting.

*Group worker is sensitive to possible group rejection. She does not reprimand the group, but counteracts the apparent group rejection by showing her interest in Ann.*

Peg asked the group worker what she thought about their laundry; Ann said it was hard work. Peg insisted on hearing the group worker's opinion.
   The group worker said that it seemed to give them a good experience in working on a job, since this is probably the first such experience for many of them.

*The group worker consciously offers the girls a new value: work experience. She does this cautiously, realizing the difference between this and the girls' values. She hopes to open new thinking—not to close the door by preaching.*

She added that she was glad that Peg had brought up this topic, because it was time for them to discuss what they were here for.

*Beginning of working with the girls and establishing the purpose of their meetings.*

She asked whether any of them knew the purpose of these meetings; three hands went up and the girls started speaking at the same time. The group worker waited a moment. Then Sue said that all the girls had gotten into trouble and were confused, and now they had an opportunity to discuss their problems with a group worker to get help with them.
   Peg said that she was told that discussion in a group helps everyone and that they should feel free to air their grievances about their stay in the home and anything else that bothered them.
   Liz said that most of them were new and did not understand everything

about the home, and so this group meeting would help them. The others nodded.

---

*The girls themselves express the focus of the group meetings.*

---

The group worker said that all these explanations were correct and that she hoped the girls would bring up any problem that affected them and that they thought could be discussed in the group. She said the girls would be helping each other and themselves.

She also discussed the confidentiality of these discussions. Peg stressed that this was important, but stated that she doubted if anyone would really do this and not discuss things with their friends. It seemed she had a particular person in mind, but everybody nodded.

---

*Group worker brings in need for confidentiality. It requires agreement among the group members to adhere voluntarily to this.*

---

Ann asked whether someone was perhaps listening through the keyhole. Everybody laughed, but Ann said it was important, and asked the group worker if she could check.

The group worker said she certainly could. Seriously, Ann opened the door, looked left and right, and then said it was all right. This time she laughed with the others.

---

*Taking concerns of a member seriously is the base for a helping relationship.*

---

Peg asked rather angrily why people referred to this home as an *institution*, since it was supposed to be a "home" for girls. The group worker wondered what she understood by "institution." Peg said that it is a place where one is taken against one's wishes because of some wrong-doing.

---

*Members now feel free to open up and discuss specific problems.*

---

The group worker asked if anyone else thought so too, or wanted to add something.

---

*Help with interaction helps members to use group process, not only member-group worker relationship.*

---

Since no one volunteered, the group worker said institution only means a building that has been set up to carry on some specific purpose, such as a school that educates or this particular home, which aims at helping girls who get into difficulties with the law.

---

*Worker gives information; also, indirectly, reassurance.*

---

Norma said that apparently, then, there is nothing wrong with this word. Peg said it may not seem so now, but it used to make her very mad when people said that she was in an institution. The group worker said that this was understandable since, like Peg, many other people associate the term "institution" with a place of punishment. She stressed again that the meaning was much broader and included places such as schools and hospitals.

---

*Acceptance of individual member's feelings.*

---

There was some expression of anger against personnel in the institution, and then the girls returned to the discussion of what this institution meant to them.

---

*More "opening up" by the girls. Expression of resentment, anxiety.*

---

Peg said that they get no choice of institutions; there is only one other place that is worse. Liz agreed with her.

Peg said that she would do much better in her own home. Sue commented that they are here because they did not do well in their own homes. Peg persisted. Ella asked Peg why she had been removed from her own home. Peg said that she had run away and stayed away for almost four months and was brought back. "For four months! What did you do while you were away!" Ella exclaimed. Peg smiled, but was unwilling to answer.

---

*Interaction between the girls shows individual differences; also, Peg is slowly compelled to move toward a fresh look at her own part in being in the institution.*

---

The group worker said that no one was compelled to answer if she did not want to. Peg then admitted that things were not so bad at the home, but she wished they were allowed to go out.

---

*Group worker establishes the right of members to withhold information. This reassurance relaxes Peg and allows her to drop some of her defenses.*

---

The group worker admitted it was hard when one could not go out at will, but pointed out that the home had certain rules, which could not be changed.

---

*Group worker conveys understanding, but stresses conformity too much.*

---

Since they cannot change the rules, it might be helpful to discuss how one can best live with them.

---

*Group worker tries to stimulate new ways of dealing with problems but not sufficiently. The opportunity to learn how to achieve changes is missed.*

---

Norma said that there were girls who bossed the newcomers and assigned them all the unpleasant jobs. The group worker encouraged her to speak about this to her housemother, who would help to assign jobs more equitably.

---

*Group worker tries to help Norma by making specific suggestions. She may have reacted too quickly here and cut off an opportunity for Norma, and others, to discuss more fully the problem of their status as newcomers in a group of peers.*

---

Ann suggested that a record be written of everything they would be discussing at these meetings; she volunteered to do this. Norma added that the recorder should also write how much help they got from this.

The group worker said it was all right to record this, but asked them where they would be keeping these records, since they were confidential. They could not think of a suitable place. The group worker suggested that they consult with their housemother, who could assign them a place.

---

*Group worker accepts and limits in the girls' interest—an important way to establish trust.*

---

Norma said that they are a group and should have a name. She wanted it to be an Indian name because the group worker was Indian; she asked the group worker to give it one.

---

*Norma increasingly shows high identification with the group worker.*

---

The group worker suggested that they think of a name in English and then she would give them the Indian translation. This was not yet picked up by the others, although they listened attentively.

---

*The group worker refuses to act for the group and so involves the girls without withholding herself.*

---

The group worker reminded them that it was time to end the meeting. The girls suggested that they see the group worker individually in-between the meetings; she agreed to this and wrote down their names.

---

*Group worker limits (use of given time for group meeting), but accepts the girls' needs for additional contacts; these are also necessary for the intensive treatment purpose of this group.*

---

They commented on the fact that she spelled their names correctly.

They tried to prolong the meeting by asking for pictures of Indian costumes, and so forth. The group worker finally stood up and said it was time to leave. The girls returned their name tags, saying they would like the group worker to take care of them.

Norma preferred to keep hers, saying she would wear it at the home.

---

*Norma shows intense identification.*

---

## COMMENT

This first meeting shows some of the same characteristics as all first ones; namely, the getting acquainted with one another and some "trying out" of the worker, but in a form different from that used by the aggressive boys in Example 1. Here the girls "try out" the group worker to see how far she will go in joining them in criticism of the institution and thus become "one of them." The group worker constantly counteracts this by her understanding and acceptance; at the same time she maintains her professional helping role.

The relationship develops comparatively fast because of the girls' great hunger for attention, typical of all institutionalized people; the attraction of the group worker's foreign background; the group worker's personal warmth; and her real group work skill. The process is also accelerated because the girls were well prepared for this experience by their housemothers.

In this first meeting, the group worker has begun to individualize the girls, establish the purpose of the group in the framework of the agency, define her own helping role, and create an atmosphere of free interaction.

Several important topics were introduced, but the group worker skillfully avoided pursuing any of them at this first meeting so as to provide all group members with an opportunity for each to express her own interests.

Several of the principles listed on pages 175–185 can be identified in this illustration. Because of the fact that this was a first meeting, the group worker was called upon to interact continually with first one individual and then another, although she also interacted with the group as a whole. When relationships are more established, she can—and must—use the interacting process more intensely. *The encouragement and enabling of helpful and cooperative relationships between group members* is an important task before her. She must find every opportunity to let the *members* be the helping persons and she must discipline herself not to be always directly in this role.

### Example 3

This example demonstrates the clarification of *group purpose* in a group that has met for a longer time. It is an excerpt from a discussion group of teenagers who are in foster families and who have difficulties getting along with other teen-agers. The group work service is provided by a family service agency.

The worker turned to Mary Lou and said, "Since you were in the group last year, I wonder if you would be willing to tell us about it—what you thought the meetings were for and some of the things you did." She laughed and said,

"You want *me* to say?," somewhat pleased to be called upon and yet a bit flustered. She explained how, at the first meeting, no one knew the others, but soon discovered all the members were being seen by the same caseworker and, although each person was different and each person's problems seemed to be different, you learned to make friends and felt free to talk about your problems. You did not always like all the members, but you learned to tolerate each other. She went on at length to explain some of the activities and made particular mention of the times she contributed the refreshments. She said they realized that what the group was, was what they made of it and June, their group worker from last year, would say things that would help them pinpoint the discussion. The group was as good as they made it by their contributions. Sometimes they got bored with just talking, so they went bowling or out for pizza. It took awhile to really understand what the group was for, but they enjoyed it and she felt that she got a lot out of it.

---

*To work meaningfully with group members, the purpose of meetings must be clear to them. Since this group has met for some time, the group worker calls on a* **member** *to explain the purpose so as to (1) establish the importance of member participation and hasten the interaction process, and (2) give special status and encouragement to a particular member.*

---

## COMMENT

The group member has explained well the specific helpfulness of the group and the role of the members and the group worker. Among teenagers, this explanation by a peer carries greater weight than would one given by an adult.

### Example 4

This example demonstrates primarily the *helpful, conscious, differential use of program according to diagnostic evaluation of individual members, group purpose, and appropriate values.*

This is a group composed of four 9-11 year-old boys on a children's psychiatric ward. The group meets for one hour twice a week in a large playroom. The group had been meeting weekly for approximately three months; during all this time, the boys continued to demonstrate their need to release aggression. They manifested this by grabbing anything in the room and throwing it at one another. Bob, one of the members, and the youngest, was especially aggressive, but also unable to participate with others. Underlying his aggression was actual fear of the other boys. He also had attached himself closely to the group worker and had difficulties in sharing him with the others.

To help Bob become more involved in group activity and also to meet the needs of all the boys for aggressive play, the group worker chose to bring to the group an attractive plastic ball, which would not hurt anyone who might get hit with it.

Before introducing the ball to the entire group, he brought it to Bob's room, where the group worker and Bob played a game of catch. This was done to give Bob the satisfaction of having seen the ball first and to not have to share immediately the beloved worker with others.

A day later, the group worker brought the ball again, but this time he played with Bob while he was in the ward with several other children. Bob was able to accept this experience in sharing the worker because the others were less involved with the group worker than he was.

Three days later, the group worker brought the ball to the group meeting and Bob asked to play with it. The group worker said that he certainly could, and that everyone would be playing with it today.

---

*Next step in helping Bob to learn how to share a toy and a friend.*

---

The other boys responded eagerly when they saw the ball. Jack suggested a game of catch. All the boys formed a circle except Bob, who withdrew into the corner and stood behind a table, working with some clay.

The group worker said that the boys would like to have Bob in their group too, and that he knew he was eager to play with the ball.

---

*Group worker understands Bob's ambivalence and lets him know that he is wanted as part of the group.*

---

In the game, George started to throw the ball in different ways; playing ball is one of George's best skills, and he is slightly more mature in his interests and skills than the other boys.

The group worker then suggested that maybe each one could think of different ways of throwing the ball; he developed a type of "follow the leader" out of this. When one person threw the ball a certain way, each of the others had to follow suit until it reached the person who had begun the game. Then the next person had a turn at inventing a new way of throwing it.

---

*Skillful inclusion of a leader so that everybody can participate.*

---

Throughout the whole meeting, the ball was the center of attention and the boys used it in many ways. George finally organized a ball game and everyone took turns batting the ball with a stick.

Bob maintained his position in the corner and continued to work on the clay, but every time the ball rolled over toward him, he grabbed it and held onto it. The group worker again recognized that he wanted to play with the ball and again invited him to join the others. He also reminded him that the other boys needed the ball for their game.

---

*The group worker does not demand that the boy participate, recognizing his deep fear and jealousy, but again encourages him and gives him attention.*

---

Several times Bob gave up the ball readily, but once he stubbornly held onto it and said he would not give it back, although he made no attempt to play with it.

The other boys came over to him and tried to get the ball away from him.

The group worker intervened to prevent its being taken away from him by force.

*The group worker protects Bob because he knows of his fear of others. He also recognizes that Bob several times has successfully overcome his impulses (he returned the ball)— quite an accomplishment. He does not want to add more frustration.*

While this was happening, George "accidentally" smashed what Bob had been making out of clay. Bob immediately flew into a rage and ran out of the room crying and screaming. He huddled with the ball in a corner of the hall outside the room. All the boys ran after him and continued to try to grab the ball away.

The worker stood between him and the others and said that Bob was very upset because he had spent a lot of time working on the clay, and that he was holding the ball because he knew the boys wanted it.

*Group worker limits and explains Bob's behavior to him and to the others, thus letting him feel he is understood and helping the others to* experience *compassion.*

Suddenly Jack ran back into the room and returned in a few minutes with an exact replica of what Bob had made out of clay. The group worker said this was very nice of Jack to do this for Bob; Bob remained unappeased. At this point, George and Jack had to leave for another activity. Sam and Bob lingered on.

*Emotionally disturbed children need to feel secure and wanted to be able to give. Jack's gesture shows that he feels this way. Since Bob cannot yet accept this, the group worker moves in for him. He knows that Jack needs this recognition.*

The worker suggested that the two of them might want to play catch for a few minutes while he was cleaning up the room. Bob did this eagerly, and both boys enjoyed the game for a short time.

*Without the preceding support, Bob would not have been able to move out to a peer.*

## COMMENT

This example shows how much must be understood about individual dynamics if the group worker is to move purposefully. Bob needs help with his feelings of sibling rivalry. It is known that people move from one developmental stage to a next one only when they gain satisfaction and see it either as desirable or as not too threatening. An infant is better willing to accept the cup instead of a mother's breast if he or she had full satisfaction in the early stage and the weaning is not done abruptly. The group worker uses this knowledge by introducing the sharing of the ball (and the beloved adult) gradually.

Movement toward a more healthy attitude is achieved (Bob finally *can* play with another boy) by careful planning of program media, by insight, and by minimum use of verbalization. This is more appropriate in this case because of the age and sickness of this child.

### Example 5

This example demonstrates mainly *the provision of opportunities for experiencing new forms of relationships, self, and ways of problem-solving.*

This group consists of seven adolescent boys who were referred to a neighborhood house because of problems in school: underachievement, emotional immaturity, shyness, withdrawal, feelings of inferiority, and insecurity. This is about the ninth meeting of the group. The excerpt describes a situation that occurred when the group worker was driving the boys in the station wagon. Unstructured discussion was taking place at this time. The boys exchanged stories and told jokes.

The group worker recorded:

Jack then said, "Did you hear about the lion who swallowed a 'niggah'?" The boy said, "No." "Yeh," Jack replied. "He swallowed a chocolate man. The boys laughed. I did not laugh and waited for the laughter to subside. The boys became aware of my seriousness and looked questioningly at me.

---

*By not doing something (by not joining in their laughter), the group worker draws attention of the boys to himself.*

---

I asked Jack what might not be "good" about that story. He looked puzzled. I asked the boys what the word "niggah" meant. They said, after a moment's hesitation, "Negro." I asked them if they felt that there was any difference in the meaning of the two words. They said nothing. I said that the word "niggah" is a derogatory term and hurts people. I illustrated this by mentioning other undesirable terms that could be applied to other groups such as our parents, friends, religious groups, and ethnic groups.

---

*Group worker works toward a change in values and relationships with another race by drawing attention to the use of derogatory terms and helping the boys to think instead of preaching to them.*

---

We discussed this during the remainder of the trip.

Somewhat later in the afternoon, we happened to see Mrs. Jones with her daughter; they are Black. I stopped to talk to them and introduced the group members to them. After introductions, Mrs. Jones and I talked a bit about our work at the Urban League; the boys raised questions about it. They seemed to be genuinely interested. Obviously many of the boys had never before met a black person.

---

*Meeting a person of another race* **alone** *does not change attitudes. "Value changing"*

*occurs through experiencing emotions. Here the helping agent was encounter with
members of a different race and the boys' identification with the group worker.*

## COMMENT

The new experience was not planned by the social group worker. He used
the opportunity when it arose, being aware of the fact that the insulting
behavior of the boys was apparently more related to ignorance and a
general racist climate than to individually acquired prejudice. He did not
preach to them, but helped them become aware of the feelings of others by
using comparisons that were familiar to them and that they could understand better. He also understood the phenomenon of identification and
used the good relationship he had with the boys by letting them feel that he
himself would not act or speak the same way that they did. At the same time
that he disapproved of their behavior he tried to understand them and not
to "shame" them. He understood that, in this case, the adolescent would
only rebel and would not be free to accept new ways of interacting with
others.

To demonstrate the helping process of social group work in time
sequence, the records of seven meetings of one formed group are presented in the following pages. (Comments regarding group work practice
are placed between lines).

It is a formed group in a treatment institution for emotionally disturbed children and adolescents. Some children in this institution go to a
public school; others do not, because they are incapable of accepting the
pressure of a public school.

This group consists of six children who can tolerate only limited hours
of tutoring and therefore are not in school. Criteria for their selection for
group work treatment were:

1.  Each one had been in the institution for some time, but had been incapable of
    accepting responsibility for his or her behavior; they blamed "the outside,"
    "the other one," as disturbed or disturbing.
2.  Each had difficulties in getting along with children and adults alike, although
    behavior patterns varied greatly.
3.  Three of the six children selected were incapable of involving themselves in
    individual treatment.

The purposes of the group were:

1.  to help them to speak more freely about their resentments, hopes, and in-
    terests;
2.  to give them the special attention of an understanding adult;

3.  to allow them support by the group or withdrawal if content of discussion became too threatening (this was expected to help the three most withdrawn members to feel more comfortable and to free them);
4.  to experience some new forms of behavior;
5.  to gain some insight into themselves; and
6.  to help them to relate more closely to each other in an environment less demanding than that of the daily living group.

Those selected were Elaine, 14 years; Susie, 16 years; Anne, 12 years; Pat, 13 years; Jim, 13 years; and Ed, 13 years.

Elaine had been in eighteen different foster homes before she was referred to the treatment center. She had been abandoned as a small child. Several times she had returned to her own home, where she was used by the parents to steal for them. Elaine was unable to make relationships in foster families; she was aggressive and cruel to siblings. She made sexual advances to the males in the foster families. She was finally placed in a mental hospital and referred from there to the treatment center. She was an intelligent, physically attractive girl who dominated the living group.

Susie's parents were divorced and there had been serious conflict in the family for several years. She had a younger sister in a foster home; she herself could not accept a foster home and showed withdrawn or hostile, almost paranoid, behavior. She had some seizures that resembled epileptic seizures. At age 15, she was hospitalized in an acute state of psychosis and received some electric shock treatment. (This author disapproves of shock treatment and is not alone in this. Unfortunately, it is still in use in psychiatric hospitals.) She was a girl of average intelligence, but incapable of involving herself in individual therapy.

Anne's parents were divorced. One younger brother lived with the mother. Anne originally displayed no behavioral problems. She had been a good student. She suddenly refused to attend school, however, and became a complete recluse. So far it had been impossible to determine any specific cause for these changes. She was referred to a mental hospital in a state of complete muteness. From there she came to the children's treatment center.

Pat's parents were divorced. She was an only child. She had been referred to the hospital a year before referral to the children's treatment center in a state of acute psychosis and with severe tics. The school reported that her behavior had been difficult for a long time previous to this, that she was stealing, lying, and constantly touching other people.

At the time of the group meetings, Pat was well in touch with reality, but she still needed to touch people. She seemed to be of average intelligence.

Jim was referred mainly because of severe temper tantrums and highly aggressive behavior. The family was generally intact. His mother seemed to have special difficulties in accepting a very active boy. The father was engrossed in his work. Jim was a handsome boy and seemed to be of average intelligence.

Ed's parents were unknown. He had been abandoned as a small infant and grew up in several foster homes and children's institutions. He acted out aggressively and was referred to a mental hospital. His comparatively low intelligence and cold indifference made treatment difficult.

### Record 1

The Assistant Director, Miss Andrews, had called the six children together for a ten-minute meeting and explained that they would meet regularly with Miss Smith, the social group worker. The children had come in, full of hostility and resistance. Every single one made remarks that showed they were coming against their will. Susie wondered whether she had "done something." Pat, who had greeted Miss Smith with great affection earlier in the morning, was apparently puzzled by the hostility of the others and did not know what to do. This meant that she was relatively quiet. She got up early because she could not sit still, not even for ten minutes. Anne was the one who tried to calm the others. Jim, Ed, and Elaine were most outspoken in their resistance, saying that they were mad at the counselors and therefore would not come to anything that was suggested by them: "If they don't cooperate with us, why should we cooperate with them?" Miss Smith explained that she had suggested these meetings so that they would have more attention and could talk about some of the reasons why they wanted to get out of the institution; she also suggested that they could do some other things if they did not want to talk.

---

*Group worker accepts hostility and explains purpose of the meetings.*

---

Elaine insisted that they talk too much with too many people already; Jim said that he sees his own doctor, although he could not remember his name; Ed complained that nobody listens anyhow. Miss Smith mentioned that she thought they were already starting quite a good meeting and it would be interesting to hear why they were so angry.

---

*Group worker accepts the children's feelings and lets them know that they have in their own way started to fulfill the purpose of the meetings.*

---

Elaine complained about not getting any decent clothes, and Ed began to talk about how wonderful the jail was and how one could tear up bedclothes, which one could not do here.

The explosion was violent, yet with the exception of Pat, they all stayed and did not walk out until Miss Andrews and Miss Smith closed the meeting.

After the meeting, Pat came up to Miss Smith and said she would like to come, but she would be just "crazy" if she did not have cigarettes during the meeting.

## COMMENT

Children in institutions usually have a long series of experiences of being pushed from one person to another. All six of these children have had demands made on them to relate to adults who then rejected them. They feel resentful and protective of themselves. In a highly authoritarian environment these children would come to such meetings without objection but with their guard up. The atmosphere of this institution is such that it allows them to express their resentment and distrust. The group worker knows that it will take time to overcome this.

### Record 2

The children were present on time. They were much friendlier than at the first meeting, and grouped around Miss Smith readily.

Miss Smith had prepared cookies and had brought some pictures for them to choose from and to use in any way they wanted to.

---

*The offering of food is not a "bribe." It gives oral satisfaction to these very immature children; it helps to create an informal atmosphere; it is a symbol of the group worker's giving interest.*

*The pictures were chosen to allow for individual withdrawal if a group member had a need for it.*

---

Ed and Jim were the first ones to arrive; they were very polite in taking only one cookie, commenting on them and saying that Miss Smith was a good baker. This was quite different from their earlier hostile attitude towards Miss Smith.

Elaine, Susie, and Anne came in next. At this point they stuffed themselves with cookies because competition started. Miss Smith had to reserve some for Pat, who had not yet come in; otherwise they would not have left any for her. This little incident is quite symptomatic of Pat's position in the group.

Miss Smith asked the youngsters whether they could give her three minutes in which she would again mention why the group was meeting, after which it would be *their* meeting. She said that she understood their anger since they meet too many people and probably could not feel free to talk openly with everybody. She suggested in this meeting that they could either do things or talk with one another about their problems; she told them she would not **press** them to reveal themselves.

---

*Explanation of group purpose while accepting the children's feelings. Also some interpretation as to the reasons for their hostility.*

---

Elaine burst out with the fact that it was true that one needed to talk to people, but then, also, something must happen.

---

*Beginning of opening up.*

---

She complained loudly and violently about having been on restriction since June just because she ran away at that time. She described, angrily, being in isolation at a mental hospital and not being permitted to go shopping now. She also complained that other youngsters who also had run away had not been put on restriction at all.

Jim contradicted this in a very calm manner, saying that these kids had been on restriction too, but for a much shorter time. Ed constantly was supporting Elaine.

---

*Group worker observes group interaction and member roles. Jim brings in reality and is able to contradict Elaine.*

---

It was evident that Elaine and Ed played into each other's emotions and increased each other's hostility. Elaine complained about Dr. Abel, the psychiatrist, and his discussing with another girl whether she [Elaine] had been involved in a sex episode involving several boys and girls. She violently denied that she had any part in it. Jim smiled and said that he could vouch for the fact that Elaine had no part in it, "but don't ask me how I know." Susie could vouch for the fact that Elaine was not involved but she, too, would not want to be asked how she knew; she asked that the others stop talking about it.

---

*Children are still guarded, but begin talking about their concerns.*

---

Ed's hostility during the meeting was directed mostly against Miss Andrews; Joanne, a counselor; and his father. He insisted that Joanne slapped people around, but did not dare do it to him anymore, as he had "once kicked her back. Now when she cannot vent her anger on me, she goes to the girls and slaps them around." (He obviously had learned about projection.)

---

*Group worker observes and listens.*

---

He talked about going to conventions with his father. When Miss Smith asked what kind of conventions they were, he said they were related to appliances; that his father had four huge business concerns; that he sits like "stupid old Carter (the director) with his feet up on the desk and does nothing."

---

*Ed's view of all persons in authority is much related to his feelings about his father. Group worker purposely encourages his talking about his father to allow him to vent feelings.*

---

Later in the meeting, just before Ed left, he refused to help Miss Smith pick up something, saying he hated women and would have nothing to do with them. He showed great resentment toward anybody representing either parent figure.

Anne was very quiet during the meeting. She was most interested in the pictures Miss Smith had brought. She checked the printing on the back of the pictures and asked Miss Smith to translate, since the writing was in French.

---

*It is significant that this "mute" girl makes her first contact through focus on a language.*

---

Susie chose a striking picture of Christ from those Miss Smith had brought and then asked her about a poem on the card that was also written in a foreign language; Miss Smith translated it. It was interesting that during the short time that Miss Smith translated poetry the children were quiet and listened. They made no remark related to the content, but they seemed to react to the sound of words. Elaine said that Susie also wrote poetry. The poetry she quoted consisted of hostile ditties, especially about Miss Andrews.

Miss Smith wondered whether they would like to start a newspaper, since some of them seemed to like to write and talk about things.

---

*Group worker channels aggression into some positive activity.*

---

She suggested that Elaine should write about how it felt to be on restriction, that that would be a good way of letting people know about it. Elaine did not react positively but, interestingly enough, Ed picked this up. He made a formal motion that Elaine should write this in her spare time since she was so much in her room. Elaine said she had a typewriter and if anybody wanted to write something, she would type it. Miss Smith did not get the impression that these were actual plans, but felt that they were quick reactions to a suggestion that seemed to stimulate them in some way.

All this discussion was interrupted constantly by a great deal of jumping up, asking for cigarettes, and unrelated talking.

---

*The stage of restlessness in which these children are, is accepted. The group worker's calm helps to allow for beginning interaction—as seen above.*

---

Miss Smith had asked the counselor whether it was permissible to smoke in that room; apparently this was all right.

---

*It is important that the person who comes into an institution from the "outside" accept the rules so that consistency is safeguarded. If the rules are considered wrong, then this must be taken up with the administration and the children.*

---

Miss Smith thought it interesting that Jim reacted very reasonably and positively when she said that as long as they wanted to smoke he should also bring ash trays and see that they were used. He accepted this without any resistance.

At one point during the meeting one of the youngsters suddenly discovered that the group was meeting in Mr. Carter's office. Susie, who up till then had been stonily silent, smiled ironically and said, "Oh! Mr. Carter!" Then she took a handful of pieces of paper that she had rolled up nervously and threw them on the floor. This hostile gesture was a signal for more hostile behavior on the part of the other children.

---

*Group worker observes "language of behavior." Susie's first open reaction is a hostile one, directed toward absent authority. It is nonverbal.*

---

Miss Smith could feel contagion start. The next minute Elaine also threw paper on the floor, Pat poised her cigarette to dump the ashes, and the two boys lifted their bottles to pour out the pop. Before this, Miss Smith had sat quietly next to Susie; now she got up in an unhurried way, walked over to Pat, with whom she had the best relationship, and turned to her but talked to everyone, saying, "We meet in a pretty nice office. Would it not be better not to get it too messed up?" Would this approach work? Miss Smith was gratified to see that neither the ashes nor the pop went to the floor. Pat used the ash tray; the boys drank the pop, as if this had been their intention all the time. No further comment was made.

*Group worker anticipates destructive action before it is accomplished. She shifts her own position (gets up), but not abruptly. Aggressive action by the group worker would arouse more hostility. Nonintervention would be seen as permission to be destructive. The group worker keeps calm and friendly—a contrast to the hostile atmosphere. She relates to the total group through one of the members who can accept her. She uses reasoning and enlists the help of the group, without "preaching." She allows for "face-saving." Hostile people feel often relieved when prevented from "acting-out," but do not want to admit this.*

They began to talk about the fact that there was a staff meeting going on and asked who was being staffed. Miss Smith replied, "Andy." (A boy in the treatment home.) Ed said that Andy had told them that he would go to public school and, if this were so, he—Ed—would never go to school. Here Elaine was helpful by saying that he wouldn't be in the same school as Andy, so he would not have to worry. The youngsters expressed hostility toward Andy, but Elaine defended him.

*Again the "group process" is allowed to work. The children help each other.*

There was much shouting against counselors—wanting to slap their faces and to kill them. At one point Miss Smith said, "Well, smash their faces, all right, but what good will it do?" This was surely the wrong thing to say. Ed quickly said that Miss Smith had given them permission to attack the counselors.

*Hostile children pick up quickly any semblance of adult sanction to be destructive. There is a great difference between the principle of acceptance and permissiveness. The latter may be harmful if the individual feels delivered to his impulses or feels encouraged to harm others.*

Jim got up and said he wanted to leave; he was given permission to do so. There was some talk about what they wanted to do the next time they met. Elaine clamored for movies; Miss Smith suggested that this was something they could do outside of the group meetings, but if they wanted to take a walk in good weather, she would find out if this was possible.

*Group worker limits the meetings to their purpose, allowing for different forms of fulfilling it. Movies present purely spectator activities and are not conducive to interaction; walks may stimulate discussions.*

After a little while, Elaine, Susie, and Ed left. (At one point, Ed asked Miss Smith if she had really been in an internment camp. This was not followed up, but apparently had much meaning to him.)

Miss Smith stayed a little longer with Anne and Pat.

---

*Group worker works with one of the subgroups—the two girls who have little ability to express themselves.*

---

At this time, Anne became more active. She was very reasonable, showed Miss Smith the pictures in which she was interested, and tried to read some of the headings that were written in English. There was, at first, a rather positive interaction between the two girls and Miss Smith. Yet when Pat reached for some of the pictures that Anne held, Anne did not want to give them to her. Anne immediately got up to leave and said she could not stand Pat.

---

*The "silent" girl can express hostility only in the intimacy of the small subgroup (pair).*

---

Miss Smith stayed with Pat another fifteen minutes. Pat spoke about the girls' not liking her. Miss Smith wondered why; Pat said she just didn't know, that she did like them. Miss Smith suggested that it could be that they felt pushed by her; she nodded her head and said this could be. She said she had come to the center originally for temper tantrums, but she felt she was much better now. She had been in a hospital and had hated it, "especially those dopey psychiatrists and dopey nurses."

---

*It is part of group work to allow the group members individual contacts with the group worker. Such contacts help the group worker to get to know members in a different situation (child/adult) and allow the group members to receive some individual attention from the group worker.*

---

Pat said she was glad we had these group meetings. She also liked several of the counselors.

---

*Pat's need to be liked by her contemporaries forces her into conforming to their expression of hostility. The individual contact allows her here to be herself—hopefully strengthening her ego.*

---

When Pat was alone with Miss Smith she could speak about positive feelings, which she did not reveal under group pressure. She was physically affectionate, but seemed to react rather reasonably to a friendly hug. She then could let go. For example, she tried to climb on Miss Smith's lap and put her arms around her. Miss Smith was friendly but did not let Pat sit on her lap; Pat was able to accept this without feeling hurt or pushed.

---

*One of Pat's problems is her constant need for physical contact. The group worker must help her to limit this without rebuffing her. This is only help on a more superficial level.*

*It is hoped that satisfactions in the group and some insight gained may lessen Pat's infantile needs.*

---

Miss Smith went to the girls' dormitory with Pat, and offered to help her clean up her dresser. The rather amusing answer was "Oh, no! Let's not do that! I must know where everything is!"

---

*The group worker shows her interest and concern by doing the "little things" mothers do for children.*

---

After leaving Pat, Miss Smith took Ed a sweater he had left at the meeting; he was very gracious and thanked her for having thought of him.

### Record 3

This morning a new boy, John, had come for a trial visit to the center. John was a 12-year-old, tall, and a very hyperactive boy. He had been afraid to stay inside the house. Miss Smith had followed the crying boy when he ran outside, and had walked around with him.

When she returned, she saw Ed sitting at the window; he had observed them. Ed said, "That kid is a pretty big baby, isn't he? What's the matter with him?"

Miss Smith asked, "Ed, have you ever been afraid of something?"

---

*Group worker enlists a boy's understanding of another boy—and also allows him to feel that one must not be ashamed of fear.*

---

Ed looked very thoughtful and said, "Yes, sometimes."

Miss Smith went on, "Well, that is what is happening here; he is afraid that he will be locked up. He has had such an experience once."

Ed got up from his chair and said, very seriously, "*I* can talk to him. I am a kid like he is. He understands *me*."

He went back to his room and got his jacket. He persuaded John to sit in his parents' car with him. The boy finally agreed to this, and Ed talked to him quietly. He explained to him that no door was locked; that the food was good; that people were not mean; and that he should not be afraid. Ed succeeded in calming this very upset newcomer.

---

*Ed is helpful to the new boy; giving help also helps Ed to see his own situation in a more positive light.*

---

At the next meeting Elaine and Anne came in first. Elaine looked unusually pretty in a new blue and white sweater. The counselor told Miss Smith that Elaine wanted to talk to her alone. Elaine said quietly that she thought the girls would like to use this group meeting to talk over a lot of things, but that it does not work because of the presence of the boys. She wished Miss Smith would let the boys go; she thought they were too agitated and loud. Also, "when boys and girls are together, one cannot talk freely."

Miss Smith explained to her that the staff had thought this might be an opportunity for boys and girls to learn to talk to one another; she added that she knew that the boys, too, needed help, yet perhaps their meeting together was really not so good. She suggested that all of them talk it through during the group meeting.

*The request of a group member is taken seriously by the group worker. She gives the reason for the agency's decision, but allows for revision. She suggests involvement of the group in the discussion because this is a serious problem concerning all of them.*

Elaine was not sure that she wanted this. (Later, during the meeting, she gave permission to bring up her concern.)

*Confidentiality is kept. The subject is brought up only when Elaine gives permission to do so.*

Pat was away shopping and was not in the group today.

Susie, Ed, and Jim arrived together. Susie brought a record player and a stack of records, but they were not used during the meeting. Ed was very quiet and still glowing with the satisfaction he had derived from his contact with the new boy. He started out by saying that he thought he had helped him. Miss Smith agreed and thanked him for what he had done. This was interesting to the other youngsters, and Ed, calmly and thoughtfully, told about the incident. He added that he thought that John was a "pretty good kid who can make it."

Miss Smith suggested that John could "make it" only if others would help him. He was scared of others because he thought they might tease him. Jim wondered why the boy should be afraid of teasing. Miss Smith threw out the question whether there was anything young people get teased about?

*Group worker helps youngsters think through their own relations with others.*

There was some talk about bringing teasing upon oneself. Ed said that this big boy surely would be good at ball playing and then nobody would tease him.

*Beginning insight (see purpose of the group meetings).*

Miss Smith said he was good at it, but that he was self-conscious about his being so tall at his age. Jim identified with this by saying that he, too, was tall when he was 12 years old, but it had only bothered him for a little while and now he thought it was fine because he could play good basketball.

*Group worker builds on the beginning insight and helps the children recognize that feelings about oneself have impact on one's actions.*

They then had a little and relatively calm discussion on the way they could help each other. Ed was the leader in this, pointing out how important it was and how he thought they all could get out much faster if they would help one another more.

Miss Smith brought up the question of Elaine's having said she felt badly about not being allowed to go out, and there, too, they could help themselves and each other.

---

*Group worker helps to focus on a member of the group who needs special help.*

---

Elaine was very quiet and calm during all of this meeting; she said that she tried to become more reasonable, but it wasn't always easy. Ed complimented Elaine on being "a recreational worker" and helping others to arrange parties and dances. Elaine mentioned that this was her intent, that she liked to cheer up people, that she had even done this when she was locked in with adults on the ward of a mental hospital; she added that this wasn't always easy because sometimes people were too mean and made it too hard for her. At this time she again expressed sharp hostility against Dr. Abel. As had happened the last time, she insisted that he called her a liar and always "just sits there."

Miss Smith raised the question of whether it wasn't enjoyable to have somebody's attention. Elaine felt that they needed attention badly, but she did not like to be stared at; Mr. Olds (the caseworker) did not do it that way. She recently had tried to stare down Mr. Olds and he didn't like it either!

---

*Group worker tries to let Elaine express some positive feelings about individual interviews, since she is aware of her ambivalence.*

*Some people need as much help with expression of warm feelings as with those of hostility.*

---

Miss Smith had again brought cookies. There was less grabbing this time and far more concern for others who wanted some. She had also brought some old Christmas cards. Anne, Elaine, and Susie were especially interested in these. There was some squabbling between Anne and Elaine when Elaine accused Anne of never participating in anything and of not even wanting to dance. Anne's response was "Oh, pooh!" Elaine and Ed told Anne that this was what she was doing all the time: her only response was, "Oh, pooh!" Anne just shook her head.

Anne had seen that Miss Smith had also brought paper and charcoal; she asked to draw. This immediately stimulated the others, with the exception of Jim. They all took paper, including Miss Smith, and sat down to draw.

---

*It is important to children that adults do things with them.*

---

Jim was restless, as usual, and jumped up to get cigarettes; he then asked for a typewriter and typed for a major part of the meeting while the others were drawing.

During the drawing period, some discussion was carried on with Elaine's trying to be serious and Ed's defeating it. With Elaine's permission, Miss Smith introduced the idea of Elaine's feeling that the boys should not participate because they did not involve themselves.

---

*Group worker remembers the promise made to Elaine to discuss her concern. It is brought up when Elaine feels frustrated.*

---

She was a bit amused when Ed objected to this on the grounds that the boys needed the meetings too, and argued that there was no reason why the girls alone should have that privilege. (What a contrast to the first meeting!) For a short time, he did listen to what Elaine was trying to say, but then he would digress and suggest that all the children band against the counselors and that way achieve what they wanted to.

At one point, Jim pulled out the paper from the typewriter and brought it over to Miss Smith, asking her to read it aloud.

It was just practice typing—no words. Miss Smith read it, however, pronouncing the funny sounds that this kind of jumble makes. The youngsters, including Jim, howled with good-natured laughter and, for a little moment, Jim was, in this way, the center of attention. He then asked for paper to draw.

---

*Group worker joins the spirit of fun. The relaxing "pause" is very necessary in meetings which have much emotional content. Also, Jim is thus drawn out of his isolation.*

---

This spontaneous drawing brought out the fact that Anne could draw very well; she drew mostly faces. Elaine drew lovely, calm landscapes; Jim, a Mexican face.

---

*Children express feelings without using words.*

---

Miss Smith commented on Elaine's calm, and she replied, "This is the way I feel right now." Susie drew caricatures of several staff members, with a delightful sense of specifics: "He always bends over the desk" or "He always puts his feet on the table." Her drawings were caricatures, but they were not hostile. She showed pride in them and wanted the staff members to see them. Miss Smith suggested they all draw what they wanted to be.

---

*This helps the group worker to understand the children better. It also frees the children to express their hopes.*

---

Susie drew a girl on a horse; Elaine, a tree; Anne, a walnut; Jim, a stiff man with a big, round stomach and a pipe in his mouth.

---

*Anne's drawing of the walnut was highly significant—a closed object one must force open to find its content.*

---

With the exception of Jim and Anne, they were verbal about their drawings and could explain what it was they wanted to be.

Miss Smith mentioned laughingly that she had always wanted to be a duck; Elaine immediately drew one, but said that she would not like it because ducks "get hunted," a very significant remark. Jim, always the least verbal, drew a picture and said that it was "a ship passing another ship." Miss Smith felt that this remark was symbolic of the way Jim relates to other people.

When all the drawing paper was used up, the youngsters became quite restless. They tried to play with the tape recorder; Miss Smith promised to find out whether they could use one the next time. They left, except for Ed. The meeting had lasted over an hour—a longer time than had been spent the previous time.

Ed stayed, working at the typewriter. He showed a surprising amount of determination to learn; he wrote his name over and over, repeating it every time he made a mistake. He told Miss Smith that he wanted to learn. He then went on to talk about the new boy, saying that he thought he was just "in a state of shock with fear." Miss Smith asked him how he knew so much about people; he replied, "I was a long time in a mental hospital—I *know* how it feels."

---

*Group worker gives Ed recognition for his thoughtfulness and understanding.*

---

### Record 4

Miss Smith came in early and met the girls at the breakfast table. Their greeting was warm.

---

*Relationship has changed considerably since the first meeting.*

---

Susie and Pat came into the meeting room a little ahead of Elaine and Anne, and used the tape recorder. A counselor came in to say that Ed and Jim had preferred not to come. Miss Smith learned later that they had gone hunting with the other boys. This seemed right for them.

The girls sat close together on the sofa. Elaine expressed her delight that they were without the boys and could finally talk things over. Miss Smith suggested that Elaine start with whatever she had on her mind. Very seriously, she said that she was annoyed with the way the girls' quarters looked. "Nobody here but Kay and I care whether the place looks decent or not. I wish we could do something about this." They talked a little about this; Miss Smith tried to help the other girls to express themselves.

Pat said she just didn't know how to fix up things. Susie said it was boring to put things together and she would just fall asleep on the bed. Elaine retorted that she slept too much anyway. Anne did not involve herself. Elaine once again expressed her frustration. Miss Smith wondered whether they wanted her to go with them and help them to clean up and, perhaps, go on from there. Elaine objected to this, saying that the kids would never learn how to do things for themselves because they get too much help now.

---

*The discussion shows beginning sense of responsibility, with Elaine's carrying the lead. The group worker gives support, but does not pressure those girls who are not ready to take on such responsibility.*

---

Miss Smith asked when they thought was the best time to clean up. Susie said, "At midnight." Miss Smith wondered if they cleaned up at midnight, when would she sleep; Susie replied, quite seriously, that she liked to sleep during the day and to be up at night, but, she added, she would try to clean up a little during the day.

Miss Smith had brought along some beautiful Hallowe'en cookies; the girls admired them and ate them quite fast. She also had brought some little gifts for them, which she had purchased on a trip to Canada. There was little reaction to them; the only overt reaction was that each one tried to exchange the one she had received for another one.

---

*Deprived children always have a fear of being "cheated." The reaction to the gifts shows this deep distrust in spite of a beginning trusting relationship with the group worker.*

---

They spotted the recorder and were very eager to begin working with it.

Miss Smith played back the recordings that Susie and Pat had made while they were alone in the room before the meeting began. Pat had talked most of the time and was unintelligible. Susie had expressed hostility toward Mr. Carter. Miss Smith had the impression, however, that the hostility was only in words, that underlying it were feelings bordering on adoration. Susie constantly begged Miss Smith not to erase the dictation so that Mr. Carter could hear it later.

---

*Again the incapacity to express positive feelings.*

---

When the girls gathered around the microphone, they saw, through the glass window, the staff meeting being held across the hall. This stimulated many remarks about staff members.

Miss Smith suggested that they record what they wanted to say and then talk it over. Elaine was immediately enthusiastic about this idea and dictated with much feeling and clarity.

---

*Group worker at this point structures the meeting to allow for a more focused expression.*

---

The other girls were very quiet and considerate of her. When she played it back, they squealed with delight, especially whenever she said something against a member of the staff.

Miss Smith tried to encourage Anne to dictate. Her extremely constricted personality was again seen in the way she used—or was unable to use—this medium. She wanted to recite the Gettysburg Address; she could say only a few words. She changed into playing a "Knock, knock" game on the tape recorder—then stopped abruptly.

---

*Children who cannot speak freely to others frequently open up when they can talk to something impersonal, as a microphone; or when they can speak through a disguise, e.g., puppets. This is the reason why the group worker uses this medium.*

---

Susie was asked to dictate. This time she spoke with real emotional expression. Pat followed. Her comments were more shallow than those of Susie and Elaine.

When Elaine reached for the recorder again, Miss Smith asked her to wait a bit. The girls clustered closely around Miss Smith; she had her arm around Susie. She told the girls that this group session had much meaning because they talked about things that really concerned them. She wondered whether it was all right for their recording to be transcribed so that they could discuss at the next meeting the problems they had raised. The girls gave this permission with great sincerity. Susie insisted, though, that she wanted to call Mr. Carter to hear it.

---

*Group worker sees progress in the way children use the group. She makes them aware of this to motivate further involvement.*

*She considers the recording valuable enough to be preserved and used as a base for more discussion.*

*Transcript must have girls' permission (ethics of the profession) since confidentiality has been guaranteed.*

---

Elaine then began to dictate about an upset in the girls' group that had happened just the day before; Susie followed her.

When the girls listened to what they had dictated, they showed the usual delight of all people who hear their own voices and their surprise at how they sounded. They laughed hysterically any time names of staff members in authority were mentioned (e.g., Dr. Abel, Mr. Dill, Mr. Carter, or Miss Andrews). They squealed and shouted.

This meeting had taken almost one and one-half hours. Ed joined the group for a few minutes toward the end of the meeting.

---

*Length of stay is significant since attention span of the children is low. To stay longer means that they were highly motivated.*

---

## Record 5

Mr. Olds told Miss Smith that there had been another upset in the girls' dormitory; he was not sure what had brought it about.

Susie, Elaine, Anne, and Ed came first. They spotted the recorder immediately and Ed and Elaine tried to do some recording. Miss Smith had this time purposely not brought along any program material; she had wanted to see how the children could handle a meeting without such. She suggested that they not use the recorder today since it was not working too well. She had brought along only the transcript of what had been recorded at the last meeting; she proposed that they discuss it.

Susie, Elaine and, strangely enough, Anne, were very outspoken and positive and wanted to talk about it and to read what had been recorded. Ed could not involve himself; this was understandable, since he had not been present the last time. He began to dictate in spite of the poor quality of the recorder. Pat came a little later and seated herself apart from the others in the group.

---

*The recording machine in the room proves to be too attractive. The children are not yet ready to move into an orderly discussion. The presence of an "outsider" (Ed) also prevents their going into the content of the previous meeting.*

---

When Ed stopped dictating and joined the girls, Elaine left and began some dictation. She talked about the "riot" in the girls' dormitory. She told how the girls had not wanted to disturb others at night; they therefore had pulled the television set into their bedroom and had turned it on very quietly. The counselors objected. Joe (a counselor) had come in and removed the television set. That had made them angry, and they had turned on their radios louder than usual. Again the counselors interfered, and the fight started.

All the children listened in while Elaine dictated this. Miss Smith asked at what time they had turned on the television set. Elaine said it was 10:30 P.M.

---

*Group worker tries to help the girls understand the reasons for the counselors' demands.*

---

Surprisingly enough, Anne, who was much more alive at this meeting than usual, spoke up loudly and with great emphasis. She agreed that there had been nothing wrong with the girls' use of the television set. She did not like to be kept awake and would have objected if it had been disturbing. The girls had it on so softly that she had slept through the whole thing until the counselors began to interfere.

---

*Anne begins to feel more comfortable in speaking up. Her support of the girls allows the discussion to become less hostile.*

---

Miss Smith wondered what late television meant in getting up the next morning when they had to go to school. Ed said that none of the girls went to school, but Elaine said—truthfully—that wasn't so, that there were several who had to go. They said they had promised that they would get up on time.

Elaine suddenly began to discuss the matter of orderliness in the girls' room. Elaine said that, in general, it is getting much better, and that the most disorderly people are Pat and Anne. Pat could not take this criticism; she got up, went outside for a moment, and seemed quite unhappy. Anne, surprisingly, once more involved herself. She said that she did not want any help with cleanup; that it annoyed her that other girls were always around. Someday she would change—but because *she* wanted it, not because of Elaine's pressure.

---

*It is not clear how transition to this subject started. It may be that Elaine, by admitting that there may be a reason for the counselors' behavior, had become uncomfortable. She needed now to turn her hostility on someone else—this time Pat and Anne. The group worker missed here an opportunity to help Elaine come to grips with her problems.*

---

### Record 6

Jim came, but stayed separated from the group. He played for quite awhile with the recorder; he disturbed the others so much that they objected to it. He was willing to stop when they told him so; however, at that moment, he also lost interest in the group meeting, and left.

The rest of the youngsters stayed together for about three-quarters of an hour. They expressed hostility against several of the counselors. This time hostility was not expressed in shouting, but in a strong plea for Miss Smith to believe them when they said that some counselors treated them badly. Only Ed screamed that he would smash them or use a switchblade or a Luger on them. Miss Smith listened, but then asked the children to give her three minutes and listen to her. She told them how, a few years ago, they had sat together—counselors and children—and had thought through the purpose of this place; that the staff members knew that they were youngsters who had been hurt in the past and that only friendship and understanding would help them. This was the intent of their work, but sometimes it was hard for the counselors to give this friendship if the children would not allow it. Did they think that something like this played a part in their relationships with the counselors right now? They did calm down, and insisted that not *all* the counselors were so cruel.

---

*Group worker takes the youngsters seriously. She does not argue against them; she explains the purpose and philosophy of the institution. She is direct in discussing relationships between the children and the counselors.*

---

Ed screamed that Mr. Carter was stuck up. Miss Smith said that she had never found this; Ed suddenly became quiet and said, "No, he really is not, but he, too, doesn't listen enough."

---

*Group worker contradicts here because she feels that her relationship with Ed is now strong enough to allow this. Ed admits that he exaggerated in his anger—a small, but important step forward for a boy who previously would not accept any limitation by an adult.*

---

They ended the meeting with Elaine's asking Miss Smith whether they could dictate some suggestions as to how the children could get along better.

---

*Elaine, too, begins to think in terms of working with instead of only fighting the adults.*

---

Miss Smith promised that the following week they would have a functioning tape recorder.

Miss Smith spent some time with Ollie and Elaine in the dormitory where they discussed Elaine's earlier recording. Elaine had asked Miss Smith to give it to Ollie. In the course of the contact, Miss Smith suggested that Elaine might want to do her dictation at the next meeting in the form of a letter to a new girl coming to the center. Elaine accepted this suggestion eagerly.

---

*Group worker realizes that Elaine is the leader in her dormitory group. She intensifies her efforts to establish a relationship with her which will help her to identify more positively with adults and use her leadership more constructively.*

*Group worker does this to give Elaine's efforts a concrete direction and to draw her away from the role of the complainer. To write a letter to a specific (even if fictitious) person allows for expression of feelings, but imposes a discipline to explain them to someone else and to think more carefully.*

---

### Record 7

This meeting consisted almost entirely of a tape recording, mostly done by Elaine. The other children listened calmly and with great interest; Miss Smith knitted.

The recording is reproduced because it shows the change toward taking more responsibility for their own actions and the development of a more positive attitude toward treatment and the center.

Elaine. A lot of kids say that this place is icky, but if you have been at the old center . . . or at the kids' unit in the mental hospital, this place is really, really nice. For one thing, we get an allowance every week and about all we have to do is just make our beds, and a lot of the kids in homes have to wash dishes, take care of brothers and sisters, and all, and they don't even get a dollar. I think we are pretty lucky to get that.

If you are going to be coming down into—if you are a girl you would be coming down into the girls' dormitory. I have got one gripe against that. The little girls' dorm is messy all the time except for Anne—she keeps her place pretty clean.

*Change in attitude toward one of the group members.*

But over in the big girls' dorm there is one pig called Joyce; she's constantly in a mess, never clean. But if you go up with the boys—if you are a boy you go up to be with the boys—well, I don't know what that's like because I am a girl.

The counselors and Dr. Abel and Carter and the nurse—well, all of the people except the two secretaries and us kids have, ah, have, ah, have what is called a staff meeting every Thursday on one of the kids. Well, I have been on restrictions for quite awhile, and they will have meetings on me to decide, you know, just how much restriction they are going to take off for awhile.

*Such staff meetings are not best practice. Today the person involved should be present throughout, or at least part, of the meeting.*

If you are a girl, I mean, and you have smoking privs and you can afford cigarettes and you don't smoke like a steam engine, you, you are allowed, well, a whole cigarette every time you smoke. But there is one girl down in our dorm—name is Pat—and she smokes like a steam engine and she is allowed only a half a cigarette at a time, because otherwise she just about has a nicotine fit if she doesn't have cigarettes all day.

*Identification with institution's limitation.*

We have some real, real nice—well, every one of the counselors is nice except, well, for one that I don't like; her name is Ella—but everybody's got their own opinion of everybody else. Well, if you're one that doesn't like to be ritzy and all, and doesn't like to follow manners, well, I don't think you're going to like Ella either.

*Elaine accepts the possibility that Ella is not all bad—that her feelings about her may be subjective.*

This isn't like being in a home because you don't have a mother and father and all,

---

*Elaine expresses her feelings of deprivation at not having a family.*

---

but the counselors—if you are feeling low or something like that—the counselors will come and try to comfort you and try to talk to you, and if you ask and you catch him at the right time you can, Mr. Olds will sometimes talk to you if you are feeling low or something like that.

---

*Elaine accepts the comforting role of the counselors and the case worker.*

---

One girl got to go out yesterday. She socked Miss Andrews in the nose and then she got to go out. Miss Andrews took her out and if you have ever been to the drugstore, you know that they have got those lalapalooza (a big dish of ice cream and fruits) things or whatever you call them; well, Miss Andrews took her out for one of those. I am just wondering what on earth would happen to me if I punched Andrews in the nose! I would probably be sent to the girls' training school!

---

*Feelings of injustice are still strong.*

---

You are allowed to, well . . . some of the kids go out to public school and then some stay here and go for anywhere from 45 minutes to half an hour with the school teacher named Miss Farrow. Eh!

Pat. I sometimes am very messy but sometimes when I feel all right, I, ah, my name is Pat. I am 13 and I am a child here, too, and, ah, I keep my place clean sometimes, but when I don't feel so well and am kind of tired 'cause I get new medication, now I try to keep it clean. 'Cause I went out last night I was quite busy deciding what to wear and that, and Elaine was nice enough to let me wear her heels and that. We went all through this one cafeteria restaurant.

---

*Pat reacts to Elaine's dictation as a standard setting device.*

---

Elaine. Well, there is something I forgot to tell you. Ah, it has to do with our money problems on allowances and like that. Well, we have this thing that is called a girls' club and we have a fund for that and each girl, you know, gets a quarter to put in every week and we go—we can use it for anything; we can go swimming, to movies, roller skating. We haven't gone roller skating yet, but we have gone swimming many, many times, and we have gone to two shows since I have been here.

Susie. My name is Susie and if you're a boy and you go into the boys' group—Oh! Let's see! I am trying to figure out! Some of us don't like two of the counselors up there. Joe, for instance. I don't think you would like him too much.

---

*The girls pressed Miss Smith to dictate too.*

---

Miss Smith. My name is Nanette Smith. I must say that every week I look forward to coming to this place because I like the kids, but especially the group I work with. If you want to know what this group is here for, well, it's a group where we sometimes talk about things that make us angry; sometimes we talk about things that we enjoy, and today you have heard some of those.

There are many other people on this staff, but they are not right here in this meeting. If you want to, perhaps the girls can introduce them to you. We could start with the director and then tell you something about the other people besides the counselors. What do you think of that?

Elaine. This is Elaine again. Miss Smith, the one who just got through talking, is very, very nice. She, ah, you won't be able to hear this tape because it's going to be typed out, but if you could listen at all you would hear that Miss Smith has an accent, and that is because I think she is part French, but the way I figure it, no matter if you got an accent, no matter what color you are or anything like that, I like you; no matter what, *what* you are.

---

*Elaine increasingly expresses positive feelings.*

---

Well, I guess I will do what Miss Smith suggested. Well, I will start off with the director, I guess. The director's name is Doctor . . . Mister—excuse me! Mr. Carter. He is English and he is very, very nice and understanding. And then, well, he is the director and he helps and sees that you come or not and puts his opinion in. Well, that's about all I can think of to say about him.

And then there is Miss Andrews. She is a very, very nice woman, and I tell you she really puts up with a lot. You got to hand it to these people. They have got a lot of patience, except there is a couple that doesn't have a lot of patience, but that can't be helped. We kind of bring it on ourselves sometimes.

---

*This spontaneous admission is very important.*

---

And then there is Mr. Olds. Excuse! I like Mr. Olds very, very much. He is pretty understanding and he is the social worker here.

---

*This is the first time Elaine allows herself to say that she likes Mr. Olds.*

---

And then there is Dr. Abel, ah . . . he is the psychiatrist here; he is one of the psychiatrists here, and he is fair in my opinion—but you may think different of him.

And then there is Mr. Crankston—Dr. Crankston; he is, I think, a psychiatrist too. I am not sure but I think he is. He's fair, too, in my opinion.

And then there is another doctor here: His name is Dr. Merton. He is a psychiatrist too. I see him and I think he is just a wonderful man. Thanks to him I am going to be going some place for Thanksgiving, and I am real thankful to him for that. At first I just . . . Oh, excuse me! I was going into my private affairs . . . I will stop there.

Oh! I have got to warn you about something! If you see Dr. Merton and you want to play chess with him, he is a very, very good chess player. And then, oh look at his beautiful, beautiful blue eyes! I tell you they are just beautiful!

And now, oh, there are two secretaries. One is, excuse me just a minute, well, excuse me, I had to consult Miss Smith on something else and she didn't know it either, but there is one fairly young secretary up here. She is very, very cute and her name is Jeannette (I don't know what her last name is). And then there is another secretary; her name is Carol. She is very, very nice, too.

Miss Smith. This is Miss Smith again: I think we should tell you something about why this place is here anyhow—maybe Elaine can do that. I also think there is one other girl in this room, Anne, who hasn't said anything, but I don't know whether she will. But maybe Elaine can tell you why we have this children's center.

---

*Group worker tries to pull in Anne, but does not press her. Anne refused to speak.*

---

Elaine. Hello! This is Elaine again! Well, I guess I will do as Miss Smith says and tell you why this place is here. Well, it's here for children that are real mixed up and that have gone through a lot of hardships through their life; they are here to get well and to be able to go out and get along in the world, get along with people. Most of the kids that have been here have been . . . have come in real, real violent and all, and have gone out real, real nice; they have just reformed—you wouldn't know them. This place is here—it may seem at times just a mean, horrid place for punishment, but it's here for only your own good—to help you. The people here do want to help you very much, although, at times, I will admit even myself that I get to thinking that it's pretty horrid, but then I get over that.

---

*Elaine explains purpose of the agency well, and yet is free to give her feelings—of thinking of it also as "mean."*

---

Oh! There is something I have to, ah . . . we have O.T. The girls have it Tuesdays and Fridays; the boys—I don't know when they have it. Our O.T. director is Miss Jones.

And then, as I mentioned awhile back, we have a school teacher here and her name is Miss Farrow. And then we have a janitor and his name is Evans. I guess that's all. He has another part to his name, but I don't know where that comes in.

And then we have a handyman—he repairs things—and his name is Mr. Keller. And then we have a laundry woman, and her name is Stella Tree.

Well, I guess that's about all I have to say here. Well, I wish you the best of luck. Your little friend, Elaine.

## COMMENT

The seven meetings presented here show movement in the social group work process. This is a *formed group,* formed by the agency with a therapeutic aim. The group members start out with expression of hostility toward and distrust of the group worker. She represents to them a symbol of all adults who are enemies. Individually and as a total group, the group members are not willing to open up with her or to accept any value presented by her. This attitude is pervasive, but, in this particular group, does not constitute a bond among the members. They are each separated from the others as if all were living on different islands. In the course of the meetings, there is general movement towards a beginning trust of the group worker and of one another. It is achieved predominantly by the group worker's complete acceptance of each individual and an honest working through of problems with them. *Insight* is achieved only to a small extent, but behavior change occurs through some insight, group members' criticizing or helping each other, and experiencing the satisfaction of less hostile behavior. *Group bond* is beginning to develop as seen in the greater concern for each other, the voluntary attendance at group meetings, and the acceptance of one member—Elaine—to act as a spokesperson for the group.

There are beginning signs of the emergence of two meaningful, self-contained subgroups—boys and girls.[9]

In the group worker/children relationship a sense of trust has developed, given by the children. Beyond that, the relationship to the group worker is quite varied, according to the needs of the different individuals.

As a group, the children have moved toward the fulfillment of some of the goals set for this group: They begin to speak more freely about their feelings; they accept the special attention of an understanding adult; and they relate somewhat more closely to one another, but not as a total group—only in subgroups.

To evaluate movement, we must also look at each individual and see whether the group has achieved some of the purposes set for it.

Elaine shows an almost dramatic movement from sharp pervasive aggressiveness toward everything and everybody to a recognition of her own part in this situation and a beginning trust in others, such as the group worker and the counselors. She emerges as a leader in the group, with drives toward more positive actions as well as verbal improvement. Her movement is somewhat too fast so that the skilled group worker will recognize it as a tenuous one and expect relapses.

Elaine's relationship to the worker is one of cautious acceptance. There is not a close identification. The relationship is still a superficial one. In view of her developmental history, one would not expect any other form in which she can relate to a woman. She had never had any close parental relationship and must have felt maternal rejection especially strongly. The group can offer to her only a motivation toward search for a closer relationship. If she is thus motivated, she may be ready for individual treatment, a deepening of insight, and a strengthening of human ties.

Susie's main progress lies in the change from silent and sullen hostility

---

[9]The reader should know that the group actually separated into a boys' and a girls' group at the request of the members when the group became increasingly meaningful to them. Disturbed adolescents seem to prefer not to meet in a heterosexual group. They struggle so hard with their feelings of sex-identification that they are more comfortable if they are not too stimulated by the presence of youngsters of the other sex in a small, intimate group. At the same time, they need some less intensive contacts with the opposite sex to try out and experience their capacity to handle those relationships.

to a capacity to speak up freely and to express ambivalence in relation to people, indicating that she has some positive feelings too. Although she starts out by showing practically no capacity to handle frustration, she begins to accept criticism of herself by the other girls (when they say she is not very orderly, for instance). She also shows the capacity to wait for her turn in recording. She begins to express herself not so much in direct verbalization as in drawings, which express her feelings and her perception, and in poetry, which she is beginning to share with this group. Susie has gone through an acute psychotic stage. Although her movement looks on the surface less dramatic than Elaine's, it actually indicates just as great a step forward toward health.

Her relationship to the group worker is a "neutral" one. She shows no warmth toward her, but does not include her in her hostile attacks on others. In fact, it seems as if this is the one person whom she exempts from her violent emotions. The opportunity to work through her feelings in the presence of someone with whom she does not have to get deeply involved means much to Susie—in fact, it makes it possible for her to become expressive.

Anne has made less progress than the other two up to this time. She had been completely mute when she entered a mental hospital and had only begun to relate when she started in the group. She frequently withdraws during group meetings into individual activities separated from the group. This is purposely supported by the group worker, who tries to convey to her the idea that she is not being pushed and can move at her own pace. Anne's history contains no clue to explain her illness. The group worker works on the assumption that whatever produced Anne's upset need not to be handled until she feels safe to do so. The group worker's attitude relaxes Anne and allows her to make beginning steps toward more interactional skills. Anne starts by asking for a translation of a foreign language, showing her struggle with verbal communication. She expresses herself in drawing—significantly by drawing faces that include the mouth, the verbal organ of the person. She draws herself as a walnut, indicating her awareness of herself as being "closed up" and perhaps her unconscious wish to have someone break her open. In the fifth meeting she interacts verbally with the others and speaks up in support of them or contradicts them. Yet, in the later recording session, she is still very inhibited and cannot use this medium to express herself.[10]

[10]At a much later meeting, Anne started it off by saying that she would use the tape recorder to "shout." The girls supported her. She first used it cautiously—but used it! In fact, she cautioned the others by mentioning frequently that "everything is recorded what we say." In the middle of the session, she began to give an account of a childish stealing episode done with her sister as an instigator. This was the first time that anything like this was expressed by her or her family. It is significant for the value of the group work method that this occurred through the support of her "equals," with the added safety of the presence of an adult who had proved acceptance through patience with her and the "unacceptable" behavior of others combined with the use of an "outside tool"—the tape recorder.

Anne's relationship to the group worker is difficult to assess because of her reluctance to express herself. One may infer positive feelings because of her regular attendance at the group sessions (which was voluntary). One has the impression that her relationship with the group worker at this time represents to Anne a safe haven from which she may venture out when she feels like it, but which makes no frightening demands on actual involvement.

Pat was farthest back in her development when she entered the group. Her behavior was no longer out of touch with reality, but was very infantile. Positive movement seen in the group meetings lies less in Pat herself than in her position in the group. She started out by being a rejected isolate in her living group as well as in the treatment group. During the group meetings her position changes and she becomes a somewhat more tolerated member of the formed group. Since Pat has been very aware of her poor relationships with her contemporaries and has suffered under them, this change has great meaning to her. She is not yet capable of basically changing her own behavior, which brings isolation upon her, but she shows a few signs of movement in regard to this: She can accept some limitations; she discusses—up to this point, only outside of the group—some of her problems with the group worker; and she is able to record some of her shortcomings.

To Pat, the social group worker is obviously a mother substitute. She wants from her much attention and affection. Her feeling toward the group worker is one of "hunger" for body contact, like the need of an infant. It has no great emotional depth, yet it is a vital necessity for her. The worker's acceptance of her need gives her some satisfaction and apparently the beginning strength to control it—at least in the presence of others. Pat, however, has a long way to go to achieve even simple maturity.

The development of the two boys, Jim and Ed, is not as significant as the development of the girls. They show definite signs of wishing to move out of the group constellation. This is seen in their spotty attendance. Jim is involved only on the surface, even when he is present. He can relate to his contemporaries and contradict them, but, in general, he has no interest in discussing problems or becoming a part of this particular group. It becomes evident that this is not a helpful group constellation for him.

Jim's relationship to the group worker is characterized by indifference. He displays neither hostility nor acceptance, nor the kind of neutrality (as Susie's) that is a positive and safe protection from which one can venture out.

Ed would probably be more involved with the group if other boys, besides Jim, were present. He has a need to express himself, to talk out anger, and to feel some sense of accomplishment. The group situation gives him that opportunity. In spite of his spotty attendance, he shows movement and some insight into his own feelings, as seen in the incident with the newcomer and in beginning identification with the group. He shows changes in feelings and behavior from angry hostility to feelings of responsibility for and liking of others. The group situation, however, which is dominated by the girls, is not the most conducive to his full development.

Ed's relationship with the group worker is meaningful. His feelings toward her are highly ambivalent. He is torn between beginning trust and a wish to be close to her and fear of involvement, which would make demands on him.

In group meetings with disturbed children such as these, seven meetings represent only a very short time period. In view of this, the development toward the goals set is remarkable. It can be explained only by the power of the group process itself, and the skillful way in which the group worker used herself and the social group work method.


## SUMMARY

Group work practice is based on an optimism that assumes that the human being can be helped to grow and change. It is not a romantic optimism, but one that drives toward action—a realistic idealism.

Its three premises are (1) social work as a profession is concerned with the enhancement of people's social functioning; (2) there is significant correlation between social functioning and group experience, and (3) people need help—sometimes professional help—to enhance social functioning.

Out of knowledge, philosophy, and skill evolve basic principles of social group work. They are:

1. Recognition and subsequent action in relation to the unique difference of each individual.
2. Recognition and subsequent action in relation to the wide variety of groups as groups.
3. Genuine respect for individuals with their unique strengths and weaknesses.
4. Establishment of a purposeful relationship between group worker and group members.
5. Encouragement and enabling of helpful and cooperative relationships between members.
6. Appropriate modification of the group process.
7. Encouragement of each member to participate according to the stage of his or her capacity and enabling the individual to become more capable.
8. Enabling of members to involve themselves in the process of problem-solving.
9. Enabling group members to experience increasingly satisfactory forms of working through of conflicts.
10. Provision of opportunities for new and differing experiences in relationships and accomplishments.

11. Judicious use of limitations related to the diagnostic assessment of each individual and the total situation.
12. Purposeful and differential use of program according to diagnostic evaluation of individual members, group purpose, and appropriate social goals.
13. Ongoing evaluation of individual and group progress.
14. Warm, human, and disciplined use of self on the part of the group worker.

In an analysis of practice we can observe these principles in action. We see the importance of time in the helping process and the complicated net of interrelationships that group workers must understand and with which they must work. The goal, help with social functioning, is not reached quickly or in a straight line, but often through several backward and forward movements.

In looking over these principles, it should become clear that social group work is not the same as some other group approaches that have been introduced either at the same time or later. I would like to enlarge on a few of them.

*T-groups* started many years ago under the leadership of Kurt Lewin and his followers. They were originally laboratory groups designed to help participants develop an understanding of their own reactions to others, as well as to learn skills in observing group process. The groups were usually quite unstructured and the "trainer" would only intervene to facilitate the process when it began to lose direction. As a learning method for qualified people with no severe emotional problems, this seems to be an appropriate method. It is a form of learning through doing. Yet this T-group approach has changed and now is a global method used to help people learn about themselves, in moving them toward optimum performance and interaction with others. *Sensitivity groups* have grown out of this, forcing all participants to do much soul searching.

The problem I see here is that these approaches are often used indiscriminately without any consideration of (1) how strong a person is to withstand group pressure, and (2) what a negative impact of group pressure can do to an individual. People with weak egos can experience serious psychological breakdown or become totally dependent on those group experiences.

Many of the sensitivity groups that have adopted T-group techniques have caused another very serious problem: They provide the illusion of warmth and intimacy to people who are deprived of these. They offer "instant" love but seldom provide the inner strength necessary to live through times of solitude or despair. They also allude that "just being open with one another" solves all problems. There is no question that openness in communication is a helpful human tool for learning, but in the reality of the world one must also be aware of times when such openness is inappropriate. One must be especially wary of "pretended" openness or that which is used mainly to hurt or to deceive. A helping person should believe in people but be a realist too. We must know that human beings can be loving, but they also may want to hurt others. We must not be overly suspicious, yet neither can we be naive and drive others into a world of illusion.

More important, it is one of the tasks of educators and social workers to help people to live in and cope with the real world with strength. Too often, group encounter or so-called "marathon" weekends serve as emotional drugs and become a flight from the hard reality of this world. I want to be understood: People who consciously choose a way of life in which weekend sensitivity groups are their recreation and marathons their personal outlets have a right to do this—just as others choose mountain climbing or visits to an art museum. But as a social work method, those approaches are neither individualized enough to be responsibly therapeutic nor do they enhance social consciousness, the two social work intents by which any social work method must be evaluated.

Another widespread group approach is based on the theory of *operant conditioning* or *behavior modification*. The theory underlying this is the assumption that the human being learns by success or nonsuccess; or, expressed differently, by reward and punishment. The teacher or social worker who uses operant conditioning is, by the nature of this approach, placed in a highly authoritarian position. This authority figure assumes that he or she knows what is best for the group members. The method is frequently manipulative—it uses reward and punishment to produce a certain kind of behavior, but *without the consent of the group members.*

In social work with people of normal intelligence, this method seems to be unacceptable, though in all of our work we use some forms of reward—we "support" a person, we give love, recognition, and so forth. Yet the principle of *informed consent* that grows out of our belief in human dignity does not allow us to manipulate people into what only *we* think is best for them. On the contrary, one of social work's, as well as education's, hardest jobs is to increase the capacity of people to think for themselves, to learn even to refuse rewards, for instance, if this contradicts their conviction, thinking, concerns. Where would social movements be if people only work for rewards? I know that the answer of the behavior modification theorists is that those people receive inner rewards. Possibly, yes, but where do those rewards come from if all through life comfort and discomfort and success and failure are the major incentives? In a democratic society people should get their motivation consciously and clearly from ethical values, not from fear of punishment or expectation of reward.

A second philosophically unacceptable part of behavior modification is the authoritarian position of the individual or group worker. Social group work asks of the group worker that he or she help others to become able to make their own decisions. This can only be accomplished by interacting with the group members in a process that lets them experience their own thoughts and feelings as well as the thinking and feelings of others.

Behavior modification points with pride to its success with mentally retarded people. It only proves that it is a good training method for people with impaired judgment, and then only if it is done gently and with more use of reward than punishment. Yet in the case of people who are able to use judgment, it defeats any development of long-range learning to make decisions. It defeats genuine "moral development."

Another group approach claimed as a panacea in work with delinquents is *guided group interaction.* It is based on the sound assumption that people can learn to help each other and that mutual help is more significant for each member than help by an outsider. This is and has always been a major premise of social group work. But guided group interaction or "positive peer culture" has unfortunately developed into a simplistic technique with specific gimmicks: Group workers, for instance, must separate themselves from groups by sitting behind desks, and all young people in delinquency institutions are required to join groups. Thus, a sound idea has been distorted because of its routine use.

*Reality therapy* is a counter movement to orthodox psychoanalysis or psychoanalytically influenced casework. It repeats what group work has brought into social work from its early beginnings, namely that help to people comes from looking at the here-and-now as well as at hope for the future. Yet social group work does not entirely reject the significance of the past and will allow a look at it when appropriate.

In reality therapy, the dogmatic singling out of *one* approach—that group members are not allowed to talk about the past—distorts an individualized and humane approach to helping people. Sometimes the past must surface and be dealt with. This does not mean that the past can serve as an excuse for present behaviors, nor that it suffices to dwell on the past. Looking at the past, however, may help to work through present problems and to prepare for the future.

Social group work is a flexible method, with respect for each human being as its pivotal point.

### *BIBLIOGRAPHY*

Basic readings for this chapter are the same as for Chapter 7 with the following additions:

KLEIN, ALAN, F.,  *Society, Democracy, and the Group.* New York: The Woman's Press, 1953.
KONOPKA, GISELA,  "Integrated Method Teaching in the Field," in *Our Commitment to Action* (three addresses for the School of Social Work on the occasion of Boston University's Charter Centennial), Boston University, 1969.

——————, "The Significance of Social Group Work Based on Ethical Values," *Social Work with Groups,* Vol. 1, No. 2 (Summer 1978). New York: The Haworth Press, pp. 123.

LEWIN, K., R. LIPPITT and R. K. WHITE, "Patterns of Aggressive Behavior in Experimentally Created 'Social Climates'," *Journal of Social Psychology,* 10 (1939), 271–299.

RUITENBEEK, H., *The New Group Therapies.* New York: Avon, 1970.

SHAFFER, J.B., and M. D. GALINSKY, *Models of Group Therapy and Sensitivity Training.* Englewood Cliffs, NJ: Prentice-Hall, 1974.

SKINNER, B. F., *Science and Human Behavior.* New York: The Free Press, 1953.

VORRATH, HARRY and L. BRENDTRO, *Positive Peer Culture.* Chicago: Aldine, 1974.

*We were pridefully serious about our jobs, but not about ourselves.*[1]

# NINE

# THE SOCIAL GROUP WORKER'S ROLE IN VARIOUS FIELDS OF PRACTICE

In the preceding chapters, we discussed the development of social group work, the movements from which it grew, the values it incorporates, and its growing identification with the profession of social work, which it, to some extent, helped to change, and by which it was changed. The review of specific cases enabled us to see group workers in action using their method and their integration of knowledge, values, and skill.

We will present now the "job," the work social group workers do in different fields. Fields of practice change because of changing needs in society—or so we would like to believe: This would be the ideal way of determining service. Yet human beings are fallible; they are not always

---

[1]Remark heard in a broadcast by Edward R. Murrow, who was speaking about the early days of broadcasting from overseas.

discerning enough to recognize needs; not always courageous enough to give up a traditional service that no longer has the importance it had in the past; not always strong enough to withstand forces that press them toward service in fields chosen by selfish interests; and sometimes they are gullible and follow fashionable fads. All this applies also to the social worker and to those fields in which group work serves. Self-knowledge and critical appraisal of one's work must apply to fields of practice and its agencies as much as to the individual practitioner. Yet agency planning is an unwieldy and complicated process because we deal with *institutions,* and one of their particular qualities is resistance to change. To remodel or create agency structures in the light of actual needs, an intelligent, informed community is necessary, along with the involvement of the professionals serving in them; of the lay boards in both private and public agencies; and of the constituency in membership organizations.

The field of "group work and recreation" is a traditional division of welfare councils all over the United States, and dates back to the early industrial revolution when group work and recreation were virtually one. The tenement districts were hiding pale children who never saw green trees or a ray of sunlight and who did not know the joy of play. Their mothers were working long days and weeks in the factories and were so tired when they returned home that they could not give much attention to their children. There was a desperate need for playgrounds and camps. Factory workers and household employees who were female were shamefully exploited. Group work was needed to help them gain confidence through meeting together and to help them stand up for their rights, including the demand for lesiure time and places where one could spend it with healthy satisfaction. Today the big cities still have slums and ghettos and a need for action to obtain additional recreational facilities. Yet, in general, the working day has been reduced, recreation is a service recognized by the public, and opportunities for it are within the reach of most of the population. Social group workers serve, and should serve, in the field of recreation where needs are still unfulfilled and where individualized group services are required, as with handicapped or upset children, or with special adult committees concerned with social action. But they do not belong only in this field. Their services are increasingly needed—and used—in other fields. In the lgiht of this need, is the traditional division of welfare councils between "Group Work and Recreation" and "Family and Children's Services" still tenable? Does it represent present needs? To this writer, this organization of private welfare services is an example of institutions' keeping alive forms that are no longer appropriate to the changing social scene.[2]

[2]On this subject see also Robert D. Vinter, "New Evidence for Restructuring Group Services," in *New Perspectives on Services to Groups: Theory, Organization, Practice* (New York: N.A.S.W., 1961).

The decade of the 1960s saw considerable changes in the whole education, welfare, and informal education field, which were related to the increasing assertion of groups that felt left out. The "Youth Revolution" also had an impact on community services. More than ever, group work's basic concepts of *participation in decision-making,* of *mutual help,* and of *informal, honest relationships* are entering wider fields. The exclusive identification of group work technique with social work has begun to wane in many countries. Education, especially, finds this method effective when the goal is educating the whole person. New community endeavors, still loosely conceived and not yet jelled into agencies, find the group work method congruent with their aims.

In the following pages a number of fields are presented in which social group work is either recognized, or is in the process of being recognized, as one of the methods by which agencies or organizations give competent service.

We will follow a given outline: We will (1) present the purpose of the given field; (2) enlarge on the needs it serves; (3) describe the functions of the social group worker in relation to purpose and needs; and (4) discuss any possible adaptation the group work method needs if practiced in this field.

## A. SETTLEMENTS AND NEIGHBORHOOD CENTERS

Originally, settlements and neighborhood centers existed to serve the social needs of persons in a given geographical and deprived neighborhood. The services were not differentiated. Neighborhood workers learned about the problems of the people they worked with by living with them, visiting them, and talking with them. They worked on whatever problems presented themselves. Thus, settlement houses can be credited with the beginning of a great variety of social services, which include well-baby clinics, school social work, recreational services, services to released mental patients, services to immigrant and minority racial groups, and nursery schools. Settlement or neighborhood houses have kept this flexibility. In 1958, the "Arden House Conference," designed to reassess the purposes of neighborhood centers, described them thus:

1. To serve as one of the few agencies in contemporary society that is not wholly formalized, bureaucratized, channelized . . . that offers a personal, face-to-face relationship in which a whole human being can be seen and talked to in something like his entire life situation.
2. To help give people roots, a sense of identification with a place, other people, existing agencies of their society, and, if they stay long enough, with the ongoing good and traditions and obligations of that society.

3. To experiment in using new knowledge and social techniques for dealing with human problems.
4. To provide decentralized services to people who need help in areas close to their homes.
5. To help promote cultural activities—"an active participant culture," countering pressures toward passivity in American life, helping to develop ways of using our increasing leisure for creative activities.
6. To provide important services in the planning and execution of programs for urban renewal.[3]

These goals are directly related to the present situation of an urban society characterized by its high mobility, mass living, and shorter working hours. The settlement houses accept these as realities and plan services to support the positives of the situation and to counteract the negatives. Such goals demand the skills of a variety of professionals. The social group worker is a major one. The practitioner's functions in a settlement house include the following:[4]

## 1. Direct Work with Groups of Children and Adults

Such groups have various purposes—increasing socialization, restoration, social action, or a combination of these. Purely recreational groups are today generally conducted by public recreation departments. Yet settlements provide such service in neighborhoods where it is not available or to groups that present special problems (e.g., mothers on ADC grants who require a short time away from their children, but who are unable to pay for baby-sitting services, need special child-care arrangements to be made; groups of mentally retarded adults or children who are unable to join other children on playgrounds). Many self-help groups have been established in communities based on a sense of responsibility for oneself and others. Such groups rarely need the constant participation of a social group worker, but group workers serve as a resource to such groups.

Since enhancement of respect for any person is one of the basic goals of the settlement house movement, practitioners work with groups of discriminated minorities (racial, nationality, religious), helping them to become more self-confident and enabling them and the majority group to experience working, talking, and living together. Group workers in settlement houses may work with homogeneous groups of Blacks or Cauca-

[3]See National Federation of Settlements, *Neighborhood Goals in a Rapidly Changing World*, A Report of the Action-Research Workshop held at Arden House, Harriman, N.Y., 1958.

[4]It should be understood that the functions described need not be carried out by one person alone. They indicate the role of the group worker, but the different functions can be divided among several people.

sians, Indians or Mexicans, or Puerto Ricans or Swedes, always with the aim of helping them to become an integral and respected part of the community. The idea is "unity through diversity," of pluralism in its best sense. Such groups are made up of children, adolescents, or adults. The program may vary from play to learning a new language or to finding out about job opportunities; from teen-agers' discussion of social customs and how to come to terms with or change them to adults' trying to find new ways of action to make their demands be heard in this complicated and often discouraging society.

Group workers usually aim toward establishment of integrated groups consisting of different races, creeds, and nationalities. Yet in the 1960s and 70s in the United States, some emphasis needed to be placed on homogeneous ethnic groups to develop their own pride and strength. This does not exclude nonsegregation as a goal as part of a truly nonracist society. The art of working toward such a society deserves a total book by itself. Settlement houses, the Urban Leagues,[5] and some Y's have been in the forefront of this work among social agencies.

Other adult groups may wish to get together and ask for consultative assistance from the group worker to help with social action in regard to specific needs of the neighborhood—housing, poor public transportation service, and so forth. Such action groups may also be initiated by the staff of the neighborhood house if the staff recognizes needs that may not yet be recognized by the neighborhood residents; for example, providing training for youngsters who drop out of scbool. It is then the group worker's task to find neighborhood leadership and to work with it so that action includes the active involvement of citizens. Indigenous leadership begins to emerge increasingly all over the world. This diminishes the need to recruit such leadership, but often such leaders want help with fulfilling effectively their new function.

Groups also may be sought out by the group worker for service even if they are not asking for it and do not welcome it. This situation is exemplified in work with young gangs and sometimes is called *street corner work* or *floating group work*. The service in this case grows out of a demand of society, not of the members themselves. They usually have become or threaten to become a serious danger to other people. Bond in these groups usually is strong because the group presents to the individuals in it the only security available and gives them a feeling of status that they cannot, or think they cannot, gain in school or neighborhood. The group as a whole provides for pleasure, for adventure, and for successfully carried out unlawful activities, which the individual alone cannot accomplish. The goal of the neighborhood worker who goes out to work with these groups is to help

---

[5]Group workers are needed in and employed by the Urban Leagues in a combination of group work and community organization capacity.

them find satisfaction in lawful, nondestructive activities and to help establish or re-establish new confidence in adult society. In addition to this, there may emerge specific goals and tangible help in relation to each member's particular needs, such as returning to school, help in finding a job, help in moving away from home if necessary, or talking with the parents to help the individual be better accepted by them. Work with gangs is probably one of the most difficult and most highly skilled forms of social group work. In this situation, there are no "props" used, no office to meet in, and no room with tools for activities. The group worker has no power over the group: He or she cannot form it, cannot choose the right combination of members, and cannot eliminate any member he or she considers too difficult or impossible to work with. The group members are not motivated to want to have a group worker with them, nor do they want any service from any kind of agency. The pratitioner usually meets indifference and hostility because of representing a society that the gang members hate. All the group worker has is the support of the settlement house of the neighborhood organization in charge of assignments, and his or her own conviction and skill.

Besides direct work with such a variety of groups, the social group worker in the nieghborhood house, and in many other fields, takes on the responsibility of teaching others to do direct group work. Another function, then, is:

## 2. Supervision of Volunteers and of Part-time Staff to Help Them with Their Group Work

Not all groups need the services of a professional group worker. Settlement houses have groups with a purely recreational purpose if public recreation agencies do not provide service in the neighborhood. Such groups can well be conducted by lay volunteers if they do not include individuals with serious problems or if their cultural composition is not too foreign to that of the volunteer. The service of the volunteer in neighborhood houses has a great value in itself since it contributes to the active involvement of the local neighborhood as well as the wider community. Work with volunteers or part-time staff, therefore, is more than a matter of overcoming a shortage of trained personnel: It requires teaching, counsulting, and group work skill with a close view toward community organization.

## 3. Neighborhood Work

This brings the group workers in contact with the basic problems and needs of a neighborhood and usually beyond its limits. It demands that they become active in behalf of such needs. Social action—participation in the collection of facts for new or changed legislation—is part of their responsibility.

Every group worker's job responsibility in each field includes more than direct work with groups alone. The settlement or neighborhood field, because of its undifferentiated function and because of the fact that the social group worker is the major professional on its staff, allows for an especially high degree of variety and flexibility of the group worker's function. A sample of a job description is presented to illustrate this (names of location, etc., have been changed):

> This position requires a social group work trained person who is able and interested in doing a varied Settlement job. It will provide opportunity for creative development of new services as well as the organization and refinement of existing services. Some of the possible assignments will be as follows:
>
> 1.   School Referral Groups—group service to children and young people in the school setting, individuals with special problems and needs around relationships and school achievement.
> 2.   West Neighborhood Services—working with a staff team and with other agencies to give neighborhood and family services in an isolated and deprived city area.
> 3.   Group Leadership in Camp Setting—utilizing Neighborhood Camp for giving special service to selected groups, referral groups, family camp, etc.
> 4.   Recruitment and supervision of leadership for leisure-time services (primarily elementary school age girls).
> 5.   Development of group services for teen-age mothers.

This same agency lists additional functions of other group work positions on its staff:

> Work with groups of mentally retarded adults.
> Services to the aging (groups; visiting).
> Services to mother's groups.
> Teen-age leadership training.
> Consultant to neighborhood youth services committees, several neighborhood planning councils, and citizen action groups.

The informal component of social group work allows for creation of new and necessary services if the administrative structure supports such creativity and does not stifle it by traditional bureaucracy. An account of such approaches was presented by group work practitioner Antonia Pantoja when she described the group worker's role in intergroup relations:

> I have chosen three examples from activities typical of the work of the New York City Commission on Intergroup Relations. They will help to prove my point that group work is the profession which can bring to such situations the

best skills and knowledge and the commitment that is necessary to function successfully and adequately in these and in similar situations.

1. *Community tension in relation to school integration.* We are all familiar with the *de facto* segregation of a large number of the public schools in New York City. As part of one of the methods used to desegregate the school system during the early summer of 1959, the Board of Education decided to transfer about 365 Negro and Puerto Rican children from schools in the Bedford-Stuyvesant neighborhood into Queens. The Queens communities have an all-white population of homeowners of long residence in the area. Although the Board of Education did not announce this move as an integration measure, the parents in Glendale and Ridgewood realized that integration was the real reason for the shift, rather than an effort to utilize better school facilities.

This situation brought about a series of disturbances carried on by Queens parents who tried to oppose the transfer of the Brooklyn children into their schools. The group which took the matter into their hands was the Glendale Taxpayers Association, composed of many local Parent-Teacher Association members and officers. Disorderly elements from the organized bigoted groups came to the area to aggravate the tension. During the summer months a job had to be done to check the negative activities, to mobilize the forces of good will, and to insure that when the children entered the schools in September, no violence would occur.

The group workers who were involved in this crisis functioned in several different roles:

a.  As professionals representing an official city agency, they attended meetings of the opposing group to help tone down actions so that the group would act only within the law.

b.  As technicians and educators, they assembled the facts, reached groups within and outside the community, and helped them to disseminate these facts to check the rumors being spread by others.

c.  As enablers, liaisons, and mediators, they called a series of meetings with the clergy in the area, with heads of organizations, with the main intergroup relations agencies of the city, with the community leaders in Bedford-Stuyvesant and in Glendale-Ridgewood. At these meetings the different groups and agencies were helped to devise programs of action.

d.  As liaison between the community and the Board of Education, they planned and conducted meetings between the parents and the principals, teachers, and officials of the Board of Education.

e.  As program experts and planners, they prepared a network of services covering the first few weeks of school, in order to prevent any violence to the children, to allay the fears of the parents who were sending their children to the Queens schools, and to help foresee any problems that would be created in the schools by this situation. These programs were all performed by volunteers, community groups, and churches.

2. *ASPIRA: the creation of a new agency.* One of the most important tasks in bringing about sound intergroup relations is that of helping the minority to develop its own resources, its own leadership. The measure of the success attained by minority groups in achieving their due place in society is directly related to the quality of their leadership. The Commission on Intergroup Relations has various programs directed to this need.

ASPIRA, a project designed to develop new leadership in the Puerto Rican community of New York through the creation of a new agency, provides my second example of the efficacy of the group worker in intergroup relations.

A group worker originated the ideas of ASPIRA. The worker offered a new concept: the training of leadership in disadvantaged or minority groups must include the motivation and guidance of those members of the groups who possess the ability and talents to enter professional, technical, and artistic fields. This is necessary in order to create a pool of persons who can function on a par with the rest of the population, give leadership to their group, and place it on an equal basis with the organizations and leadership of the majority groups.

As an organizer, the worker has brought together a board of directors to administer the project. The worker has also played the role of technical advisor to the chairman of the board and other officers to secure from foundations the funds necessary to sustain and fully develop the project. (ASPIRA has received two grants from two foundations.)

When it opens its doors for service ASPIRA will be a private agency, staffed primarily by Puerto Rican professionals, with a Puerto Rican board of directors. It will represent a self-help effort. It will be in itself a symbol of its own purposes.

3.  *The neightborhood clinic.* My last example is that of a service offered by the Community Relations Division of the Commission on Intergroup Relations.

The neighbrohood clinic offers consultative services and guidance to groups from neighborhoods that are having intergroup problems. In cases where the group does not have the appropriate structure to work with the problems faced, the worker can help them to organize an intergroup relations committee. The worker will enable the group to identify and diagnose the problems that beset their area and will help them to secure the necessary facts and materials, including a survey of existing resources that they could use.

The worker helps the group to devise a practicable plan or action to solve or alleviate their problems. As an expert, he brings in program aids and makes referrals to other agencies. Using the prestige of his agency, the worker helps the citizens' group take their problems to the proper city agencies and officials.

These are not the only programs which the Commission offers, but they indicate the kinds of problems with which people need help if they are to find answers and solutions.

When the relationship among groups breaks down, the Commission staff find themselves propelled into dealing with tension and violence in local neighborhoods. We also enagage, at the top levels of governmental and private agencies, in negotiations that will change, create, or modify policies and administrative decisions that affect minorities. We train minority leadership in the fields that govern their fate and progress, and we train "majority" leadership in techniques and programs that will help their own groups learn how to live with people who are different. We work with neighborhood organizations to help integrate newcomers into homogeneous neighborhoods, to prevent changing neighborhoods from becoming ghettos, to involve the minority leadership in the decision-making structures, and to handle local incidents of prejudice and bigotry.[6]

The preceding example presents a partial model of the group worker's function in *community development*. The major skills in this field are the

[6]Antonia Pantoja, "The Social Worker in Intergroup Relations," *Community Organization 1961* (New York: Columbia University Press, copyright by National Conference on Social Welfare, 1961), pp. 126–131.

capacity to discover and to help develop indigenous leadership and the ability to work with conflicts in groups.

## B. YOUTH SERVICES

This field is difficult to discuss as a unit because it involves a wide variety of clientele and is under different auspices—public and private, sectarian and nonsectarian. Some of the services are mostly building-centered: the Jewish Centers, the different Y's, the Boys' Clubs and the various church- or synagogue-sponsored youth organizations. Others provide a wide net of group services in different meeting places: the Scouts, Camp Fire Girls, 4-H Clubs, and so forth. Most youth services are movements that subscribe to a common purpose or philosophy. Members frequently carry several roles: They are part of the policy-making body; they give direct service as volunteers or paid staff; and they are members receiving a service. Group participation is usually voluntary. The designation of "youth services" is not quite accurate since membership consists also of adults who participate actively in these agencies or organizations.

In a democratic society the youth services are one of the major ways the society helps its youth perpetuate a democratic way of life—not just a political form—and are also a means by which adults carry out their responsibilities toward the younger generation outside the one given to them as individual parents or as teachers and professional youth workers. The goals of youth organizations are to increase the mental health of their membership, youth and adults alike; to help them assume responsibility for the welfare of others; to enable them to participate intelligently in the life of their community; and to improve creatively the total culture of a given society. Services are predominantly group services. These agencies were the first ones, together with the settlements, to develop social group work. Group work as the core of their work appeared in numerous statements, of which the following is a representative sample:

> Members take part in developing the life of the Association through the democratic process of shared responsibility and cooperative effort. Through group experience, opportunities are provided for individuals to grow and become responsible leaders and citizens.[7]

In spite of the traditional close association between youth-serving agencies and social group work in the past, this association had become problematic during the 1950s and 1960s. There were two major reasons for this:

[7]"Deep Roots and World Reach," *Work Book 21st National Convention YWCA of the U.S.A.,* St. Louis, 1958 (New York: YWCA National Board), p. 126.

1. Certain youth-serving agencies have taken on exclusively a recreational function, and therefore see little need for the services of social group workers.
2. Social group work, by virtue of its increasing identification with the profession of social work, has limited its own sphere of action in some instances to the restorative services and has neglected those other services represented by the youth-serving agencies.

There are signs, however, that these two impediments to integration of group work in youth services are being removed to the benefit of adults and youngsters who participate in them.

Youth agencies widen their work to include qualitative services for *all* people so as to include those who are capable leaders as well as those who have special problems and those who deviate for one reason or another from the average youngster who can make his way into the community without special help. In 1961, Luada Boswell presented a paper at the National Conference reporting on two Girl Scout projects that had as their purpose:

> To broaden the reach of Girl Scouting to include a better cross-section of the community. Specifically, we proposed to carry it out by organizing troops for the daughters of migrant workers and the urban hard-to-reach, at places convenient for them to meet, with leadership indigenous to their neighborhoods.[8]

Y's work with groups of hard-to-reach young people, provide group work services for released mental patients, etc. Today Y's and other youth agencies are increasing their work with young people in the inner cities, with youth action groups and with self-help youth groups related to the drug scene.

The Center for Youth Development and Research at the University of Minnesota, started in 1976 the National Youthworker Education Project. One of its purposes was to bring together personnel from a range of youth-serving organizations, including the field of corrections, to increase understanding and cooperation across organizational lines. It was significant for youth workers to learn that whether they worked with so-called "normal" youth or with those in conflict with society, they needed the same understanding of people.

Group workers in youth-serving agencies rarely work directly with youth groups, since one of the purposes of the agencies is the involvement of adult volunteers. They do work with groups, but they usually are not *youth* workers. They work with *adult* groups for the purpose of helping them to lead youth groups intelligently and with regard to group work

---

[8]Luada Boswell, "A Report on Two Girl Scout Pilot Projects: Migrant Agricultural Workers and Urban Hard-to-Reach Groups," *New Perspectives on Services to Groups: Theory, Organization, Practice; Social Work with Groups, 1961* (New York: N.A.S.W., 1961), p. 81.

principles. They also help adults to learn about community problems, to accept differences in the population, to help with the integration of various groups, and to meet intelligently pressures of public opinion that may have direct bearing on youth as, for example, the wave of accusations against teen-agers.

The social group worker's functions in these agencies usually include:

1.  Group work with adult committees.
2.  Supervision of individual group leaders.
3.  Teaching in-service training courses.
4.  Occasional group work with specialized youth or children's groups.
5.  Consultant for or participant in community committees concerned with youth services.
6.  Ongoing research into the needs and concerns of young people in a given community.

The social group worker's role in the youth services or youth groups that emerged in the 1960s is somewhat different. He or she also works directly with groups who want someeone with expertise to help (1) with interpersonal problems; (2) with community action projects; and (3) with conflict-solving in several areas.

## C. CHILD WELFARE SERVICES

The field of child welfare is a widespread one with many branches. "It encompasses services provided directly to children and is also concerned with the preservation and strengthening of family life and the bringing about of the kind of community life which makes for wholesome child development."[9]

The role of the group worker must be described separately in the different branches of this field:

### 1. Aid to Children in Their Own Homes

This covers a wide field of child welfare services. Originally these were seen exclusively as the domain of the caseworker. Yet the recognition of group needs of children—especailly of adolescents—as well as adults, has opened the way for the use of groups in those services. Action groups of mothers on Aid to Dependent Children grew out of meetings with social group work services originally provided by social agencies. One can trace

---

[9]Maurice O. Hunt, "Child Welfare," in Russell H. Kurtz, ed., *Social Work Year Book, 1960,* (New York: N.A.S.W., 1960), p. 141.

the origin of this movement to some groups started in Denver, Colorado, by a social group worker, Ethel Lunde, who worked in the public school system, but saw a need for mothers of dependent children to meet, to discuss their plight, and to gain strength through such group discussions and through the action that followed. Meanwhile most of these groups act autonomously without agency sponsorship.

Other groups of adults serve to gain insight into the parents' own problems or the behavior of their children and move toward a bond that allows them to feel more secure and protected. The latter is something that many of these mothers need desperately.

In one such group, a mother, for instance, described how she did not ever dare to go out without her children, not even to a store. Once she had left them alone for a very short time and one of the girls had cut her finger. She was desperately concerned with the well-being of her children. In addition, she feared that "the welfare" would take the children from her if there was any suspicion that she was being neglectful. There was no one who would support her in this difficult task of rearing children. This young woman became more and more disturbed and almost a recluse. The group not only gave her a place where she could talk about her concerns, but also conveyed to her compassion and gave her relief from her guilt about being selfish because she, a young woman, wanted not to be tied down all the time. The group members also gave tangible help by forming a mutual baby-sitting pool, thus freeing mothers for a few hours each day. The group worker's role was first to establish a free and comfortable atmosphere in the group and to help members to accept themselves, their feelings and those of others. At a later stage the group worker introduced the question of community action: Could they, with their knowledge of the situation of single parents, testify to the need for nursery schools? They wanted to do this. With this project started a new life for the women. They experienced a real involvement in community life and established relationships with people they never would have met otherwise. There was increased self-confidence and a sense of satisfaction.

Group work services are used with adolescents in foster homes who feel a bond because of their particular situation and their age group. These groups are mostly "talking groups," with the group worker's role that of listener and helper, bringing problems out into the open. The group worker also assesses together with the young people the group needs of individual members and helps them to move into other group constellations in the community. Similar services are provided with younger children in foster homes or in adoptive homes who have shown particular problems in relation to their situation.

With the practice of letting adopted children know about their heritage and the many people now seeking their biological parents, postadoption services have become necessary. Those are frequently conducted in groups to increase understanding and to help with feelings of anxiety.

## 2. Care of Children Away from Home

This care is given in two forms: foster care in families and care in children's institutions. A new form, group boarding homes, is emerging.

The major contribution of the group worker lies in the institutional area or in the group boarding home. Institutional care is the oldest service given to children.

Social workers made a great contribution to child welfare in stressing the need for foster care for any child who is capable of living in a family. Unfortunately they neglected institutions completely for a long period, and did not help to improve their services. This has changed, though not yet sufficiently. Institutions are often still used only as a "last resort." They are looked upon as poor replicas of family living, which sometimes have a few clinical services attached to them.

Children in institutions need a group life that allows for balance between activities and, as Fritz Redl once called it, "constructive loafing," and between group living and privacy. They need all the services given to children in their own homes and some additional ones related to their anxieties, loneliness, and planning for life outside the institutional services. The quality of group living is therefore as vital as the clinical, educational, and other specialized services attached to the institution.

The persons who have most contact with the children, who take care of them during most of the twenty-four hours of the day, are the child-care workers (sometimes called houseparents); they are no longer considered custodial personnel. They are group workers with a strong additional function of "parenting." They work with children who have been hurt, who are anxious and defiant; they must be understanding in order to be helpful to them.

In addition to the child-care workers, the institutional team consists usually of the caseworker, who maintains the continuity between the child's home, the institution, and the return to the community and who helps the child individually with specific problems; the teachers, who are responsible for individual or group schooling, dependent upon the child's capacity; other clinical workers—such as psychologists or psychiatrists—as necessary; and the social group worker. Some larger institutions employ special service personnel such as recreation workers and art teachers. The functions of the social group worker on the institutional team are twofold: to help with the group living situation and to conduct clinical groups. The tasks include:

1.  Direct group work with formed groups of children inside the institution—through both house councils and therapeutic groups.
2.  Work with parent groups, where possible.
3.  Supervision of child-care workers.
4.  Supervision of volunteers who work with groups of children placed in the institution.

5. Responsibility for referral to resources for group association in the community, when the child is in the institution as well as when planning for his or her release.
6. Responsible participation in diagnosis of individuals and in decisions regarding placement in the institution, grouping of children, treatment plans, and plans for after-care.
7. Responsibility for better public understanding of the new concept of institutional care, of needed improvement in the totality of its services.

Here the term "institution" means any group living situation that is different from a family context. This includes group homes.

### 3. Services to Unmarried Mothers

Those have changed greatly in the United States since the 1960s. Sexual activity is no longer considered a sin to be hidden. After interviewing thousands of teen-agers who do not consider unmarried motherhood a crime or a horrible shame, but who look at sexual relations as something that should include affection among partners, this author concluded that there is not rampant promiscuity in our society.[10] Most services to unmarried mothers are now given in the community. I myself consider it most important to regard children as children and mothers as mothers— regardless of the situation in which a child is conceived. Sexual relations should be discussed as *human* relations based on mutual respect of partners and any possible future life created. I find it regrettable that most services are limited to young women instead of to both sexes. It is very important that men and women *together* discuss their emotional and physical well-being as well as their mutual responsibilities. Group discussions of this kind are most important.

Since more unmarried mothers keep their children than ever before, it is also important to discuss child rearing as human relations and look toward the *growing* child. Too many preparations of young mothers concern themselves almost exclusively with infant care, thus leaving the women frequently helpless and angry when the infant grows into an independent child.

### D. FAMILY SERVICES

The concept of the family as an institution that regulates the responsibility for offspring is a universal phenomenon, but it changes in time and place. The 1970s and '80s have seen a change within the North American culture mostly due to a new perception of each family member—as significant

---

[10](See Konopka, Gisela, *Young Girls: A Portrait of Adolescence* (Englewood Cliffs, NJ: Prentice-Hall, 1976.)

members of their unit with equal rights and responsibilities. As always, transition in human institutions is somewhat confused and painful. There is great danger for any professional to accept unquestioningly generalized indictments of change. Public media speak about the breakdown of the family and compare this era with the "good old times." Any student of history knows that those "good old times" were, indeed, not so good and that hypocrisy, especially in family relations, was rampant. It behooves the family worker to accept changes in family structure, to not consider all of them as pathological, and then to give help with specific problems the family group encounters. Problems lie mostly in the economic and socioemotional areas. Both public and private agencies offer services to families. For a long period, private agencies took responsibility for social service help with marital relations problems, the rearing of children, or other crisis situations—such as sickness, death, desertion—that threatened the family, while public agencies provided for economic assistance. This separation between the functions of public and private agencies is disappearing. Public agencies accept more and more service functions in addition to those of financial help. Financial support will be increasingly separated from any additional service a family wants. But the distinction will not be between "public" and "private."

Basic family problems in a given society do not change greatly, but certain aspects of these problems are stronger at any given time. At present, there is an increased need to help single-parent families, whether they are due to divorce, the death of a spouse or no marriage having been contracted. Whatever the reason, there is pain, though not always pathology. There is also the awesome task of child rearing that is not shared with another person; this lack of sharing is a major concern. Groups are therefore most important because they allow for exchange with people who are "in the same boat."

A longer life span in our times is of special significance to family life. Again, as with all changes in human society, it brings with it advantages and problems. It frequently allows the younger generation to rely more heavily and for a comparatively longer time span on the protection or support of parents who can afford this; but it may also place a burden on grown children to support parents who may live for many years with diminished physical or mental capacities.

The changing form of the family, with less emphasis on the ruling power of the father, may make for happiness and security through a feeling of mutual appreciation and support, but it may also bring about serious problems of confusion and conflict. Open expression of changing values in regard to sex, drugs, success orientation, and so forth, often cause problems in communication within the family.

Most literature on adolescence discusses the period in a person's life as though the growing child lives in isolation. It is important to realize the specific relationship of the adolescent to parents who, especially in a family in which child bearing was deferred for a number of years, are in the late phase of maturity: An age of enormous physical and psychic energy hits against an age of diminishing energies. Also, the doubts and insecurities of adolescents have their parallel in an adult stage fraught with new questions about life and one's own place in the universe. All this need not present serious problems when those relationships are understood. Yet problems do arise when the family members are unprepared to deal with their differences and therefore blame one another. Again, group associations with people who live through similar problems relieve the situation and enhance family living.

Poverty has always produced many problems for a family. It means additional hardship in an abundant society because the contrast between "have" and "have-not" is so great and one lives in such close proximity to goods and opportunities that are unreachable. The answer the individual may choose can be constructive group action to improve one's situation and that of others, but it can also be delinquency or withdrawal expressed in many different forms.

Such are some of the problems with which family agencies must concern themselves. Traditionally, family services are rendered through the use of social casework. Yet, in most instances group work has become an important part of these services. Use of group work has come about through:

1.  The concept of the family as a group. This includes a new diagnostic understanding of family problems as problems partially caused by the group process in the family and also a realization that treatment of interpersonal problems is sometimes more effective when working with the family as a group than when working individually with each member.
2.  The general recognition that some people gain more through interaction in a group.
3.  The recognition that certain social work activities with an educational emphasis are more economically carried on through groups.

Family agencies work today with the following kinds of groups:

1.  The total family group.
2.  Groups consisting of couples, whose focus is on general family life education.
3.  Groups consisting mostly of single parents who work on problems of child rearing.
4.  Groups of present or prospective foster or adoptive parents, who discuss agency requirements and procedures as well as the problems encountered in being a foster or adoptive parent.
5.  Groups of children and adolescents who work through a variety of problems that these youngsters face at home, in school, or with their peers.

With the increasing use of groups in family services, social group workers are employed in such agencies. Their functions are:

1.  Direct group work with the variety of groups named previously.
2.  Training of other staff members in the use of the group work method.
3.  Consultation to the agency in relation to community resources offering socialization services for children or adults.
4.  Work on community action as it relates to the problems encountered by the agency. This may include leadership or participation in committees established by the family service agency or by other community organizations.

Group work method needs some adaptation when it is used in the family interview. The role of the group worker in this particular group usually must be a less active one than in almost any other group he or she conducts. The helper must avoid appearing as an arbiter in family conflicts; each family member then may tend to call upon the social worker as a judge and an ally. Conflicts in the family group are especially fraught with emotion. It takes a special skill to give each member present the feeling that the group worker is a warm listener concerned with every one of them and yet also with the total unit.

A word must be said about the use of co-therapists in family group work as well as in other settings. This has become a routine practice without enough consideration of group dynamics. Those knowledgeable about group process know the difficulty of shared leadership for both those in the helping position and for the members. There has been a myth that female and male co-therapists provide a helpful simulation of family. This is not the case, as members are perfectly aware of the fact that this is not a family. Co-therapy is useful only for educating group workers (with the group advised that one of the two therapists is in training) or for research (again, with the group members informed of this). Otherwise the responsibility of a single group worker is the most desirable in any group work situation.

## E. SERVICES TO THE AGING

In 1971 the *Encyclopedia of Social Work* stated under *Group Services:*

> These have been offered to older people both in institutional settings and in the community (e.g., in churches, settlement houses, community centers). There is an increasing number of senior centers specifically geared to the elderly. Programs include recreational, occupational, and educational activities and groups formed on counseling and therapy. In general, group services to community dwellers are accessible to those who are relatively intact mentally, physically, and functionally. There is a need for the development of group services for the impaired that include transportation and medical and nursing supervision.[11]

[11]*Encyclopedia of Social Work* (New York: N.A.S.W., 1971) p. 68.

In our society, youth has been stressed as the most desirable period of human life. Youth has been equated with being attractive, being productive, being able to learn, and therefore being an asset in a society that must constantly live for the future. Old age, then, was considered the reverse of all these desirable qualities. This general attitude of society toward the aged was—and possibly still is—frequently intensified by the shrinking personal income of the aged and by their possible loss of physical or mental capacity. As parents, they usually have fulfilled their task of child rearing and feel a loss of importance as heads of families. They have lost friends through death. The older person often feels alone, unwanted, and an outcast of the community. This realization has changed social services.

Social group workers serve as consultants in the establishment and improvement of services for the aged as well as in social programs, frequently in self-help support groups, and in institutions for the aged. The activities of these clubs have moved from being purely recreational to adding aspects of education and serving particular psychosocial needs of their participants. Jean Maxwell lists the special dimension of need for group participation in older people:

1.  Changed physical and psychological capacities require understanding and acceptance of these changes, necessitating substitutions and reorganizations of behavior. Peers who have lived or are living through such changes give a support and understanding most helpful to individuals.

2.  Groups offer the opportunity to renew old friendships and develop new ones to replace the losses from death of old friends.

3.  Community groups and organization memberships increase in importance as a means of providing identity for older people. A person's identity is closely tied to his group affiliations. The question "Who is he?" is directed to family, occupation or profession, company or organization worked for, organization represented. With the growth of larger urban and suburban areas and more moving from place to place, family names are less easily recognized and carry less identity value for the individual than in earlier days. With retirement, identity through the employing agent, occupation, or profession decreases or is lost. There are few doors open to "Joe Smith, retired." Group identification promotes a sense of self-worth and worth in the eyes of others.

4.  Groups are the means by which an older person belongs to something larger than himself or his family. They serve as a channel through which the individual can act in unison with others to express a point of view, accomplish tasks, enjoy experiences possible only through groups, and make his voice heard in the community and the world—feel useful, alive.

5.  Status and recognition are elements achieved by the individual within a group, or through a group in the broader community. In our society self-esteem is so closely related to the job one does and the money one earns from it that retirement can easily mean a loss in self-esteem. To be valued by a group for what one contributes to its success, to be rewarded by members' respect for what one is like as a person, to be praised for what one can make, all rebuild self-esteem.

6.  Every group requires its members to meet a set of specific expectations.

These may concern ways of behaving, dress and grooming, manners, beliefs, type and quality of activity and so forth. We have seen that older people are often left completely on their own as to what they shall make of their retired or older years. Group membership helps to undergird and broaden, focus and define, these expectations.

Thus we see that group participation represents far more than filling in time or having fun. . . .[12]

The functions of the social group worker in community agencies giving service to the aged are:

1. Working out a program of different kinds of groups related to the highly varied needs that this age group presents, from relatively self-directing persons to those who need much support. The common designation of being "aged" does not really present common characteristics. Groups must be, therefore, specifically formed and consideration must be given to their different constellations as well as to diversified programs. This function is partially an administrative one.
2. Direct work with certain groups of the aged, especially those who present problems in relationships.
3. As in all group work, some contact with individuals outside of the group, but more intensively in this particular age group. Home visits are indicated.
4. Supervision of volunteers or part-time workers in programs for the aged.
5. Consultant to committees of older citizens in relation to social action in their own behalf, if requested to do so.

Many of the problems of the aged are intensified when they enter an institution. As all institutionalized people, they feel that they are removed from the normal community life, which centers around the family. They frequently are also those who have some impairment of their capacities. Self-respect is especially threatened.

It is important that they feel that they are truly "senior citizens" in a community which accepts them as capable human beings. The social group worker's contribution to the institutionalized aged is to enhance this possibility by offering opportunities for making such contributions and to relate the older person more satisfactorily to the group which has taken on the vital replacement of the family.[13]

In the institution for the aged, the functions of the social group worker are:

1. Direct work with formed groups for the purpose of specific help to those who cannot easily enter the group life of the institution.

[12]Jean M. Maxwell, "Group Services—Well-being for Older People," in Kurtz, ed., *Social Work Year Book, 1960,* pp. 83–84.

[13]Gisela Konopka, *Group Work in the Institution* (New York: Association Press, 1954), p. 285.

2.  Responsibility for the stimulation of a rich and varied program in the institution designed to allow for satisfaction of individual needs, as described by Jean Maxwell, and to counteract the feeling of segregation from the community, which may appear in an institution. This may be done by either being a consultant to the staff of one particular institution or by serving several smaller institutions at the same time.

In the community service for the aged, as well as in the institutional service, an additional function is to help with the change of community climate toward old age. From direct knowledge of aged people in social interaction grows a wealth of information in regard to their needs, which must be transmitted to the community. In informal contacts, people speak freely about their concerns even if they otherwise may be too proud to ask for help. While playing cards, the members of a group may talk freely of their worries about medical care, the impossibility of getting housing that they can afford, their yearning for contact with younger people and the wish to do something for them, or difficulties in finding a decent nursing home for a member of a discriminated-against minority. All this calls for action in relation to medical care for the aged, housing developments, foster grandparent plans,[14] and action to fight discrimination.

The social group work method needs no particular adaptation to this field. It must be pointed out, though, that practitioners involved with the aged must work consciously through their own emotional responses to this group. They have been reared in an environment where the prevailing culture places little value on older people, and group workers are part of this culture. This may influence them. They also work with people in a period in human life that they themselves have not yet experienced. When working with senior citizens helpers must learn to project themselves into an age group that is still before them but which they usually do not happily anticipate. Self-knowledge and insight are necessary to overcome this.

## F. MEDICAL AND PSYCHIATRIC SERVICES

The fields discussed up to this point are indigenous to social work, although all of them also require the services of other professions. There are a number of fields, however, where social work has taken a prominent part in the given service, but whose major function lies within the scope of other

---

[14]There are many children who have never known grandparents and who would enjoy and profit by the kind of relationship grandparents offer to a child. On the other hand, there are those older people who yearn for contact with children, but who have no grandchildren of their own. The foster grandparent plan brings the two together.

professions. Such fields are called in the literature "host settings" for social work. The four fields presented in the following pages—medical social work, psychiatric social work, corrections, and school social work—will fall into this category. One of the oldest ones in which social work has been practiced is the health field; it has led to two specializations: medical social work and psychiatric social work. Both represent general social work practice adapted to those particular settings.

> During the past twenty years mental health professionals have shifted their concerns from the individual (typified by psychoanalysis) to the group (typified by group therapy and family therapy) to the community (typified by community health centers). This is not to say that the individual has been abandoned....[15]

And there are new insights:

> The public health model does not work too well with mental health because cause and effect are a myth. Yet there are factors that show a relationship between certain environmental (human and otherwise) influences and a person's reaction to them. And we must be aware of the infinite variety among people.[16]

Sick people need more than direct medical services. A physically ill patient in a hospital, for example, may be concerned with mounting bills, with holding his job, or with the emotional well-being of his family. Youngsters worry about school and the classes and social contacts they miss. They wonder whether they have done something wrong for which they have been removed from the family. An epileptic in the community suffers still under an old stigma and frequently does not dare to make social contacts, even though her seizures may be controlled by medication. The handicapped child in a camp may receive physical therapy, but may feel so hopelessly inadequate and "ugly" that the effort to improve is made only halfheartedly, or he may try to control everybody by tantrums because of the nagging fear of being unattractive. Relatives of a long-term sick person need practical help with arrangements for care of the patient. They also need help with their feelings about the person's illness. A physician may recommend and insist upon institutionalization of a woman because of increasing physical deterioration caused by a serious sickness; someone is needed to help her husband with his anguish. Is he institutionalizing her too soon? Or maybe not soon enough? The parents of a child with a cardiac

---

[15]Philip M. Margoli, M. D., and Armando R. Favazza, M. D., "Mental Health and Illness," *Encyclopedia of Social Work* (New York: N.A.S.W., 1971), p. 782.

[16]Gisela Konopka, "Social Change, Social Action as Prevention," Justin M. Joffe and George W. Albee, eds., *Prevention through Political Action and Social Change,* (University Press of New England, Hanover and London, 1981), p. 229.

disease may be told about the disease in detail, but what meaning does it have to them? Do they blame themselves? So much of what they will do depends on how they relate to the sickness and to the child.

Mental and emotional illness present even more problems of this kind. Aside from the stigma still attached to them, they involve so much more of the total personality than most forms of physical illness.

Both medical and psychiatric social work were originally conceived of as casework services, mostly with relatives of the patients. Social group work was introduced later (see Chapter 1). Group workers usually work directly with patients. This has at times retarded group work's identification with social services. A milestone in the development of clinical group work was the Waveland Conference of 1955, a conference conducted by what was then known as the American Association of Group Workers and made possible by a grant of the National Institute of Mental Health. It was directed toward group work in the psychiatric setting, but had implications for the total helath field. One of the observers at this conference, Joseph W. Eaton,[17] summarized the general contributions of the social group worker to psychiatric treatment:

> ... recovery is a social process and ... group workers have demonstrated this in the following way:
> A. By preparing patients to accept help through social channels, relationships, and group encouragement.
> B. By gathering data for diagnosis from the social behavioral dimension.
> C. By helping patients to be more comfortable.
> D. By demonstrating treatment through milieu-group treatment.
> E. By helping patients to help themselves.[18]

The conference report states:

> Dr. Eaton made reference to our problem of professional identification. He pointed up concern with our development as a branch of social work, a branch of the helping professions in general, or as a new entity. He voiced the feeling of the group that it was important to maintain our identification with social work, but he also indicated the need for us to contribute much of our learning to the fields of education and administration.
> Dr. Eaton went on to point up the potential of meeting a vast amount of presently unmet needs for treatment through the use of the group work method.[19]

---

[17]Eaton was involved with the Russell Sage Foundation, and Visiting Professor of Sociology, Western Reserve University, School of Applied Social Sciences, at the time the conference was held.

[18]Joseph W. Eaton, Dr. Raymond Feldman, and Eileen Blackey, "Evaluation and Plans for the Future," in Harleigh B. Trecker, ed., *Group Work in the Psychiatric Setting* (New York: Whiteside and Morrow, 1956), pp. 171–172.

[19]Ibid., p. 172.

Another observer at the same meeting, Dr. Raymond Feldman,[20] stated:

> ... that social group work in treatment settings can be of tremendous value to the psychiatrists because there is so little emphasis on the group in their training. Particularly in our state hospitals, there is a lack of knowledge as to how to make the most effective use of group experience. He stated in this regard that extension and expansion of group work is certainly in order.[21]

Both comments point to the major responsibilities of the group worker in this field, namely, direct service to patients, consultation, and in-service teaching.

In both psychiatric and medical settings there is great variation from agency to agency and from one patient population to another. Work with adult mental patients in a state hospital is different from work with children in an out-patient child guidance clinic; residential treatment for emotionally disturbed children demands a different approach than do services to people who come to a community rehabilitation agency in search of help with vocational planning.

Job descriptions, therefore, will be only samples of possible combinations of services the group worker is asked to perform. We will begin with in-patient work. The rationale of the group worker's contribution to in-patient work was so well presented by Fritz Redl at the Waveland conference that his remarks are reproduced here:

> The contribution of group work as a method in residential therapy is important. We should get over our "professional neurosis" which arises from our being a minority group. This produces the tendency to swallow everything wholesale or the tendency to overidentify with the so-called higher status groups and leave our skills behind.
>
> We don't yell loud enough about what we know regarding design. There is a readiness to hear more than group work assumes. Group workers do not talk enough....
>
> ... What does a group work program in a residential setting mean?... Group work must be a part of the total design of the institution.
>
> *The Therapeutic Ingredients:*
>
> 1. The group worker can provide the diagnostic assessment of group relevant data and secondary individual characteristics of high treatment relevance....
> 2. The group worker is highly important in figuring group composition—

---

[20]Feldman was with the Veterans Administration Central Office, Department of Medicine and Surgery, Psychiatry and Neurology Division, and was Representative, American Psychiatric Association at the time of the conference.

[21]Eaton, Feldman, and Blackey, "Evaluation and Plans for the Future," p. 172.

the clinician and the group worker as a team make the decisions. This is the framework within which group and individual treatment can function....

3.  *Treatment* is a multidefined term. Whenever you talk of a residential treatment center you speak not of an educational polishing process but of an "unpacking" process. This process must be related to particular phases of individual therapy. The group worker must design group life to support the individual therapy process and must also indicate to the individual therapist where the individual therapist's limits must be placed at any one time. Because of the interrelatedness of the two on the life process of the child, there must be constant cooperation between group life development and individual therapy development at any one time.

4.  The group worker must take responsibility for the total hygiene of the program. He has a responsibility to protest when program is not hygienic. Every part of life in the institution must be coordinated....

5.  Rules, regulations, routines and policies have great importance. They are just as relevant as individual therapy. Group work must contribute to the plan....

6.  There is a tendency to forget that *what* you do with people is important, not only how you feel about them. It is frequently up to the group worker to see that handling remains hygienic—not only the affects on what we do on one child, but the group psychological hygiene is important as well.

7.  We need to develop the use of the "life space interview" and learn to interview a child when something has stirred him, in close proximity to the event. This must be done by someone who "smells like" the others in the child's environment. The group worker needs to decide, "What will I pick up; what will I leave?" He needs to help make decisions about timing.

8.  The group worker can contribute his knowledge about climate, group atmosphere, contagion pile-up, build up of we-feeling and the like.

9.  The group worker has to raise his voice about the functioning of the staff group....

10. The group worker must assist in the role distribution and the function of the team. Not only is what you do important, but in what role you do it....

11. The group worker must understand group pathology as well as individual pathology. Group pathology may or may not be related to individual pathology.

12. It is the group worker's job to evaluate the group's help to a child. Sometimes the child does not need a group. The group worker must make a professional judgment as to when to withdraw the child or lower the level of group life intensity. In free life children may drop out of groups. In the residential center, they are psychologically forced into groups—it is our responsibility to determine exposure to or relief from group activity.[22]

[22]Fritz Redl, "The Therapeutic Ingredients in the Group Work Program in a Residential Treatment Center for Children," in Trecker, ed., *Group Work in the Psychiatric Setting*, pp. 43–46.

The responsibility of a social group worker in a children's treatment center may therefore be:

1. Supervision of the child-care workers (sometimes called group counselors, houseparents, and so forth). The child-care worker is the person with whom the child has contact during most hours of the day. Since the living situation is a group situation and must provide for the needs of a growing child as well as help these particular children to overcome their problems, the child-care worker must be capable of translating understanding of the individual and the group into everyday practice. It is the group worker's responsibility to help with this through individual or group supervision and to provide for continued in-service involving other members on the team.
2. Direct work with children in formed groups.
   A. Newcomer or diagnostic groups in larger treatment centers. Such groups must offer the children the opportunity to freely discuss their anxieties and expectations and give information about the treatment center. The group worker offers in this group a relationship with an adult whom the children have to share but who gives each of them a high degree of individual attention. The helper can observe the children in their interaction with others for the purpose of helping to work out proper placement of the children and a purposeful treatment program.
   B. Discharge groups. In these groups the practitioner helps the children face the problems of moving out of the protective institutional environment and work through reactivated anxieties. This may be done through discussions, through role-playing, or through planned activities, such as trips which allow the child to experience the new environment.
   C. Treatment groups. The group worker helps select the children to work through their problems in interaction with contemporaries in a structured group. Such groups may be discussion groups or activity groups.
   D. Group living councils. These are groups that help the child to gain the feeling of participating responsibly in the life of the institution and to have a place where the child can express feelings about institutional living and suggest changes.
3. Life space interviews, as Fritz Redl called them. The group worker does not take over the role of the caseworker or the psychiatrist, but is available for short individual contacts to handle serious problems that may arise in the reality of the living situation.
4. Responsible team participation in relation to intake of children. The group worker's responsibility is (1) to help with assessment of the social capacity of the individual child and to determine his or her degree of readiness for group life; and (2) to help with the assessment of each cottage group or other sub-unit in the treatment center, and to determine its capacity to accept newcomers and the kind of newcomers it can absorb.
5. Responsible participation in the consideration for discharge. The group worker's responsibility here is to consider particularly the child's social ability and to know what informal group life the particular child will need after leaving the treatment center. The group worker must be aware of community resources that are appropriate for those needs and must help to prepare the child and the family to use them.
6. Work with the family. Occasionally parents' groups are considered necessary

and possible. Selection of parents for such groups usually will be made by the caseworker, but the group worker is responsible for the composition of such groups and for direct work with them. The purpose of such groups is to help parents share their concerns in regard to their children or foster children, to help them understand the work of the treatment center, and to prepare them for the return or entrance of the child into their homes.

7.  Consultation to special service staffs. Most of the need for play in a child's life should be fulfilled in the cottage and through the creative efforts of the child-care worker. Larger treatment centers do employ special service staffs concerned with this area of the child's life. Swimming instructors, art teachers, recreation workers, and so forth, are professionals in their own right, but they may want consultation from the group worker as to the group process occurring in those activities and how to make it most helpful to individual children.

8.  Supervision of volunteer group leaders. Whenever possible, treatment centers must keep open the channels to the community. Volunteers help with this. They also bring specific skills that are not always available on the staff. If they work with groups, the group worker must take responsibility for helping them with their task.

9.  Continuous re-evaluation of the total group living situation. The social group worker is the person on the team who must be particularly sensitive to the total atmosphere of the treatment center. This includes staff relations as well as relations among the children.

As in every other institution where teamwork is indicated, social group workers must responsibly share information with other members of the team and, in turn, make responsible use of the information team members share with them. They also may be asked to pass on to other team members their specific knowledge and skills, which they may have been taught by others.

There has been increasing recognition of the vital importance of the hospital environment and the relationship of patients with each other. Most state mental hospitals are vastly understaffed. It is impossible to give psychiatric services to all patients. Individual treatment can reach only a small minority of them. The greatest effort at this time must be directed toward the making of a "therapeutic community." One of the functions of the social group worker therefore—as always when he or she becomes part of institutional work—must be participation in hospital programs for in-service training of those members of the staff who are directly responsible for the daily living situation of the patient. In addition to this, the group worker carries the responsibility for working with formed groups. Marion B. Sloan presented these functions in the following outline:

A.  *Direct work with patients in small formed groups:*
    Patients are referred for group experiences by their doctors, social caseworkers and other professional personnel. Referrals and selections of these patients for group experiences are based on specific problem areas and/or

common treatment experiences. Frequent conferences with other professional personnel help the group experiences to become an integral part of the total treatment plan for each patient.

The program for each group includes both discussion and informal activities, determined in each case according to the needs, interests and readiness of the individual group members and the treatment objectives for the particular group. . . .

Groups which have demonstrated their usefulness in meeting the needs of patients . . . have been developed around the following:

1. *Patients with common treatment experiences:*
    a. *Admissions:*
       A short-term group experience for new patients which is focused on helping the patient with his initial adjustment to the hospital milieu, acceptance of mental illness and the need for treatment.
    b. *Insulin and Electrocoma:*
       Fear is a common element among patients on physical treatment. Sometimes this is realistic, but often fears, apprehensions and anxieties arise from misconceptions about treatment. Emphasis in these groups is on developing collective support, clarification and understanding through common social experiences and discussions. The observations of these group interactions are shared by the staff and used in effectively structuring the treatment of experience with other members of the treatment team.
    c. *Pre-discharge:*
       Through support and identification the group offers help in handling difficulties which arise in the process of discharge from the hospital and return to family and community. The group serves as a medium of helping one another face realistically their common concerns and problems related to having been mental patients, seeking employment, meeting friends and re-entering family life.
2. *Patients with common psychosocial problems:*
    These are planned, directed group experiences for patients whose mental illnesses are complicated by psychosocial problems associated with age, sex, and marital status. These groups include:
    a. Adolescents
    b. Older Adults
    c. Young Mothers
    d. Young Single Men
3. *Patients with common activity interests:*
    These are groups where common interests serve as a basis for the formation of positive social relationships. Purposes for such groups include need satisfaction through success and recognition, channeling of physical and emotional energies, encouragement of self-expression through creative activities and the development of social skills.
4. *Suggested groups to be developed in the future are:*
    a. Post-discharge
    b. Pre-transfer
    c. Relatives of patients.[23]

[23]Marion B. Sloan, "The Role of the Group Worker in the Adult Psychiatric Hospital," in Trecker, ed., *Group Work in the Psychiatric Setting*, pp. 58–60.

It may be added that a group worker must also know when groups are not appropriate—when they are either harmful or not helpful. Patients selected for special groups must be grouped with this knowledge in mind. It must be realized that hospital life in itself means constant exposure to other people who were not chosen by the individual patient. This means that the one part of working on constructive social environments in the hospital lies in the provision for privacy, if patients so desire and if this does not contradict treatment aims.

Group workers frequently are not used in general hospitals serving patients with short-term physical illnesses. The living situation has neither the same purpose nor the same impact on a patient who is hospitalized only for a limited time. Group workers have worked, though, in children's wards for the purpose of relieving the childrens' feeling of isloation. Children's general hospitals have gradually accepted the fact that they must provide for special needs of children in addition to the necessary medical care. These special needs, however, are more likely to be met through recreational specialists, occupational therapists, and so forth, than through group workers.

Group work services are needed more in hospitals or camps for patients with long-term illnesses or with serious physical handicaps, such as summer camps for handicapped children and adults. Their functions in such camps parallel those in children's institutions and treatment centers.

Out-patient services that employ social group workers include child guidance clinics, societies for the deaf, societies for the blind, general rehabilitation centers, organizations for released mental patients, and, occasionally, general or psychiatric hospitals that give out-patient service. To diagnose children's behavior correctly, experts are agreed that one needs to observe children in interaction with their contemporaries as well as in interaction with adults. Also, most children show difficulties in their relations with contemporaries and need to work them through in a protected environment. Younger children especially are incapable of working out problems in interviews and need activities to work through them. The responsibilities of the group worker in child guidance clinics are usually:

1. Work with diagnostic groups: Every child coming into a clinic is automatically referred to such a group in the same way that he or she is referred for psychological and psychiatric interviews. Such groups meet for a limited period—about once a week for three or four consecutive meetings. This equals the period during which the child is seen by other members of the team. On the basis of such observation, the group worker then participates responsibly in diagnosing the child and in working out an adequate treatment plan.

2. Work with formed treatment groups: Children are referred to these groups after a decision is made by the total treatment team. They are either activity or discussion treatment groups or a combination of both. They usually meet once a week over a longer period of time. These groups may have a changing

membership, since some children recover earlier than others. The group worker is responsible for assessing the individual's need for referral to or discharge from the group, as well as the total group situation and its capacity to let go of an individual member or accept a new one. During school vacations, such groups may meet more frequently or for a full day instead of the usual two-hour sessions.

3.  Intimate knowledge of and referral to appropriate community agencies that can give the child or adolescent helpful and healthy group experiences when he or she is ready to leave the protected and therapeutic atmosphere of the clinic.

4.  Work with parents' groups: Such groups serve to provide the parents with information, afford them relief from anxiety, and develop some insight into themselves and their relationships with their children. Such groups may be short-term or long-term.

Permanent physical handicaps require an inner adjustment by the person who is afflicted by them. The feeling about such handicaps is highly related to the social environment. This is based partially on the nature of the handicap and partially on the attitude of society toward it. Blindness, for instance, is socially handicapping because of the restrictions it imposes on the blind person until the individual learns to accept it and then to deal with it. Yet blindness is a socially accepted handicap and there are few prejudices toward the blind.

The deaf or hard-of-hearing person, on the other hand, frequently faces individual hostility in addition to the restrictions stemming from the handicap. This handicap is not visible and therefore someone who meets a deaf person may consider him or her unfriendly or conceited. Communication with the deaf or hard-of-hearing is difficult, and after some effort people often withdraw from an individual with a hearing impairment. The deaf person needs special help to overcome a sense of isolation.

Epileptics and former mental patients may be handicapped little by their present or former illness, but the social stigma of it alone may drive them into isolation. Out-patient group work services, therefore, are directed toward resocialization of people with such handicaps by helping them to increase their skill in meeting others and by helping nonhandicapped persons to understand them better and to integrate them into community groups. This means that the social group worker is involved directly with out-patient groups and is responsible for community interpretation of those handicaps. Such workers help to change community climate.

## G. CORRECTIONS

The field of correction involves the operation of prisons, reformatories, training schools for boys and girls, and the administration of probation and parole systems. These correctional agencies are charged with a two-fold objective:

that of maintaining the secure custody of offenders committed to their care, and that of providing such treatment as will direct their behavior into more law-abiding channels. The achievement of these two objectives requires the skills of trained custodial administrators in combination with the services of many professional groups including psychiatrists, social workers, psychologists, educators, and chaplains. In meeting the many needs of any correctional institution, one of the major administrative problems is to mobilize and integrate the specialized skills required for the custody and treatment of the inmate population.[24]

The field of correction includes not only a variety of services, but also a variety of philosophies that determine those services. In addition, the clients of this field represent every kind of human being and every category of human problem. They have in common only the fact that they have violated the law.

A clear understanding of crime and delinquency is still in its beginning stage. The older theories of explaining them by heredity or environmental influences alone are no longer accepted. It is understood that a large complex of factors is involved in triggering a delinquent act. Whatever the person or the problem, crime and delinquency always include a component of a *social* disorder. They are violations of human interaction. In treatment of the offender, not enough attention has yet been paid to this. Group situations in which offenders find themselves are not used purposely to change their modes of relating to others. Group associations in prisions are too frequently left to the hazard of daily encounter of inmates with each other.

In 1946, the National Conference on Prevention and Control of Juvenile Delinquency recognized the need for group treatment. Several of its deliberations, which were later published, stressed this. It was stated:

> Group work services should be provided for those apprehended for delinquent behavior, for those in institutions for detention, and for long-term treatment of juvenile delinquency.[25]

The standards for detention care of delinquents place group work in the core of its service. Group work functions are presented on two levels:

1.  Group Work Staff:
    The most important staff members are those who have direct contact with children. These persons are variously known as group supervisors, group counselors, child care workers, group leaders, etc. The term "group worker"

---

[24]James V. Bennett, "Corrections," in Kurtz, ed., *Social Work Year Book, 1960,* pp. 205–206.

[25]"Case Work-Group Work," A Report of the National Conference on Prevention and Control of Juvenile Delinquents, Washington, D C, Nov. 1946, p. 38.

is used throughout this book because of the professional standing which ought to be given this type of work. Group work functions are not confined to supervision, counseling, care or leadership. The distinguishing mark of a good group worker is his ability to meet individual and group needs with knowledge and skill. The trend in detention homes is toward the employment of college-trained personnel for this work. Few have had graduate training in social group work; they should be supervised by one who has. Group workers should be encouraged to secure graduate training in social group work just as many caseworkers in the field of probation have acquired graduate training in social casework....[26]

2. Group Work Supervisor:

Institutions with nonresident personnel should have a trained and experienced group worker to supervise and assist the group workers on each shift. In *single-unit* institutions for fifteen or twenty children, the superintendent, assistant superintendent, and caseworker may perform this function. However, constant coverage must be given during the hours of the two day shifts with at least an "on call" resident available to those on duty at night. *Institutions of two or more units* should have, for each "group worker shift," a group work supervisor free of other responsibilities or attachments to a particular group. Where possible, the group work supervisor (head of shift) should have graduate training in social group work. In *institutions of four or more units,* the head of each shift should have experienced assistants so that there is at least one "roving group worker" for every two units.[27]

Group discussions, planned and unplanned, should be encouraged, but should be conducted only under the guidance of a social worker trained in ground discussion techniques.[28]

There are other signs also, in the institutional field for delinquents, that the need for social group work is beginning to be recognized. Functions of the social group worker in these parallel closely those of the treatment centers and institutions in child welfare. Resistance to adults and refusal to accept personal responsibility are especially strong among the youngsters in delinquency institutions. August Aichorn understood this when he wrote in 1935:

To the dissocial child we are a menace because we represent society which he is in conflict with.... They do not tell the truth.[29]

Group workers in the institution work only rarely with voluntary groups; more often they work with living groups or with groups formed for treatment purposes. Groups with relatives have also been comparatively

---

[26]National Council on Crime and Delinquency, *Standards and Guides for the Detention of Children and Youth,* 2nd ed. (New York: N.C.C.D., 1961), p. 48.

[27]Ibid., p. 49.

[28]Ibid., p. 88.

[29]August Aichorn, *Wayward Youth* (New York: Viking 1935), p. 125.

rare in corrections, although there have been some experiments with group work with wives of long-term inmates who are scheduled for parole or discharge. These sessions prepare the wives for the problems and discouragements they will have to face. Simultaneously the inmates themselves have group sessions.

In probation and parole services some attempts have been made to use the group work approach. The function of group workers in this service include:

1. Direct work with groups of probationers or parolees for the purpose of discussing their present adjustment or for the purpose of offering constructive group activities to those who are not yet ready to enter into community group services.
2. Summer programs for youth probationers or parolees who are still in school, but who cannot find employment during the summer and who are not yet ready to participate in other youth camps.
3. Weekend programs for the same kind of youngsters.
4. Discussion groups with parents of children and adolescents adjudicated delinquent to help them understand court services, to allow them to express concern, anxieties, and hostilities, and to enable them to become more helpful to their children.
5. Helping children or adults under their supervision to become aware of and to use different community resources.
6. Casework services.
7. Work with family units, which should include home visits as friend, not investigator.

In the correctional field especially, the same person must often be able to use both casework and group work methods and to use them judiciously.

There has been much discussion as to whether group work needs much change in an authoritarian setting such as the court. Group work method includes the constructive use of limitations. It definitely is based on the value of respect for individual integrity. This unfortunately is often violated in the correctional systems all over the world. The group worker's task is as much to change such abuses as to work directly with groups in corrections. The increasingly punishing climate is dangerous to all human relations. In working in the field of corrections, any professional must learn to be equally concerned with the victim as with the one who has committed a crime. We must learn not to retaliate with cruelty nor be unconcerned.

> ... Deny them humanity, and for your luxury you will pay with the bodies of your own children. It is easy to forget one's own vanity and evil and cruelty.[30]

[30]Joanne Greenberg, *The King's Persons* (New York: Avon Books, 1972) p. 56.

## H. SCHOOL SOCIAL WORK

School Social Services represent some of the efforts being made in education to meet the needs of certain individual children who have social and emotional problems which interfere with their school functioning and achievement. These services have increased and expanded as new knowledge has enhanced the understanding of behavior and of the needs of children when learning difficulties are encountered.

Social services, an integral part of the total school program, may include psychological service, psychiatric service, attendance service, vocational counseling, and school social work service. The teacher uses these resources to supplement her own work with children in the classroom in order that her teaching efforts may be more effective. Social services help by working directly with children who have school adjustment problems and with their parents. Opportunity is provided also, through consultation, for the teacher to gain a deeper understanding of the children in her classroom—understanding of their feelings, attitudes, and behavior that may be thwarting or enhancing the opportunity for learning which the school provides.[31]

The school setting is definitely a group setting, and teachers work with groups. When group work was more closely related to informal education, it was not part of school social work programs as it is understood today, but those informal groups were widely used by the schools to help youngsters. School social work, as developed in this country, was more traditional casework combined with the task of the "truant officer." This was symbolized by the designation of the school social workers as "visiting teachers." The function of the school social worker has changed, and with the change has come an appreciation of possible contributions to be made in this field by the group worker. Representatives of this field of social work are especially open to experiments with group work services as part of their specialization. Some departments have employed social group workers. Their function has included:

1. Direct work with groups of children who have shown school difficulties.
2. Consultation with teachers to help them with the handling of children who are difficult in the classroom situation.

School social work using the group work method is frequently done outside the formal school system. Outstanding examples of this are Big Sisters organizations and neighborhood houses, which serve school referral groups. They meet usually over a comparatively long period of time.

Social group workers have also entered the field of higher education. Offices of Student Affairs may use the knowledge and skill of group workers in the areas of student housing (dormitories are group living situa-

---

[31]Opal Boston, "School Social Services," in Kurtz, ed., *Social Work Year Book, 1960,* p. 517.

tions); outreach of the university to its immediate geographical environment through student involvement; student union and other activities; and work with foreign students. Practitioners work in close cooperation with student counselors and other academic staff and faculty.

## I. DRUG EDUCATION

The use of drugs has increased in the last ten years, and a wide variety of agencies have been established to work with young people who are drug abusers. Some of those are small group homes, others are out-patient services. There is still very little knowledge of how to combat drug abuse. We do know that it is often related to group pressure, though not exclusively so. Group work, therefore, seems to be appropriate with its strong individualization and creation of an atmosphere that allows for frank exchange among members.

### *SUMMARY*

In looking over the fields in which the group work method is used, certain trends can be ascertained:

1. A trend toward the use of the group as a conscious helping-tool in *all* social services, including those that formerly used the casework method alone.
2. A widening of the traditional social work function toward inclusion of the educationally-oriented functions as exemplified in the youth services.
3. A concern with social action, not only *on behalf* of clients, as has been traditional in social welfare, but with involvement of group members as allies of the professional social worker.
4. A concern with the individual, the group, and necessary cultural change.

Activities of the social group worker in different fields are not always the same. They include a wide variety consisting of:

1. Work with client or membership groups.
2. Work with committees, boards, or other community groups.
3. Work with individuals related to group services.
4. Supervision of volunteers or part-time staff.
5. Consultation with other professionals working with groups.
6. Participation or leadership in social action.
7. Continuous research into the psychosocial phenomena that confront the group worker.
8. Evelution of group worker practice.

The wide range of agencies in which group work is practiced raises questions of agency structure and education, which are not yet wholly answered. For instance, the separation of casework and group work originally indicated different agency functions; now they are methods often used in the same agencies. Should social work keep the separation in professional training?

At the time the first edition of this book was written, the social work profession had not yet answered this question. That was in 1962. The next decade saw development that began to produce an answer. Social work increasingly became problem, not method, oriented. Practitioners recognized the need for being capable of using a variety of skills and to work in various human contexts: one-to-one, group, community. It took educators longer to accept what this author had written in 1961: the fact that all social work methods are based on common knowledge, philosophy, and principles, though skills differ. I wrote in 1961:

1.  Every teacher in social work must be thoroughly informed about the other basic method, must *know* it and have at least some contact with its practice in whatever setting.
2.  The same applies to leadership in our profession, executives, supervisors, etc.
3.  Gifted social workers who are interested must have the opportunity to take additional courses to learn actual skill in the other method—because of our commonness this is not too difficult to achieve, and is done already in many parts of the United States and Canada.
4.  While we are not yet educating the generic social worker, we must imbue every new student with high appreciation of the other method he himself is not yet practicing and make him feel strongly that he belongs to *one* profession.
5.  We must in the future be able to educate the generic social worker who can use both methods, and we must not indefinitely continue to demand specialization in method before the student knows what he chooses.
6.  We must keep our ears open to hear the plea of our clients, the call of our disadvantaged groups, the angry words of our young people, to use ourselves creatively and give our help with all the thinking and discipline each one of us has learned, but free from fetters of a too narrow concept of such help.[32]

Social work education became more generic, yet it frequently fell back into exclusive casework teaching or it began to teach group work techniques without the underlying humane philosophy indispensable to social group work. There is a reawakening in the 1980s, especially in countries that have experienced the horror of very inhuman situations.

---

[32]From Gisela Konopka, "Needed—A Generic Social Work Method," *The Social Worker,* 30, No. 2 (Apr. 1962), 18–30.

## BIBLIOGRAPHY

### Settlements and Neighborhood Centers

ADDAMS, JANE, *Forty Years at Hull House.* New York: Macmillan, 1935.

BERRY, MARGARET, "Settlements and Neighborhood Centers," in Russell H. Kurtz, ed., *Social Work Year Book, 1960*, pp. 523–528. New York: N.A.S.W., 1960.

CARPENTER, H. DANIEL, "The Neighborhood-Grass Roots of American Democracy," *Ethical Frontiers.* New York: New York Society for Ethical Culture, 1948.

CHAMBERS, CLARKE, *Seedtime of Reform; American Social Service and Social Action, 1918–1933.* Minneapolis: University of Minnesota Press, 1963.

DILLICK, SIDNEY, *Community Organization for Neighborhood Development—Past and Present.* New York: Woman's Press and Morrow, 1953.

HILLMAN, ARTHUR, "Experimental Approaches in Deprived Areas," *Community Organization 1961*, pp. 109–123. New York: Columbia University Press, 1961.

——————, "Settlements and Community Centers," in Harry L. Lurie, ed., *Encyclopedia of Social Work, 1965*, pp. 690–695. New York: N.A.S.W., 1965.

International Federation of Settlements, *The Building of Human Relationships in Our Times*, Conference Report of the 6th International Conference of the International Federation of Settlements, Amsterdam, Holland, June 1952; Utrecht, Holland, 1953.

KONOPKA, GISELA, "The Present Crisis in Perspective," University of North Carolina, Chapel Hill, North Carolina, May 17, 1968 (pamphlet).

MIDDLEMANN, RUTH R., "The Use of Program: Review and Update," in *Social Work with Groups*, Vol. 3, No. 3 (Fall 1980). New York: The Haworth Press, Inc.

National Federation of Settlements, *Neighborhood Goals in a Rapidly Changing World*, A Report of the Action-Research Workshop held at Arden House, Harriman, New York, 1958.

PACEY, LORENE M., *Readings in the Development of Settlement Work.* New York: Association Press, 1950.

TAYLOR, GRAHAM, *Pioneering on Social Frontiers.* Chicago: University of Chicago Press, 1930.

WOODS, ROBERT A., *The Neighborhood in Nation Building.* Boston: Houghton Mifflin, 1923.

### Youth-Serving Agencies

Basic Standards for the Triennium, 1958–1961, "Deep Roots and World Reach," Work Book 21st National Convention Y.W.C.A. of the U.S.A., St. Louis, 1958. New York: Y.W.C.A. National Board.

BOSWELL, LUADA, "A Report on Two Girl Scout Pilot Projects: Migrant Agricultural Workers and Urban Hard-to-Reach Groups," *New Perspectives on Services to Groups: Theory, Organization, Practice.* New York: N.A.S.W., 1961.

Center for Youth Development and Research, University of Minnesota, *Dialogue on Youth.* Minneapolis, 1970.

COYLE, GRACE L., *Group Work and American Youth.* New York: Harper & Row, Pub., 1948.

—————, "Social Group Work in Recreation," *Proceedings of the National Conference of Social Work,* 1946, pp. 202–208. New York: Columbia University Press, 1946.

FISHER, GALEN M., *Citadel of Democracy.* Berkeley, CA: Howell-North Press, 1955.

HEIGHT, DOROTHY I., *Step by Step with Interracial Groups.* New York: Publications Services, Y.W.C.A. National Board, 1955.

KONOPKA, GISELA, *Effective Communication with Adolescents in Institutions,* p. 13. New York: Child Welfare League of America, 1965.

—————. *Young Girls: A Portrait of Adolescence.* Englewood Cliffs, NJ: Prentice-Hall, 1976.

MAHONEY, ANNE R., "Gifted Delinquents: What Do We Know About Them," *Children and Youth Services Review,* Vol. 2, No. 3 (1980). New York: Pergamon Press, Ltd.

—————, "Barriers Between Generations—The Issue in Perspective," in *The Function of Rebellion—Is Youth Creating New Family Values?* New York: Child Study Association of America, 1969 (1968 Child Study Conference proceedings).

—————, *Being Young.* A television program of six one-half hour segments sponsored by the University of Minnesota Extension Division, KTCA-TV, Jan. 8, 15, 22, and 29, and Feb. 5 and 12, 1969.

—————, "The Nature of Adolescence in Our Time," *Sisters Today,* 42, No. 1 (Aug.–Sept. 1970), 20–30.

—————, *The Teenage Girl.* Albany, NY: New York State Division for Youth, 1967 (pamphlet).

—————, "Youth and Freedom," published in the *Congressional Record,* Apr. 19, 1966.

New York City Youth Board, *Reaching Teen-Agers through Group and Recreation Programs.* New York: N.Y.C. Youth Board, 1954.

SEROTKIN, HARRY, "Youth Services," in Russell H. Kurtz, ed., *Social Work Year Book, 1960,* pp. 607–617. New York: N.A.S.W., 1960.

SHIFFMAN, BERNARD M., "Youth Services" in Harry L. Lurie, ed., *Encyclopedia of Social Work, 1965,* pp. 843–850. New York: National Association of Social Workers, 1965.

SOLENDER, SANFORD, "The Place of the Jewish Community Center in Jewish Life," *Journal of Jewish Communal Service,* Fall 1957.

## Child Welfare Services

BETTELHEIM, BRUNO, *Love is Not Enough.* Glencoe, Il: The Free Press, 1950.

Child Welfare League of America, Inc., *Group Method and Services in Child Welfare.* New York, 1964.

COLE, MINERVA G. and LAWRENCE PODELL, "Serving Handicapped Children in Group Programs," *Social Work,* 6, No. 1 (Jan. 1961), 97–104.

JONES, HOWARD, *Reluctant Rebels.* New York: Association Press (copyright 1959 by Tavistock Publications, Ltd.).

HUNT, MAURICE O., "Child Welfare," in Russell H. Kurtz, ed., *Social Work Year Book, 1960,* pp. 141–157. New York: N.A.S.W., 1960.

KEANE, SISTER M. CHARLES, R.S.M., *The House Mother.* Washington, D C: National Conference of Catholic Charities, 1954.

KONOPKA, GISELA, *A Changing Culture Asks for Changed Services.* Chicago: Florence Crittenton Association of America, 1967 (pamphlet).

——————, "Attention Must Be Paid," *American Journal of Orthopsychiatry,* XXXIV, No. 5 (Oct. 1964), 805-817.

——————, "Enriching the Role of the Social Worker in Child Welfare," *The Conference Bulletin,* 63, No. 4 (Summer 1965).

——————, "Executive and Staff—A Responsible Treatment Team," (The I. G. Greer Anniversary Lecture), *Chapel Hill Workshops,* 1964, Part 2, Workshops for Executives of Children's Institutions, July 27-31, 1964, pp. 48-58.

——————, *Group Work in the Institution,* (rev. ed.) New York: Association Press, 1970.

——————, "Part 4. The Role of the Group in Residential Treatment," Symposium 1954, The Role of Residential Treatment for Children, *American Journal of Orthopsychiatry,* XXV, No. 4 (Oct. 1955), 679-684.

——————, "Re-Thinking from the Beginning—What is Absolutely Essential in a Child Care Program Today," *Chapel Hill Workshop Reports,* 1969, Part 2, University of North Carolina, Chapel Hill, North Carolina, July 27-31, 1969.

MAIER, HENRY, ed., *Group Work as Part of Residential Treatment.* New York: N.A.S.W., 1965.

MAIER, HENRY W., "The Meaning of Repeated Adult Requests," *Child Welfare* (Dec. 1958), Vol. XXXVII, No. 12, 7.

REID, JOSEPH H. and HELEN R. HAGAN, *Residential Treatment of Emotionally Disturbed Children.* New York: Child Welfare League of America, 1952.

SCHULZE, SUSANNE, *Creative Group Living in a Children's Institution.* New York: Association Press, 1951.

SCHWARTZ, WILLIAM, "Characteristics of the Group Experience in Resident Camping," *Social Work,* 5, No. 2 (Apr. 1960), 91-96.

SEABLOOM, WILLIAM, "Group Therapy with Emotionally Disturbed Adolescent Boys," *Lutheran Social Welfare Quarterly,* 1, No. 1 (1961), 22-28.

TODD, T. and J. BARCOME, "Use of Groups at Intake: Impact Upon Clients, Staff, and Programs," in *Social Work with Groups,* Vol. 3, No. 3 (Fall 1980). New York: The Haworth Press, Inc.

TRIESCHMAN, A. E., J. K. WHITTAKER, and L. K. BRENDTRO, *The Other 23 Hours.* Chicago: Aldine, 1969.

TURITZ, ZITHA R. and REBECCA SMITH, "Child Welfare," in Harry L. Lurie, ed., *Encyclopedia of Social Work,* 1965, pp. 137-144. New York: N.A.S.W., 1965.

## Family Services

BLACKBURN, CLARK W., "Family Social Work," in Harry L. Lurie, ed., *Encyclopedia of Social Work,* 1965, pp. 309-318. New York: N.A.S.W., 1965.

Family Service Association of America, *Use of Group Techniques in the Family Service Agency.* New York: F.S.A.A., 1959.

KONOPKA, GISELA, "CMAC Group Counselling Workshop," Report of Workshop sponsored by Catholic Marriage Advisory Council, 502 Caritas House, Caine Road, Hong Kong. Dec. 27-30, 1969.

——————, "Group Work Techniques in Joint Interviewing," *Social Welfare Forum, 1957.* New York: Columbia University Press, 1957.

PARSONS, TALCOTT and ROBERT F. BALES, *Family, Socialization and Interaction Process.* Glencoe, IL: The Free Press, 1955.

SEABLOOM, WILLIAM, "Group Therapy with Emotionally Disturbed Adolescent Boys," *Lutheran Social Welfare Quarterly,* 1, No. 1 (1961), 22-28.

SHOEMAKER, LOUISE,   "Use of Group Work Skills with Short Term Groups," *Social Work With Groups, 1960,* pp. 37–51. New York: N.A.S.W., 1960.
THOMAS, CAROLYN,   "The Use of Group Methods with Foster Parents," *Children,* 8, No. 6 (Nov.-Dec. 1961), 218–222.
WEIL, RAE C.,   "Family Social Work," in Russell H. Kurtz, ed., *Social Work Year Book, 1960,* pp. 251–257. New York: N.A.S.W., 1960.

## Services to the Aging

FARRAR, MARCELLA and NELIDA FERRARI,   "Casework and Group Work in a Home for the Aged," *Social Work,* 5, No. 2 (Apr. 1960), 58–62.
HOGE, EVELYN B.,   "Developing Clubs for Older People," Pamphlet No. 3, *How Public Welfare Serves Aging People.* Chicago: American Public Welfare Association, 1954.
KAPLAN, JEROME,   *A Social Program for Older People.* Minneapolis: University of Minnesota Press, 1953.
_____, "Mobilizing Community Resources," Pamphlet No. 5, *How Public Welfare Serves Aging People.* Chicago: American Public Welfare Association, 1955.
KUBIE, SUSAN H. and GERTRUDE LANDAU,   *Group Work with the Aged.* New York: International Universities Press, 1953.
McCARTHY, HENRY L.,   "Day Centers for Older People," Pamphlet No. 4, *How Public Welfare Serves Aging People.* Chicago: American Public Welfare Association, 1954.
McGOWEN, VIRGINIA A.,   "Helping Older People Find Good Nursing Home Care," Pamphlet No. 8, *How Public Welfare Serves Aging People.* Chicago: American Public Welfare Association, 1955.
MARGOLIN, LILLIAN,   "Residential Camping Services for Older Adults," *New Perspectives on Services to Groups: Theory, Organization, Practice,* pp. 133–142. New York: N.A.S.W., 1961.
MATHIASEN, GENEVA,   "The Aging," in Russell H. Kurtz, ed., *Social Work Year Book, 1960,* pp. 95–102. New York: N.A.S.W., 1960.
_____, "The Aging," in Harry L. Lurie, ed., *Encyclopedia of Social Work, 1965,* pp. 73–80. New York: N.A.S.W., 1965.
MAXWELL, JEAN M.,   "Group Services—Well-being for Older People," *Social Work with Groups, 1960,* pp. 74–85. New York: N.A.S.W., 1960.
MONK, A.,   "Social Work with the Aged: Principles of Practice," *Social Work,* Vol. 26, No. 1 (January 1981) New York: National Association of Social Workers.
National Association of Social Workers, *Social Group Work and Older People.* New York: N.A.S.W., 1963.
SHAPIRO, SIDNEY,   "The Old Cronies," in Harleigh B. Trecker, ed., Group Work—*Foundations and Frontiers,* p. 172. New York: Whiteside, Inc., 1955.
TIBBITS, CLARK, and WILMA DONAHUE, Compilers,   "A Handbook for Group Members," Vol. 1, *Aging in the Modern World,* Ann Arbor: University of Michigan, Division of Gerontology, 1957.
_____, "Guidebook for Leaders," Vol. III, *Aging in the Modern World,* as cited above. 1957.
TINE, SEBASTIAN, KATHERINE HASTINGS, and PAUL DEUTSCHBERGER, "Genetic and Specific in Social Group Work Practice with the Aging," *Social Work with Groups,* 1960, pp. 86–99. New York: N.A.S.W., 1960.

## Medical and Psychiatric Services

BLACKEY, EILEEN, "Social Work in the Hospital: A Sociological Approach," *Social Work*, 1, No. 2 (Apr. 1956), 43–49.

COCKERILL, ELEANOR E., "Medical Social Work," in Russell H. Kurtz, ed., *Social Work Year Book, 1960*, pp. 375–382. New York: N.A.S.W., 1960.

COYLE, GRACE L., "Group Work in Psychiatric Settings: Its Roots and Branches," *Social Work*, 4, No. 1 (Jan. 1959), 74–81.

COYLE, GRACE L. and RAYMOND FISHER, "Helping Hospitalized Children through Social Group Work," *The Child*, 16, No. 8 (Apr. 1952).

FELIX, ROBERT H., et al., *Mental Health and Social Welfare*. New York: Columbia University Press, 1961.

FISHER, B. A. and WAYNE S. WERBEL, "T-Group and Therapy Group Communication: An Interaction Analysis of the Group Process," *Small Group Behavior*, Vol. 10, No. 4 (Nov. 1979). Beverly Hills, CA: Sage Publications.

FREY, LOUISE A., "Social Group Work in Hospitals," *New Perspectives on Services to Groups: Theory, Organization, Practice*, pp. 92–103. New York: N.A.S.W., 1961.

GUZIE, FRANCES P., "Psychiatrically Oriented Groups," *Use of Groups in the Psychiatric Setting*, pp. 123–129. New York: N.A.S.W., 1960.

HARLOW, MINNIE MAUDE, "Group Work in a Psychiatric Hospital," in Robert H. Felix, *Mental Health and Social Welfare*, pp. 152–174. New York: Columbia University Press, 1961.

HARM, CARL S. and JOSEPH GOLDEN, "Group Worker's Role in Guiding Social Process in a Medical Institution," *Social Work*, 6, No. 2 (Apr. 1961), 44–51.

HERMAN, MELVIN, "Reintegration of Handicapped Persons in the Community," *New Perspectives on Services to Groups: Theory, Organization, Practice*, pp. 70–78. New York: N.A.S.W., 1961.

IMPALLARIA, CONSTANCE, "Some Contributions of Therapeutic Group Work in a Medical Setting," *Selected Papers in Group Work and Community Organization*, National Conference of Social Work, 1952.

JONES, MAXWELL, *The Therapeutic Community*. London: Tavistock Publications, 1952.

KAPLAN, IRVING H., "Some Aspects of Group Work in a Psychiatric Setting," *Social Work*, 5, No. 3 (July 1960), 84–90.

KONOPKA, GISELA, "Group Treatment of the Mentally Ill: Education for Life," *Canada's Mental Health*, Supplement No. 54, Jan-Apr., 1967.

—————, "Implications of a Changing Residential Treatment Program," *American Journal of Orthopsychiatry*, XXXI, No. 1 (Jan. 1961), 17–39.

—————, "Self-Respect: The Basis of Treatment," *Chapel Hill Workshops*, Part II, Chapel Hill, North Carolina, July 24–29, 1966, pp. 68–79.

—————, "Team Relationships and Operations in Social Group Work," in Marjorie Murphy, *The Social Group Work Method in Social Work Education*, Vol. XI, *A Project Report of the Curriculum Study*, Werner W. Boehm, Director and Coordinator, pp. 106–114. New York: Council on Social Work Education, 1959.

—————, "The Generic and the Specific in Group Work Practice in the Psychiatric Setting," *Social Work*, 1, No. 1 (Jan. 1956), 72–80.

—————, *Therapeutic Group Work with Children*. Minneapolis: University of Minnesota Press, 1949.

——————, "The Role of the Group Worker in the Psychiatric Setting," *American Journal of Orthopsychiatry*, XXII, No. 1 (Jan. 1952), 176–185.

LANE, DOROTHEA M., "Psychiatric Patients Learn a New Way of Life," *New Perspectives on Services to Groups: Theory, Organization, Practice*, pp. 114–123. New York: N.A.S.W., 1961.

LINDSAY, DOREEN, "Group Placement of Long-Term Mental Hospital Patients," *New Perspectives on Services to Groups: Theory, Organization, Practice*, pp. 104–113.

MAIER, HENRY W., "Group Living: A Unique Feature in Residential Treatment," *New Perspectives on Services to Groups: Theory, Organization, Practice*, pp. 124–132.

National Association of Social Workers, *Use of Groups in the Psychiatric Setting*. New York: N.A.S.W., 1960.

O'KEEFE, DANIEL E., "Psychiatric Social Work," in Russell F. Kurtz, ed., *Social Work Year Book, 1960*, pp. 451–460. New York: N.A.S.W., 1960.

PENNOCK, MARY and GRACE WEYKER, "Some Developments in the Integration of Casework and Group Work in a Child Guidance Clinic," in Harleigh B. Trecker, ed., *Group Work—Foundations and Frontiers*, p. 76. New York: Whiteside, Inc., 1955.

PERLMAN, BERNICE, "Group Work with Psychotic Veterans," *American Journal of Orthopsychiatry*, XIX, No. 1 (Jan. 1949), 69–78.

SLOAN, MARION B., "Factors in Forming Treatment Groups," *Use of Groups in the Psychiatric Setting*, pp. 74–86. New York: N.A.S.W., 1960.

——————, "The Special Contribution of Therapeutic Group Work in a Psychiatric Setting," in Harleigh B. Trecker, ed., *Group Work—Foundation and Frontiers*, p. 208.

TRECKER, HARLEIGH, B., ed., *Group Work in the Psychiatric Setting*. New York: Whiteside, Inc. 1956.

——————, "The Hospital, the Ward, and the Patient as Clients: Use of the Group Work Method," *Social Work*, 4, No. 4 (Oct. 1959), 57–64.

WHITE, GRACE, "The Distinguishing Characteristics of Medical Social Work," *Medical Social Work*, 1, No. 1 (Sept. 1951), 31–39.

WILSON, GERTRUDE, "Hospital Group Work," Pittsburgh: University of Pittsburgh, mimeographed, No. 677, undated.

WILSON, GERTRUDE and GISELA KONOPKA, "Social Group Work in a Psychiatric Setting," *The News-Letter of the American Association of Psychiatric Social Workers*, XIV, No. 2 (Autumn 1944), pp. 35–43.

WOODRUFF, ROBERT R., "Group Work in a Children's Hospital," *Social Work*, 2, No. 3 (July 1957), 56–61.

## Corrections

AUSTIN, DAVID M., "Goals for Gang Workers," *Social Work*, 2, No. 4 (Oct. 1957), 42–50.

BENNETT, JAMES V., "Corrections," in Russell H. Kurtz, ed., *Social Work Year Book, 1960*, pp. 205–211. New York: N.A.S.W., 1960.

BLAKE, MARY, *Youth Groups in Conflict*. Washington, D C, U.S. Department of Health, Education and Welfare, 1958.

CLOWARD, RICHARD A. and LLOYD E. OHLIN, Delinquency and Opportunity. Glencoe, IL: The Free Press, 1960.

DONOHUE, JOHN K., *Baffling Eyes of Youth*. New York: Association Press, 1957.

FENTON, NORMAN, "The Prison as a Therapeutic Community," *Federal Probation*, XX, NO. 2 (June 1956), 26–29.

JERECZEK, GORDON, "Gangs Need Not Be Delinquent," *Federal Probation*, XXIV, No. 2 (June 1960).

KONOPKA, GISELA, "Adolescent Delinquent Girls," *Children* II, No. 1 (Jan.-Feb. 1964), 21–26.

——————, *Adolescent Girl in Conflict.* Englewood Cliffs, NJ: Prentice-Hall, 1966.

——————, *Group Work in the Institution* (rev. ed.) New York: Association Press, 1970.

——————, "Institutional Treatment of Emotionally Disturbed Children," *Crime and Delinquency*, 8, No. 1 (Jan. 1962), 52–57.

——————, "Our Outcast Youth," *Social Work*, 15, No. 4 (Oct. 1970), 76–86.

——————, "The Group Worker's Role in an Institution for Juvenile Delinquents," *Federal Probation*, XV, No. 2 (June 1951), 15–23.

——————, *Therapeutic Group Work with Children.* Minneapolis: University of Minnesota Press, 1949, 2nd printing, 1965.

——————, "The Social Group Work Method: Its Use in the Correctional Field," *Federal Probation*, XIV, No. 1 (Mar. 1950).

LERMAN, PAUL, "Group Work with Youth in Conflict," *Social Work*, 3, No. 4 (Oct. 1958), 71–77.

McCLEARY, R. D., "Group Work with Delinquents," *The Group*, VIII, No. 4 (June 1946), 1–4.

National Conference on Prevention and Control of Juvenile Delinquents, Reports of the National Conference on Prevention and Control of Juvenile Delinquents, Washington, D C, Nov. 1946.

National Council on Crime and Delinquency, *Standards and Guides for the Detention of Children and Youth* (2nd ed.) New York: N.C.C.D., 1961.

New York City Youth Board, "Pattern for Prevention," New York: N.Y.C. Youth Board, Jan. 1953.

NOLTE, ROBERT E. and JOHN J. FALLON, "Delinquency Treatment by a Public-Private Agency Team," *Social Work with Groups, 1960*, pp. 100–107. New York: N.A.S.W., 1960.

RAHM, HAROLD J. and ROBERT J. WEBERT, "Office in the Alley," report on a project with gang youngsters, The Hogg Foundation for Mental Health, 1958.

REDL, FRITZ and DAVID WINEMAN, *Children Who Hate—Controls from Within.* Glencore, Il: The Free Press, 1951.

SARRI, R. C. "Adolescent Misconduct and the Juvenile Justice System," *Children and Youth Services Review*, Vol. 2, No. 3 (1980). New York: Pergamon Press, Ltd.

SMITH, ALEXANDER R. and ALEXANDER BASSIN, "Group Therapy with Adult Probationers," *Federal Probation*, XXIV, No. 3 (Sept. 1960), 15–21.

STUDT, ELLIOT, "The Nature of Hard-to-Reach Groups," *Children* (Nov.-Dec. 1957), 219–224.

——————, "Correctional Services," in Harry L. Lurie, ed., *Encyclopedia of Social Work, 1965*, pp. 219–229. New York: N.A.S.W., 1965.

TOLMAN, NORMAN G., "Approaching the Institutionalized Female Delinquent through Group Therapy," *Federal Probation*, XXV, No. 2 (June 1961), 34–40.

WITMER, HELEN L. and RUTH KOTINSKY, *Personality in the Making.* New York: Harper & Row, Pub., 1952.

## School Social Work

BENNETT, MARGARET ELAINE, *Guidance in Groups: A Resource Book for Teachers, Counselors and Administrators.* New York: McGraw-Hill, 1955.

DELGADO, M. and S. SIFF, "A Hispanic Adolescent Group in a Public School Setting: An Interagency Approach," *Social Work With Groups,* Vol. 3, No. 3 (1980). New York: The Haworth Press, Inc.

JOHNSON, ARLEEN, "Schools," in Harry L. Lurie, ed., *Encyclopedia of Social Work,* pp. 672–678. New York: N.A.S.W., 1965.

MERL, LAWRENCE F., ed., *Work With Groups in the School Setting.* New York: N.A.S.W., 1965, 60 pages.

POOLE, FLORENCE, "An Analysis of the Characteristics of School Social Work," *Social Service Review,* XXIII, No. 4 (Dec. 1949), 454–459.

QUATTLEBAUM, VIRGINIA, *School Social Work Practice: Proceedings of the Lake Forest Workshop.* New York: N.A.S.W., 1958.

WRIGHT, BARBARA H., *Practical Handbook for Group Guidance.* Chicago: Science Research Associates, 1948.

FORT, JOEL, "Youth and the Drug Crisis," in David Gottlieb, ed., *Youth and Contemporary Society.* Beverly Hills, CA: Sage Publications, 1971, pp. 191–210.

KONOPKA, GISELA, *Young Girls: A Portrait of Adolescence,* Chapter 5, Drugs and Alcohol. Englewood Cliffs, NJ: Prentice-Hall, 1976.

WIDSETH, J. C. and J. MAYER, "Drinking Behavior and Attitudes Toward Alcohol in Delinquent Girls," *International Journal of the Addictions,* Vol. VI, No. 3, September 1971, pp. 453–461.

*I believe that we should make room in our outlook for tested knowledge about human nature and social behavior. But if we are wise we shall also provide for the revision of this knowledge—for what we know, or think we know, is not the last word. And I am equally convinced that we should find out how to make more constructive use of the knowledge we have.*[1]

# EPILOGUE

We have described the particulars of one of the helping methods in social work, its change in the course of history, its underlying values, its view of individual, group, and society, its principles and techniques, and the fields in which it is practiced.

A 13-year-old girl exclaimed after a group meeting in which the youngsters had worked through many conflicts, "I feel so much better— and we begin to like each other! You surely have done this, Miss Summer. Alone, we would just have bickered around; you did it!—Oh no, you didn't! We did it, We!"

She put in a nutshell the basic helping intent of social group work.

[1]Merle Curti, *Probing Our Past* (New York: Harper & Row, Pub., 1955), p. 170.

Out of the group worker's understanding and skill had emerged the essential totality of helping people to help themselves.

Work with human beings seems simple on the surface—something anyone can do. Yet the history of thousands of years of human life has shown how difficult it is. The aim, the demand for living together harmoniously, has been pronounced by all the great philosophers, religious leaders, and statespeople. Practice has not yet been able to follow them. The human being is one of the most complicated entities in the world. Help with human relationships is not easy, as relationships among people produce conflicts, problems, and satisfactions. Knowledge and theory about human beings is in constant development. A helping profession is dependent on this knowledge, since it is actively engaged in change—change of the individual, the group, the community. This is a difficult and responsible task, and must therefore be harnessed by disciplined use of available knowledge. *Discipline* here means an honest understanding of oneself, so that one does not misuse the helping position for one's own purposes; it also means an open and searching mind to participate in better and deeper understanding of people. While the group worker must place a major effort on practice, he or she must also take on responsibility for raising questions growing out of this so that new insights can be obtained. Progress in understanding human beings cannot come from the laboratory alone. It is incumbent upon the practitioner to raise questions, to observe, to analyze and thus contribute to knowledge and better practice. As in the science concerned with "matter"—physics—an effort has to be made to analyze for the purpose of finding new ways of working effecitvely. And just as in the natural sciences, this must be the work of many, not only of one genius.

There is sometimes a reluctance to analyze on the part of professionals who work with people and who have an intuitive gift to help. They are afraid they may destroy the essential totality of the phenomenae with which they work. If they dare to become more conscious of what they are doing, they will discover that their work becomes enhanced by this, that they can be of greater help.

The botanist dissects the flower to discover its secrets of color, of reproduction, of life cycle. The parts are obvious, but in the end the botanist knows that it was a flower that was studied, not just petals, stamens, and pollen. In understanding human beings, the same applies. Beyond the parts necessary for analysis, the total human being in his or her environment must be seen and experienced. The final work of the group worker must not show the parts, the technique, the effort. It uses all of them, but it becomes valuable only because of the fusion of the parts in the fire of creativity.

Social group work is a helping process that becomes increasingly significant in the social welfare field. The skill of individualization in a group is desperately needed in a world with a growing population and with much awareness of its interdependence. Eduard C. Linderman's words, written into one of his notebooks, summarize its essence:

> Group Work is a mental hygiene experience—a venture in sanity. Small groups, conscious discipline in human relations, nuclear democracy, leadership laboratory....

To practice in accordance with this goal, much knowledge and learning are needed. To the student of social group work who works through this to arrive at an integrated capacity to help, the old Zen saying may apply:

> To a man who knows nothing, mountains are mountains, waters are waters and trees are trees. But when he has studied and knows a little, mountains are no longer mountains, waters no longer waters and trees no longer trees. But when he has thoroughly understood, mountains are once again mountains, waters are waters and trees are trees.[2]

---

[2]Bryan Holme and Thomas Forman, *Poet's Camera* (New York: Studio Publications, Inc., 1946), p. x.

# INDEX

227

233    **Index**